The Power of

Business Process Improvement

Second Edition

The Power of

Business Process Improvement

10 Simple Steps to Increase Effectiveness, Efficiency, and Adaptability

Second Edition

Susan Page

AMACOM

American Management Association

New York • Atlanta • Brussels • Chicago • Mexico City
San Francisco • Shanghai • Tokyo • Toronto • Washington, D.C.

The following are registered trademarks:

> Adobe Acrobat Reader®; Adobe PDFAcrobat®; Microsoft Office Access®; Microsoft Office Excel®; Microsoft Office Outlook®; Microsoft Office PowerPoint®; Microsoft Office Project®; Microsoft Office SharePoint®; Microsoft Office Visio®; Microsoft Office Word®; SmartDraw®; Winshuttle; IBM Blueworks Live; iGrafx Flowcharter; Promapp

Library of Congress Cataloging-in-Publication Data

Page, Susan (Susan Ann)
    The power of business process improvement : 10 simple steps to increase effectiveness, efficiency, and adaptability / Susan Page.
        pages   cm
    Earlier edition: 2010.
    Includes bibliographical references and index.
    ISBN 978-0-8144-3661-5 (hardcover) — ISBN 978-0-8144-3662-2 (ebook)
1. Workflow—Management.   2. Organizational effectiveness.   3. Management.   I. Title.
HD62.17.P34   2016
658.5'1—dc23

                                                                        2015008792

About AMA
American Management Association (www.amanet.org) is a world leader in talent development, advancing the skills of individuals to drive business success. Our mission is to support the goals of individuals and organizations through a complete range of products and services, including classroom and virtual seminars, webcasts, webinars, podcasts, conferences, corporate and government solutions, business books and research. AMA's approach to improving performance combines experiential learning—learning through doing—with opportunities for ongoing professional growth at every step of one's career journey.

To Greg . . .

without his encouragement and ongoing support,

this book would never have happened

Contents

CHAPTER 1

The Roadmap: Learning How to Navigate 1

Can You Do It? 5
The Journey 6
The Ten Simple Steps to Business Process Improvement 9
    Step 1: Develop the Process Inventory 9
    Step 2: Establish the Foundation 9
    Step 3: Draw the Process Map 10
    Step 4: Estimate Time and Cost 11
    Step 5: Verify the Process Map 11
    Step 6: Apply Improvement Techniques 12
    Step 7: Create Internal Controls, Tools, and Metrics 13
    Step 8: Test and Rework 14
    Step 9: Implement the Change 14
    Step 10: Drive Continuous Improvement 15
The Executive Summary 16
Business Process Management 16
Case Study 1: Training and Development 16
Case Study 2: Recruitment Process in Hong Kong 16
Chapter Summary 17

CHAPTER 2

Step 1: Develop the Process Inventory: Identifying and Prioritizing the Process List 18

The Process Inventory 19
Process Prioritization 23
    Developing Criteria 23
    Determining Scale 29
    Applying Weighting 43
Chapter Summary: Step 1 48

Time Estimate   48
Build the Business Process Inventory   48
Sponsor Meeting   49
Establish Categories, Criteria, Scale, Weighting   49
Complete the Process Prioritization Table   50
A Second Sponsor Meeting   50
What You Have Achieved   50
Knowledge Check   50

CHAPTER 3
Step 2: Establish the Foundation: Avoiding Scope Creep   52

The Eight Sections of the Scope Definition Document   55
Section 1: Process Name   57
Section 2: Process Owner   57
Section 3: Description   58
Section 4: Scope   63
Section 5: Process Responsibilities   67
Section 6: Client and Client Needs   69
Section 7: Key Stakeholders and Interests   70
Section 8: Measurements of Success   72
Chapter Summary: Step 2   72
Time Estimate   76
First Project Team Meeting   76
Sponsor Meeting   77
What You Have Achieved   77
Knowledge Check   77

CHAPTER 4
Step 3: Draw the Process Map: Flowcharting and Documenting   79

Process Map Overview   80
Drawing the Process Map   84
Box 1   85
Box 2   89
Box 3   92
Boxes 4–8   95
The Cross-Functional Process Map   95
Continuing the Work from Meeting to Meeting   98
Documenting the Process   103
Process Mapping Tools   105
Microsoft Visio   106
SmartDraw   107

Chapter Summary: Step 3   107
Time Estimate   109
    Second Project Team Meeting   109
    Postmeeting Work   110
    Follow-on Project Team Meetings   110
What You Have Achieved   111
Knowledge Check   111

CHAPTER 5

Steps 4–5: Estimate Time and Cost and Verify the Process Map: Introducing Process and Cycle Time and Gaining Buy-In   113

Business Process Timing   113
    Process Time   114
    Cycle Time   116
Process Cost   120
    People Costs   121
    Tool Costs   127
    Overhead Costs   129
Putting It All Together   130
Alternative Cuts of the Data   130
    Analyzing the Cost Estimate Columns   132
Verify the Process Map   136
    Process Workers   136
    Stakeholders   137
    Sponsor   137
Chapter Summary: Steps 4–5   138
Time Estimate   139
    Project Team Meeting   139
    Postmeeting Work   139
    Sponsor Meeting   140
    Verify the Process Map   140
    Postvalidation Work   140
What You Have Achieved   140
Knowledge Check   141

CHAPTER 6

Step 6: Apply Improvement Techniques: Challenging Everything   143

Eliminate Bureaucracy   146
Value Added   149
Eliminate Duplication   153

Simplification 155
Reduce Cycle Time 158
Automation 161
Impact Analysis 164
Chapter Summary: Step 6 166
Time Estimate 168
Project Team Meeting 168
Postmeeting Work 169
What You Have Achieved 169
Knowledge Check 170

CHAPTER 7

Step 7: Create Internal Controls, Tools, and Metrics: Making It Real

Step 7: Create Internal Controls, Tools, and Metrics: Making It Real 171
Internal Controls 171
Tools 176
Job Aids 178
Custom Email Forms 178
Excel Tools 184
Metrics 185
Chapter Summary: Step 7 190
Time Estimate 191
Project Team Meeting 191
Postmeeting Work 192
Project Team Meeting 192
What You Have Achieved 192
Knowledge Check 193

CHAPTER 8

Step 8: Test and Rework: Making Sure It Works

Step 8: Test and Rework: Making Sure It Works 195
The Five Steps in Testing the Business Process 198
Step 1: Create the Test Plan 199
Step 2: Develop Test Sets 203
Step 3: Implement the Test Plan 207
Step 4: Summarize Feedback and Rework 209
Step 5: Retest 210
Chapter Summary: Step 8 210
Time Estimate 211
Create the Test Plan 211
Create Test Sets, Gain Resource Approval, Develop Feedback Tool 211
Implement the Test Plan and Rework 211

What You Have Achieved 212
Knowledge Check 212

CHAPTER 9
Step 9: Implement the Change: Preparing the Organization 214
The Implementation Plan 215
Overview of the Three Phases of the Implementation Plan 218
The Design Phase 219
The Development Phase 219
The Implementation Phase 220
The Four Tracks in the Implementation Phase 220
Change Management Track 221
Testing Track 221
Communications Track (Communication Plan) 221
Training Track (Training Plan) 224
Chapter Summary: Step 9 229
Time Estimate 230
Develop the Implementation Plan 230
Refine the Impact Analysis 230
Develop the Communication Plan 231
Develop the Training Plan 231
Gain Sponsor Buy-In 231
What You Have Achieved 231
Knowledge Check 232

CHAPTER 10:
Step 10: Drive Continuous Improvement: Embracing the
New Mindset 234
The Continuous Improvement Cycle 236
Evaluate 237
Test 242
Assess 243
Execute 245
Continuous Improvement Plan 246
Chapter Summary: Step 10 249
Time Estimate 250
Develop the Continuous Improvement Plan and Schedule 250
Gain Sponsor Buy-in 251
Test, Assess, Execute 251
What You Have Achieved 251
Knowledge Check 252

CHAPTER 11
Create the Executive Summary: Getting the Recognition 253

The Six Sections of the Executive Summary 254
    Section 1: Project Focus 255
    Section 2: Goals 257
    Section 3: Summary 258
    Section 4: Key Findings 265
    Section 5: Deliverables 265
    Section 6: Appendix 266
Chapter Summary 267
Time Estimate 267
    Create Analytical Tables 267
    Write the Executive Summary 268
What You Have Achieved 268

CHAPTER 12
Business Process Management: BPM and Other Improvement Techniques 269

Business Process Management 270
Business Process Modeling (BPM) 272
Business Process Model and Notation (BPMN) 273
    Gateways 274
    Pools 275
    Swim Lanes 276
    Events 276
    Activity 277
    Loops 277
    Flow Lines 277
Software Products 277
    IBM Blueworks Live 278
    iGrafx Flowcharter 279
    Promapp 279
Other Process Improvement Techniques 280
    TQM (Total Quality Management), Continuous Improvement, and
      Kaizen 280
    Hoshin Kanri 281
    Reengineering 282
    Six Sigma 284
    Lean 285
    Lean Six Sigma 286

Chapter Summary 286
What You Have Achieved 287

CHAPTER 13
Case Study 1: Training and Development 289
Background 289
Step 1: Develop the Process Inventory 290
Step 2: Establish the Foundation 294
Step 3: Draw the Process Map 298
Step 4: Estimate Time and Cost 302
  Part 1: List Process Activities and Process Time 305
  Part 2: Identify Annual Volume 309
  Part 3: Determine the FTE Formula 313
  Part 4: Determine Employee Costs 315
Step 5: Verify the Process Map 315
Step 6: Apply Improvement Techniques 316
  Benchmarking 316
  A New Approach 322
Step 7: Create Internal Controls, Tools, and Metrics 326
  Internal Controls 326
  Tools 326
  Metrics 329
Step 8: Test and Rework 331
Step 9: Implement Change 333
  Communication Track 333
  Training Track 333
  Change Management Track 334
Step 10: Drive Continuous Improvement 336
Chapter Summary 336
What You Have Achieved 338

CHAPTER 14:
Case Study 2: Recruitment Process in Hong Kong 340
Background 340
Step 2: Establish the Foundation 341
Step 3: Draw the Process Map 343
Step 4: Estimate Time and Cost 351
  1. List Process Activities and Process Time 351
  2. Identify Volume 353
  3. Determine FTE Formula 353
  4. Determine Employee Costs 355

Step 5: Verify the Process Map   355
Step 6: Apply Improvement Techniques   355
Step 7: Create Internal Controls, Tools, and Metrics   356
Step 8: Test and Rework   356
Step 9: Implement Change   357
Step 10: Drive Continuous Improvement   357
Chapter Summary   358
What You Have Achieved   358

INDEX   361

CHAPTER 1

The Roadmap

Learning How to Navigate

Have you ever had a problem that you know little or nothing about land on your desk at work? Does the problem make you feel overwhelmed and uncertain as to where to begin? Challenges like this usually occur when you already have a full workload, unrealistic deadlines, and limited resources. What can you do when you feel lost, like Hansel or Gretel trying to find the way out of the forest?

Learning to navigate through unfamiliar territory goes a long way toward easing the burden and can help you feel comfortable dealing with the unknown. *Business process improvement* (BPI) work, the systematic examination and improvement of administrative processes, can seem scary and overwhelming because no one teaches this navigation skill in school. But once you give it some thought, *everything is a process*, from making breakfast for yourself in the morning to building the space shuttle. In both cases, you follow a series of actions or steps to bring about a result. Making breakfast, no matter how informal, is still a process. You brew the coffee, cook the eggs, and toast the bread. If Vince Lombardi had run a business instead of a football team, we might remember him today for saying that process isn't everything, it's the only thing.

The techniques covered in this book help smooth the path to successful BPI by clearing away the unknowns and delivering the power of process improvement directly into your hands. Whether you consider yourself an expert on the subject or do not see yourself as a process person, you will appreciate learning how to tackle process improvement work in a bottom-line, straightforward approach. For the inexperienced, The *Power of Business Process Improvement* guides you along a proven, step-by-step approach to a successful result; for the expert, it becomes a handy A-to-Z reference guide to help you engage an organization in a process improvement effort.

This guide cuts through the long, confusing, and difficult-to-comprehend explanations regarding BPI and takes you directly to the core of what you, the business professional, want to understand. It describes a pragmatic approach to business process improvement that I developed over the years and that anyone can use in real time to solve real problems. The ten simple steps to increasing the effectiveness, efficiency, and adaptability of your business processes start with the creation of a process inventory and end with how to keep a business process continually delivering value to the business.

If you want to evaluate how your company hires employees, secures sales, or manufactures a product, examining the underlying processes helps you better understand how the business works. Every day we experience challenges with inefficient or ineffective processes, and, after you start thinking of business processes as the foundation for the business, you begin to see the power of having a process focus and wonder why you waited so long to change your perspective.

Bill Gates wrote several years ago, "A rule of thumb is that a lousy process will consume ten times as many hours as the work itself requires." This truth has not changed in all that time. We have all seen bureaucracy and red tape continually added to a business process. Bureaucracy happens not all at once but incrementally over time. A business process can easily become bloated, leading to an ineffective, inefficient, and inflexible process.

Improving business processes enables you to stay competitive and to increase your responsiveness to your customers, the productivity of your employees doing the work, and your company's return on investment. The expertise to examine and understand how business processes work sets you apart from the rest because you have the power to demonstrate the value that the process delivers, its importance to your company, and the effect that a single change can produce.

People become interested in process improvement for any number of reasons. Do any of these scenarios sound familiar?

▶ Your customers, clients, or suppliers complain about the business process.

▶ You find that your department makes numerous errors and/or makes the same one again and again.

▶ You want to understand how your department can improve its efficiency so your employees can spend their limited time on more valuable work.

▶ You have accepted responsibility for a new organization or department, and you want to understand the work.

▶ You want to understand the end-to-end processes across your company.

▶ You discovered challenges with the handoffs between departments.

▶ You want to increase your department's productivity.

▶ You noticed duplication of data or tasks in multiple departments.

▶ You started a new job and want to understand how the department works.

If you encountered one or more of these experiences, then BPI can help. It improves your ability to meet your customer's needs, helps you eliminate errors, identifies opportunities to yield a more effective and efficient process, assists you in learning the end-to-end process for a new part of the business, makes clear the relationship between departments and the roles and responsibilities of each, improves your organization's productivity, and eliminates redundancy.

Working on business processes helps demystify the process and makes a seemingly complex process less intimidating. Process improvement work also gives you the chance to engage a cross-functional team in the work so that everyone can learn the end-to-end business process, instead of simply focusing on his or her own piece of the process. You will find that, as you do the work, few employees understand the end-to-end process. Employees may understand their own piece but not how the entire process works from beginning to end. When a team works together on improving business processes, the work itself provides a means for colleagues to talk about common topics, and the team effort promotes an understanding of the interconnectivity of the work.

When you focus on a business process, it appears less threatening to colleagues than focusing on the employees who do the work. The process of finding challenges and linking those challenges to the process instead of to a particular employee leads to easier, less threatening solutions. No one employee or group of employees has to worry about repercussions.

On the other hand, BPI does affect the entire business system, including the employees who do the work; the information technology systems that support the process; the measurements established to assess the effectiveness, efficiency, and adaptability of the process; and reward and recognition programs that exist in a company.

If you still find yourself wondering whether you should undertake a process improvement effort on one of your processes, ask yourself four questions. If you answer no to any of these questions, you should start examining your business processes:

- ▶ Does your process include a high level of customer/client interaction?
- ▶ Does every step in your process add value for the customer/client?
- ▶ Have you established customer- or client-focused metrics for the business process?
- ▶ Are your employees evaluated on their contribution to the business process?

Throughout this book, the term *customer* refers to someone external to a company who pays money for a product or service. The term *client* denotes an internal customer within a company.

If you work as an internal consultant in your company, then you probably work with clients. The client's business processes should support the company's business goals, which in turn should support the paying customer. Remember, in business process work, the customer is king, and you should always focus on the customer.

Can You Do It?

Many of the process improvement books on the market support the myth that business process improvement must be time-consuming and complex. *The Power of Business Process Improvement* shows that nothing is further from the truth. It presents you with numerous tools and examples that you can use to make the work simple and yet maintain high standards.

Perhaps you have shied away from process improvement because it looks like something that only an expert can do. In reality, you can do this work without having to learn the ins and outs of total quality management, reengineering, or business process management. This book shares my own unique approach to BPI, an approach influenced by many quality-related techniques that works for me every time. I have successfully used the approach outlined with every employee level in different and complex situations. It works. It works even with people who start out as skeptics.

As you apply the ten simple steps introduced in this chapter and covered in depth in the chapters that follow, you will find yourself adopting several of the quality-related philosophies because the focus on the customer is at their core, but you use them in a seamless way that makes the work palatable to the business.

I geared each step toward ease of use. This book answers basic questions and elaborates on how to perform each step by demonstrating its application. It explains topics that no one ever bothers to tell you about, either because authors, consultants, or colleagues assume that you already know about them or because they do not want you to know the full story, believing that knowledge is power and wanting to hold onto that power. The various BPI books on the market remind me of getting a favorite recipe from a restaurant, but with some key ingredient missing. This book tells you the whole story and gives you the power of knowledge.

You will feel comfortable with the formulas that I use throughout the book because they are the ones commonly used in business. You do not have to understand complicated statistical measurements of process capability or know how to use Six Sigma, Lean, or other quality methods. You have everything you need right now, so let us begin the journey.

The Journey

Anyone who has ever driven on vacation or taken a business trip knows how to follow a navigation system or read a roadmap to follow the best route to reach a destination. Roadmaps or driving directions are easy to follow. To help you navigate through the ten simple steps to BPI, I developed the roadmap in Figure 1-1. Join me as I take you on a trip through process improvement, using the roadmap as a mental model of the ten steps.

The roadmap becomes a meaningful tool for you to use with your colleagues when engaging them in the work. Business professionals like to know what the voyage looks like and how long it will take; the roadmap describes the journey.

The objectives of BPI are:

▶ **Effectiveness:** Does the process produce the desired results and meet the customer's/client's needs?

▶ **Efficiency:** Does the process minimize the use of resources and eliminate bureaucracy?

▶ **Adaptability:** Is the process flexible in the face of changing needs?

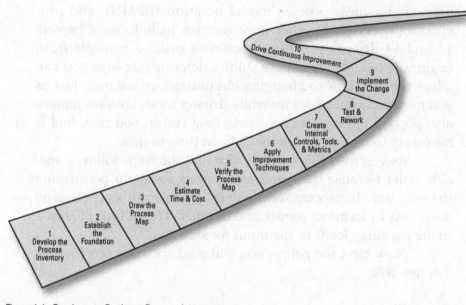

Figure 1-1 Roadmap to Business Process Improvement

These three terms appear frequently throughout this book:

▶ *Effectiveness* focuses on the customers/clients and whether the process delivers what they want.

▶ *Efficiency* focuses on the employees responsible for the overall process, the workers in a department or departments, and how easily they can use the business process.

▶ *Adaptability* evaluates how easily you can modify the business process on the basis of changing business requirements.

Chapters 2 through 10 focus on the ten steps in the roadmap, describing each step and explaining how it works. Each chapter includes tools that I created to help with the step, summarizes the key points in the chapter, and ends with a time estimate, so you can see how long it takes to finish each step. Chapter 11 then helps you to gain recognition for your work. Chapter 12 introduces business process management (BPM), presents business process model notation (BPMN), and provides an overview of other improvement techniques. Chapters 13 and 14 discuss two of my business process projects from beginning to end. These case studies demonstrate how you can adapt the ten steps to changing circumstances because, just as you may encounter detours while driving a car, course changes also pop up during process work. As a result, you may find it necessary to alter your approach from time to time.

As you read this book, notice that the steps follow a specific order because the result of one step assists in performing the next step. In process terminology, you hear this progression described in terms of *inputs* and *outputs*. The output of step 1 in the roadmap leads to the input for step 2.

Now meet the people you will read about on our journey through BPI:

► The regional sales manager who did not feel that his sales team brought in a sufficient number of new customers

► The buyer who could not get her orders filled in a timely manner

► The marketing director who took too long to bring her product to market

► The training and development manager who wanted to reduce her team's course development time

► The human resource bank vice president who could not decide which business process to focus on first

► The human resource information system manager who wanted to understand how system funding worked and how system costs hit his budget

► The compensation director who wanted to learn the head count requirements for his business processes

► The workforce analysis manager who wanted to understand why multiple groups in her company produced similar reports

► The vice president who wanted to know how to develop a recruitment process for his company's expansion in Hong Kong

The Ten Simple Steps to Business Process Improvement

Although each chapter focuses on a step in the roadmap, I briefly explain each of them here so you have a snapshot of what is ahead.

Step 1: Develop the Process Inventory

Every department has numerous business processes to manage, but how do you decide which process to examine first? Take the simple process involved in joining a health club: First you identify the available clubs in your neighborhood, and then you list your key selection criteria. Do you care more about the distance from your home, the age of the facility, the type of equipment, or the qualifications of the staff? You choose the health club to join based on what is most important to you.

Step 1 in the roadmap introduces the process inventory to help you decide where to start. The inventory lists the entire complement of business processes in a department, business area, or company. The chapter describes how to:

▶ Identify the business processes.
▶ Create prioritization criteria.
▶ Apply the criteria to each business process in the inventory.
▶ Create a process prioritization table so that you can contrast a group of business processes to determine which business process you should address first.

At the end of this step, you have a list of the business processes and you understand the order of priority, so you know where to start.

Step 2: Establish the Foundation

Once you create the process inventory in step 1 and select the business process to focus on first, step 2 introduces the *scope definition document*, your blueprint or foundation that guides you through the rest of your process improvement work.

Before starting a home improvement project, you develop a plan so you know the tools and materials you need. Whether building a deck on your house or simply painting a room, you always do prework to avoid those time-consuming trips back to the home center to pick up what you forgot. Likewise, in BPI you have to establish the boundaries associated with a process before you begin the in-depth process work, so you avoid future time-consuming discussions about the beginning and end of the business process.

This is the role of the scope definition document, which includes the process boundaries and other baseline information about the business process you selected, and thus keeps you on track. The document works like a contract, but it does not seem as formal or as threatening to the business. It helps you avoid scope creep, whereby you veer away from the original purpose of the work without an increase in time, resources, or money.

At the end of this step, you have the basic information required to start the process improvement work, as well as specific boundaries to help you stay on track.

Step 3: Draw the Process Map

Drawing the process map enables everyone involved to understand how the business process works and where handoffs occur between departments.

The hardest part of many projects is getting started—taking that first step. You will find it no different when it comes to drawing the process map. Whether you work alone or with a project team, you may find yourself questioning where to start, how to handle conflicts that arise with a project team, and how to keep everyone interested and involved in work that can seem tedious at times. The scope definition document that you created in step 2 helps you get started with this step because it identifies where the process starts and ends.

In most cases, unless you own the process and work alone, you need other colleagues to help you build the process map. It helps to have a project team work with you throughout the ten steps or at least to have resources that you can go to with questions.

The process map you create in this step provides the information you require for step 6, when you apply the improvement techniques, and it assists in setting improvement targets. This step gives everyone involved in the work a better understanding of how the process works from beginning to end by educating the project team on the end-to-end process.

At the end of this step, you and the project team understand how the process works.

Step 4: Estimate Time and Cost

To measure an accomplishment, you need to know where you started. Whether you want to lose weight or run a marathon, you need to establish a baseline to know how much you have improved. How much do you weigh today, or how quickly do you run a marathon today? In process work, to establish an improvement target, you have to know how long a process takes and what it costs.

After drawing the process map in step 3, you understand the activities involved in a business process; step 4 assists in identifying what the process costs today. In step 4, you learn about process time and cycle time. *Process time* helps you summarize the labor required to deliver a business process, and *cycle time* identifies how long the process takes from beginning to end, a key metric that customers/clients usually list as a top concern. Identifying the employee, overhead, and tool expenses associated with a business process brings a financial dimension to your work.

This step helps you define the process cost and cycle time, parameters you can use to set improvement targets.

Step 5: Verify the Process Map

In the United States, before adding a deck to your house, you would talk with your town's or county's code enforcement office and seek opinions from family members to ensure that you meet the town's setback requirements and keep family members happy. Similarly, you want to review the process map with the appropriate colleagues to validate that the map accurately reflects the existing process. Performing this review validates the baseline for your improvement targets and eliminates the possibility of any future challenges. It provides you with a solid foundation to start the next step, improving the business process.

By completing this step, you gain sponsor and stakeholder support, and you build a solid foundation on which to start the improvement work.

Step 6: Apply Improvement Techniques

If you weigh 200 pounds and want to lose 15 pounds in three months, you know that you have to make changes in your daily routine. You may change your eating habits and eliminate dessert, add an exercise like jogging, or partner with a friend for motivation. The same type of evaluation has to occur to improve a business process.

The *improvement technique wheel* provides an organized approach to improving a business process by introducing key methods to use, including:

► Eliminating bureaucracy
► Evaluating value-added activities
► Eliminating duplication and redundancy
► Simplifying the process, reports, and forms
► Reducing cycle time
► Applying automation tools

You learn how important it is to apply the techniques in a specific order and how applying the six improvement techniques, one at a time, aids in evaluating the business process in a planned and thoughtful approach.

You also learn how to create an impact analysis, a tool

you can use to capture the changes that have to occur to ensure the success of the new business process.

By the end of this step, you have changed the business process so that it delivers business value.

Step 7: Create Internal Controls, Tools, and Metrics

Once you establish your plan to lose the extra pounds, how do you keep track of your progress so that you keep moving toward your goal? You probably weigh yourself at regular intervals and perhaps use an online tracking tool, or mobile application, to view your progress. Without frequent measurement, you might easily gain the weight back. The same is true of a business process: Without regular measurement, it gets outdated, and without internal controls, human errors occur.

To bring the process to life—to move it beyond just creating a process map—you establish internal controls; you create tools to increase the effectiveness, efficiency, and adaptability of the business process; and you create metrics. Specifically:

▶ *Internal controls* identify points in the business process where mistakes can occur and explains how to prevent them.

▶ Creating *tools* to support the business process streamlines the process and assists in avoiding errors and training new employees on how to perform their jobs.

▶ Developing *metrics* shows you whether the process works as planned.

This book sticks to simple tools that anyone can use; it does not discuss large system implementations that you have no control over. In Chapter 7, I discuss using the tools that you no doubt already have on your desktop computer and that you are now using every day.

This step helps you to minimize potential errors, create tools to automate the business process, and identify process metrics.

Step 8: Test and Rework

Before you purchase new software or join a health club for a year, you might want to accept a 30-day trial offer and test it out to make sure it meets your needs. Likewise, before introducing a new, improved process to an organization, you should test it and work out any bugs before implementing the change on a wide scale.

In this step you learn how to create a plan to test the new business process. The details included in the plan help you to confirm that the new process and tools work as planned and to resolve any bugs before fully implementing the change. In creating a test plan, you answer questions like whom to involve in the testing, what items to test, what steps are involved, where you should conduct the testing, and the best time to conduct the test.

Testing the business process evaluates how well the business process performs, so that you satisfy project goals such as increased productivity or minimizing errors.

At the end of this step, you should feel comfortable that the business process, tools, and metrics work as planned.

Step 9: Implement the Change

When companies introduce a new product, they create a marketing plan that identifies the product price, customer base, distribution channels, and promotion strategies. Likewise, when you change a business process, you have to identify who has to know about the change, what they need to know, and how to communicate the right information to the right people.

Now that you have validated the business process and tools work, this step explains how to introduce the change to the organization. Chapter 9 introduces a sample implementation plan that helps you successfully introduce the changes to the business process. The implementation plan includes design, development, and implementation phases and further organizes each phase into tracks. For example, the implementation phase can have these four tracks:

1. **Change Management Track:** This track includes the impact analysis created in step 6, which identified the orga-

nizational changes required to ensure the success of the new business process.
2. **Testing Track:** The steps in this track confirm that the process and tools work as expected.
3. **Communication Track:** This track identifies whom to notify of the change, what they need to know, when they need to know it, and the audience's preferred communication vehicle(s).
4. **Training Track:** This identifies who requires training on what, when the training should occur, who delivers the training, and the preferred training method.

At the end of this step, you have introduced the new process.

Step 10: Drive Continuous Improvement

Now that you have lost weight, can you relax and allow old habits to creep back into your life? Not if you intend to keep the weight off for good. The maintenance phase of a weight loss program should lead to lifestyle changes that become part of your everyday life. Likewise, once you improve a business process, you cannot simply relax. Just as you need to keep weighing yourself to maintain your weight loss, you have to continually measure the business process to retain the strategic gains.

Continuous improvement means achieving a new mindset by which ongoing improvement is the natural course of business instead of an event. The *continuous improvement cycle wheel* introduces four phases—evaluate, test, assess, and execute—to help you attain the new mindset. Each phase in the wheel provides you with a degree of structure to help you think through how to keep the business process up to date on an ongoing basis. Continuous improvement validates that the business process continually delivers effectiveness, efficiency, and adaptability to the organization.

You now have a plan in place to evaluate the business process on an ongoing basis, so that it stays relevant to your customer's/client's needs.

After covering steps 1–10, additional chapters include the

executive summary, business process management, and two case studies.

The Executive Summary

Chapter 11 assists you in gaining recognition for your efforts. After all your work, this chapter shows you how to gain the credit you deserve. An executive summary is a tool that allows you to present your work to senior management in the natural course of business. In this chapter, you learn how to write an executive summary and present statistical information in a thought-provoking manner. By the end of this chapter, you have a concise summary of your work, appropriate for senior management to read.

Business Process Management

Chapter 12 introduces business process management, presents business process model and notation, and provides an overview of other process improvement techniques such as total quality management, reengineering, Hoshin Kanri, Six Sigma, Lean, and Lean Six Sigma.

Case Study 1: Training and Development

Chapter 13 presents a case study from beginning to end. You see the ten simple steps applied to a training and development case that I worked on for a financial institution. You can follow my journey past the detours I had to take and all the way through to implementation.

When you reach the end of this chapter, you will know how adaptable you can make the ten steps.

Case Study 2: Recruitment Process in Hong Kong

Chapter 14 presents a case study for a U.S.-based company expanding in Hong Kong. You learn how I built a process where no process existed and how I adapted the ten steps to create a business process from scratch.

When you reach the end of this chapter, you have another example of the adaptability of the ten steps.

Chapter Summary

The journey to improving business processes should not appear threatening. I assure you that you can do the work. Just as Hansel and Gretel found their way out of the forest, you will quickly find that you are a business process person just by following the ten simple steps to business process improvement.

You can use the ten steps whether you work with a project team or on your own. If you work with a project team, the roadmap helps the team members understand what to expect, keeps them interested, and makes them feel part of the journey. If you work alone, the roadmap helps you keep track of your progress.

You can adjust the time spent on each step, spending as much or as little time as you see fit, depending on your goal. Always keep in mind the return on investment of your time. Expend as much effort as required to achieve your goal. That may mean delving deeply into a business process or simply skimming the surface.

This book puts the power of business process improvement in your hands. You can make your business processes more effective in delivering what your customers/clients want, more efficient for the employees who perform the processes, and more flexible so the processes can adapt to changing business needs.

CHAPTER 2

Step 1: Develop the Process Inventory

Identifying and Prioritizing the Process List

Kendall Smith, senior vice president of human resources for a bank in the midst of a merger, wanted to improve the bank's human resource processes. He had recently received complaints from the bank's executives claiming that they did not have enough money in the budget to give their employees salary increases. The annual salary planning process ended six months ago, and, in all previous years, the compensation department had always put aside money to handle ongoing salary increases throughout the year. The senior managers at the bank demanded that compensation explain why the budget had been depleted.

To add to Kendall's concerns, his vice president of recruitment came to him complaining about process inefficiencies at their last job fair and wanted to introduce process changes. At the same time, his vice president of training and development felt that the training delivered to new employees as part of the hiring process required improvement to support the bank's upcoming acquisition.

Kendall was at a loss as to where he should start. Which business process should receive top priority? Should his management team address compensation's budgeting process first? Should they focus on increasing the efficiency of their job fairs?

Or should they worry more about ensuring the appropriate integration of new employees into the business?

The process inventory and the process prioritization table introduced in this chapter helped Kendall to prioritize the work, and these same tools will help you rank your organization's business processes so you know where to start your improvement efforts. In this chapter, I describe three steps:

1. Build the process inventory.
2. Develop prioritization criteria and scale.
3. Build a table that merges the inventory and criteria so you know which business process to improve first.

Figure 2-1 shows the framework for a table I build throughout this chapter. The list of business processes appears in the left-hand column (the stub), and the prioritization criteria are listed horizontally as column headings. As we move through the three steps, you will see how all the pieces fit together.

Process	Criterion 1	Criterion 2	Criterion 3	Criterion 4
Process 1				
Process 2				
Process 3				

Figure 2-1 Process Prioritization Table Framework

Let us start by examining how to go about building a process inventory.

The Process Inventory

The *process inventory* is a list of the business processes that a company or department owns, and you have to build one if you find that such a list does not exist. You can identify business processes by reviewing the work done by a department, by scanning job descriptions, or by talking to colleagues to identify their roles and responsibilities.

If you ask human resource managers, for example, what they do, they may tell you that they handle employee performance problems, help with change management, write or interpret policy, manage the recruiting strategy, or perform similar tasks. You can then translate those responsibilities into business processes. In this example, you may define the following business processes that come from talking to a human resource manager:

▶ **Performance Management Process:** Defines how to handle employee performance problems.

▶ **Change Management Process:** Defines how the organization deals with change from both the employee and organizational perspectives.

▶ **Policy Development Process:** Defines the steps required to write and gain approval on employee-related policies.

▶ **Recruitment Process:** Defines how to move from sourcing candidates to hiring the right employees.

These four processes become part of the process inventory. Now, let us use another example: talking to sales representatives. You may discover that they spend a great deal of time generating leads, cold calling, or managing existing accounts. You can then translate these responsibilities into the following business processes:

▶ **Lead Generation Process:** Defines how the sales group generates, assigns, and evaluates leads.

▶ **Sales Process:** Defines the steps involved in calling on potential customers and closing sales.

▶ **Account Management Process:** Defines how to manage a strategic customer account on a day-to-day basis.

These two examples demonstrate how easily you can develop a process inventory simply by talking to colleagues. Figure 2-2 provides additional examples of business processes for the human resource, sales and marketing, finance, and information technology (IT) areas. If you look at the first group of processes under human resources, you see that it lists three main business processes: hiring, training, and compensation and benefits.

Since a single business process can have multiple subprocesses, you can further break down each main process into subprocesses. In this example, I broke the hiring process into four subprocesses: requisition, sourcing, job fair, and orientation.

As you build the process inventory, break major processes into subprocesses to make sure you do not overlook any business process.

Another way to organize the process inventory is to group all business processes under general category names. If you work with an information technology department, you could group their business processes under fairly general categories that should work in most cases. For example:

1. **People/Organizational Processes:**
   - Performance management
   - Succession planning
   - Communication
   - Recognition
2. **Financial Processes:**
   - Capital budgeting
   - Five-year plan
   - Annual operating plan
3. **Client-Facing IT Processes:**
   - Client relationship management
   - Change order
   - Issue resolution
4. **Internal-Facing IT Processes:**
   - Network administration
   - Security administration
   - Software development

The technique of grouping business processes under a few major headings works well when you have a long process

Business Process

Human resource processes:
Hiring
 ➢ Requisition process
 ➢ Sourcing process
 ➢ Job fair process
 ➢ Orientation process
Training
 ➢ Need identification process
 ➢ Course development process
 ➢ Evaluation process
Compensation and benefits
 ➢ Salary planning process
 ➢ Budget process
 ➢ Job-leveling process
 ➢ New hire pay process

Sales and marketing processes:
Portfolio management
Market planning/segmentation
Advertising
Distribution
Lead development
Account management
Sales and marketing administration
Revenue generation

Finance processes:
Budgeting and forecasting
Payroll
Tax planning
Risk management
Cash management

Information technology processes:
Application development
Change order
Client relationship
Portfolio management
Program management
Incident management

Figure 2-2 Sample Business Process Inventory

list because grouping the processes helps manage the inventory and makes it easier to decide where to start. For example, you may decide to start with the collection of client-facing processes because they will improve the effectiveness of the organization's business processes.

So, now that you know how to build the process inventory, let us move to the next step and discuss how to develop the appropriate criteria so you can prioritize the process inventory and pinpoint where to start.

Process Prioritization

Whether you have a list of specific business processes or just general categories, develop criteria and apply them to the items in the process inventory.

Remember Kendall Smith at the beginning of this chapter? He had to decide whether to focus on compensation's budgeting process, the job fair process, or their training process to better integrate new employees into the company. I had to find a way to help him prioritize his business processes so he and his management team could easily decide where to start. The next section explains how to develop criteria to prioritize a process inventory.

Developing Criteria

The following four general categories help you determine the relative importance of one business process over another. Of course, you may have to vary these categories depending on the situation, and you should feel free to identify additional criteria if doing so helps to reach a better decision on where to start your improvement effort.

1. **Impact:** How much does the business process affect the business?
2. **Implementation:** How feasible is it to make the change?
3. **Current State:** How well is the process working today?

4. **Value:** What is the benefit, or return, of improving the process?

Figure 2-3 shows the continuation of the table framework with the four general categories of criteria added across the first row as column headers.

Process	Impact		Implementation			Current State			Value	
Process 1										
Process 2										
Process 3										

Figure 2-3 Process Prioritization Table Framework

The next step involves deciding how to measure each of the categories of criteria. For example, what does *Impact* mean? What does *Implementation* mean? To demonstrate how to accomplish this task, I will use two typical business processes one might find in a compensation and benefit department: the annual salary planning process and the budgeting process.

Impact

Let us start with the *Impact* category to define how we might measure the impact of a business process on the business. Two common criteria used for this category are *Number Affected* and *Client Level*. Figure 2-4 shows the *Salary Planning* and

Process	Impact		Implementation			Current State			Value	
	Number Affected	Client Level								
Salary Planning										
Budgeting										

Figure 2-4 Process Prioritization Table Framework: Impact

Budgeting processes in the left column and the two criteria added in the second row (note the shaded areas in the figure).

➤ **Number Affected** refers to volume, and it includes the number of employees affected by a business process. If a business process affects a large number of employees, it has a greater impact on the business than if it affects only a handful of employees.

  For example, in a compensation and benefits department, how many employees are affected by a company's annual salary planning process compared to the budgeting process? Generally, you find a higher number of employees affected by the salary planning process because more employees receive a pay increase and fewer employees manage budgets. As a result, the salary planning process receives a higher score for this criterion because it affects a larger number of employees.

➤ **Client Level** refers to the level of employees affected by the business process. As pointed out in Chapter 1, the term *client* denotes an internal customer in a company, whereas *customer* refers to a person external to the company who pays for a product or service. For demonstration purposes, let us categorize client levels as executive or senior level, midmanager level, professional level, and hourly level. Let us further decide that the higher the employee level is, the higher the score.

  In the example, the employee level for the salary planning process can consist of all four levels because each category of employee usually receives a pay increase, whereas the employee level for budgeting probably includes only the executive and midmanager levels. As a result, the budgeting process receives a higher score for this criterion because of the senior-level visibility to the business process.

Remember to include any criteria in this category that defines the impact of the business processes on the business. You must also weigh political criteria, as in the level of employee example, against other criteria in terms of the overall effect on the business to achieve the proper end result.

Implementation

Implementation, the second prioritization category, refers to elements that measure the feasibility of a successful execution. Again, feel free to define additional criteria besides these three common ones: *Time to Market*, *Funding*, and *Timing of Next Cycle*. Figure 2-5 shows these three criteria added to the second row in the table framework.

Process	Impact		Implementation			Current State			Value
	Number Affected	Client Level	Time to Market	Funding	Timing of Next Cycle				
Salary Planning									
Budgeting									

Figure 2-5 Process Prioritization Table Framework: Implementation

▶ **Time to Market**, in marketing terminology, denotes the total time it takes to move from product conception to product availability. In business process work, it refers to how long it takes to proceed through the ten steps to business process improvement. Estimate the time on the basis of your understanding of the business process. Think about potential problems like:

- The complexity of the process
- Whether you expect delays
- Anything unusual about the process that adds time
- The availability of knowledgeable resources to answer questions
- The number of people you have to include in the work

These factors all contribute to the length of time the work takes, and you should weigh them accordingly. For example, one group I worked with wanted to create a process map to explain how a particular business process worked, but it was a complex process that few people understood; so multiple gaps existed in the team's knowledge at different points in the process. As a result, it took a long time to draw the process map due to the complexity and lack of knowledgeable resources.

The score that this criterion receives depends on your estimate of how long it will take to move through the ten steps. On this criterion, the shorter the time to market, the higher the business process will score.

▶ **Funding** refers to whether you require a budget and its size. Although you may not know the exact cost associated with any technology investment, in most cases you do have an idea of the size of the investment (small, medium, large) and know whether you have to pay for additional services or resources. If you expect to require funding, this criterion receives a negative, low score because of the time-consuming nature of gaining budget approval.

▶ **Timing of Next Cycle** refers to the time lapse before the organization plans to use the business process again, that is, ongoing, almost daily, or cyclical (quarterly, semiannual, or annual). In the annual salary planning process example, this process receives a low score on this criterion if the annual process just occurred because it will not happen again for another year. On the other hand, an ongoing process receives a high score because any improvements immediately affect the business.

Current State

The third prioritization category, *Current State*, refers to how well the business process works for the customers/clients and for the internal department or area that owns the process. Three common criteria used to assess the current state are *Customer/Client Satisfaction*, *Pain Level*, and whether a *Process Exists*. Figure 2-6 shows these three criteria added to the table framework.

▶ **Customer/Client Satisfaction** evaluates how well or poorly the business process currently works from the customer's/client's perspective—the effectiveness of the process. As you recall from Chapter 1, we define effectiveness from the customer's/client's perspective. Answer the question, "How

Process	Impact		Implementation			Current State			Value
	Number Affected	Client Level	Time to Market	Funding	Timing of Next Cycle	Customer/ Client Satisfaction	Pain Level	Process Exists?	
Salary Planning									
Budgeting									

Figure 2-6 Process Prioritization Table Framework: Current State

delighted are your customers/clients with the current process?" If you score *Customer/Client Satisfaction* as low, this criterion receives a high score.

▶ **Pain Level** refers to how well or poorly the business process currently works for the department responsible for delivering the process results. This criterion evaluates the efficiency of the existing process, and we define efficiency from the process owner's perspective. Answer the question, "How easily can the department manage the existing process?" If you score the process as an extremely manual one and feel that it requires too much work, this criterion receives a high score.

▶ **Process Exists?** simply refers to whether a process exists or not. Even when no formal process exists and employees just do whatever it takes to get the job done, a process does in fact exist, albeit an informal one. If no formal process exists, this criterion receives a high score because you should document the process.

Value

This final prioritization category can have a myriad of definitions. *Value* can denote economic value, personal value, or cultural value. A frequently accepted criterion for value is the size of the *Benefit/Return*, or return on investment, and this definition works well for business processes. Again, feel free to add more criteria to this category. Figure 2-7 shows this last criterion added to the table framework as well as a *Total Score* column.

Process	Impact		Implementation			Current State			Value	
	Number Affected	Client Level	Time to Market	Funding	Timing of Next Cycle	Customer/ Client Satisfaction	Pain Level	Process Exists?	Benefit/ Return	Total Score
Salary Planning										
Budgeting										

Figure 2-7 Process Prioritization Table Framework: Value

> **Benefit/Return** refers to either a quantitative or qualitative measure of the value of improving the process:
>
> ■ *Quantitative* signifies a number or quantity, usually a measurement represented in numerical terms (like turnover rate or error rate).
>
> ■ *Qualitative* denotes quality, usually a measurement represented in softer terms (like responsiveness or the ability to make decisions).
>
> Quantitative value often speaks louder to the business because it is associated with a number. However, in business process work, qualitative value becomes increasingly important because of the positive results that an effective business process can have on customers/clients.
>
> The *Benefit/Return* criterion requires further discussion to come to a common understanding and agreement about how to evaluate the benefit or return of a business process. Think about value relative to the status quo, which means leaving a business process in the existing condition. What merit do you associate with taking action versus doing nothing?
>
> **Total Score**, at the far right in Figure 2-7, shows the overall score for each business process once we populate the table with numbers.

Determining Scale

Now that we created the process inventory and defined the criteria, we have one more step before filling in the process prioritization table with the scores for each business process: determining the scale for the criteria. To determine the score for a business process, the first step is to settle on the scale to use for the criteria. You can use a 1–3 scale, a 1–10 scale, or any other scale that makes sense for your business. I generally like to use a small scale to reduce the degree of interpretation available to people. I use words like *small*, *medium*, *large*, and others to explain what the numbers mean in my example.

Figure 2-8 shows the process prioritization table, with the scale included on the third row. To avoid confusion, take a careful look at the scales used in Figure 2-8, and remember that the highest number is assigned to the item with the greatest impact on making a decision. In *Number Affected*, the largest number of people affected gets a 3 because in this case it has the greatest impact. Now look at *Funding*. A score of 3 for *Funding* goes to the business process that requires the least amount of funding because not having to go through an approval process to obtain a budget is a good thing.

So, in this example:

▶ If the number of employees affected by the business process (number affected) scores high, then this criterion should contribute more to the final total score: in this case, a score of 3.

▶ If we do not require much funding to improve the business process, then this positive fact should contribute more to the final total score: in this case, a score of 3.

While building the scale, make sure that it depicts what you intend. To clarify the importance of developing an appropriate scale, let us take a deeper look at the criteria in the four general categories to eliminate any confusion. I am using an intentionally simple explanation to help everyone follow along. If you happen to be a math enthusiast, you may want to use another method for scaling.

Process	Impact		Implementation			Current State			Value	
Row 1 = Category										
Row 2 = Criteria	Number Affected	Client Level	Time to Market	Funding	Timing of Next Cycle	Customer/Client Satisfaction	Pain Level	Process Exists?	Benefit/Return	Total Score
Row 3 = Scale	3 = large number 2 = average number 1 = small number	3 = senior 2 = management 1 = other	3 = short 2 = average 1 = long	3 = small 2 = medium 1 = large	3 = close/ongoing 2 = intermediate 1 = far	3 = low 2 = medium 1 = high	3 = high 2 = medium 1 = low	1 = no 0 = yes	3 = high 2 = average 1 = low	
Salary Planning										
Budgeting										

Figure 2-8 Process Prioritization Table Framework

Scaling for Category 1: Impact

Remember that *Impact* refers to the effect that the business process has on the organization, and Figure 2-9 shows the scale for this category.

Impact	
Number Affected	**Client Level**
3 = large number	3 = senior
2 = average number	2 = management
1 = small number	1 = other

Figure 2-9 Impact Category

▶ **Number Affected:** For this criterion, the larger the number of employees affected by a business process, the higher the score the process receives. Figure 2-10 explains how the scale supports this decision.

Score	Description
1	The business process affects few employees.
2	The business process affects an average number of employees.
3	The business process affects a high number of employees.

Figure 2-10 Scores for Number Affected

▶ **Client Level:** In this criterion, the higher the management level of the employees affected by a business process, the higher the score the process receives. Figure 2-11 provides an example of the application of the scale for this criterion.

Once you develop the scale, as we just did for the Impact category, apply it to the process prioritization table by giving each business process a score. To show how this works, Figure 2-12 shows the process prioritization table with the impact scale

Score	Description
1	The business process affects the *other* group, mostly composed of professional or hourly employees.
2	The business process affects the midlevel managers.
3	The business process affects the executive or senior-level employees.

Figure 2-11 Scores for Client Level

and scores applied to the salary planning and budgeting processes.

Figure 2-12 shows that the salary planning process receives a higher score for *Number Affected* because it affects a larger number of employees than the budgeting process, which applies only to managers and above. The budgeting process receives a higher *Client Level* score than the salary planning process because of its visibility to the most senior-level employees in the organization, even though it pertains to fewer employees. After applying the scores for the *Impact* category, the salary planning process seems to take precedence, relative to where to start an improvement effort, over the budgeting process because it has a total score of 5.

But we have three more categories to add to the table before making a final decision. The next three sections follow the same method used for the Impact category to incorporate the implementation, current state, and value categories.

Scaling for Category 2: Implementation

Now let us look at the scale for the *Implementation* category, which refers to the feasibility of a successful execution. This category consists of three criteria: *Time to Market*, *Funding*, and *Timing of Next Cycle*. Figure 2-13 shows the scale for the Implementation category.

▶ **Time to Market:** This criterion states that the longer you estimate it will take to improve the business process, the

Process	Impact		Implementation			Current State			Value	
	Number Affected	Client Level	Time to Market	Funding	Timing of Next Cycle	Customer/ Client Satisfaction	Pain Level	Process Exists?	Benefit/ Return	Total Score
	3 = large number 2 = average number 1 = small number	3 = senior 2 = management 1 = other	3 = short 2 = average 1 = long	3 = small 2 = medium 1 = large	3 = close/ongoing 2 = intermediate 1 = far	3 = low 2 = medium 1 = high	3 = high 2 = medium 1 = low	1 = no 0 = yes	3 = high 2 = average 1 = low	
Salary Planning	3	2								5
Budget	1	3								4

Figure 2-12 Process Prioritization Table

	Implementation	
Time to Market	**Funding**	**Timing of Next Cycle**
3 = short	3 = small	3 = close/ongoing
2 = average	2 = medium	2 = intermediate
1 = long	1 = large	1 = far

Figure 2-13 Implementation Category

lower the score will be, and the low score negatively impacts the Implementation category. Figure 2-14 shows the explanation of the scoring.

Score	Description
1	It will take a long time to examine and improve the business process, for whatever reason. This includes items like complexity, expected delays, uniqueness, lack of knowledgeable resources, and the number of employees involved in the work.
2	It will take an average amount of time to improve the business process.
3	The business process appears easy to improve. When the process seems simple and does not involve many people, you will sometimes hear this referred to as a "quick win."

Figure 2-14 Scores for Time to Market

▶ **Funding:** A lengthy approval cycle lowers the score because it adds time to the work. Figure 2-15 explains this scoring.

Score	Description
1	The business process requires significant funding.
2	The business process requires a reasonable amount of money that will not include a long approval cycle.
3	The business process requires little or no money.

Figure 2-15 Scores for Funding

▶ **Timing of Next Cycle:** The more frequently the business process is used, or if the process will be used soon (for cyclical processes), the higher the score will be because it becomes more critical to improve this business process sooner than others. Figure 2-16 explains the scoring logic.

Score	Description
1	The process is a cyclical one, and the timing of the next cycle for the business process is far out.
2	The process is a cyclical one, and the timing of the next cycle is not too close and not too far away.
3	The timing of the next cycle appears imminent or the process is an ongoing one.

Figure 2-16   Scores for Timing of Next Cycle

Now that we have defined the implementation scale, Figure 2-17 shows the updated process prioritization table, with the scale and scores from the Implementation category added for the two business process examples. Notice in Figure 2-17 that the budget process now has the higher total score of 13 at this point, assuming the following:

▶ It will take considerable time to work on the salary planning process because of its complexity and the number of people involved. (These considerations affect the time to market.)

▶ Technology will help improve both processes, but we assume that a software package to handle budgeting will not cost as much money as a tool to plan compensation. (This affects the funding criterion.)

▶ The annual process for salary planning has just ended. (Thus the timing of the next cycle is affected.)

▶ The budgeting process is ongoing because of the different pay programs available throughout the year. (Again, the timing of the next cycle is affected.)

As these assumptions show, any of the scores can change based on the evaluation of the criteria.

Process	Impact		Implementation			Current State			Value	
	Number Affected	Client Level	Time to Market	Funding	Timing of Next Cycle	Customer/ Client Satisfaction	Pain Level	Process Exists?	Benefit/ Return	Total Score
	3 = large number 2 = average number 1 = small number	3 = senior 2 = management 1 = other	3 = short 2 = average 1 = long	3 = small 2 = medium 1 = large	3 = close/ongoing 2 = intermediate 1 = far	3 = low 2 = medium 1 = high	3 = high 2 = medium 1 = low	1 = no 0 = yes	3 = high 2 = average 1 = low	
Salary Planning	3	2	1	1	1					8
Budget	1	3	3	3	3					13

Figure 2-17 Process Prioritization Table

Scaling for Category 3: Current State

The *Current State* category refers to how well the business process works for the customers/clients and for the internal department or area that owns the process. Figure 2-18 shows the scale for the *Current State* category.

	Current State	
Customer/Client Satisfaction	**Pain Level**	**Process Exists?**
3 = low 2 = medium 1 = high	3 = high 2 = medium 1 = low	1 = no 0 = yes

Figure 2-18 Current State Category

▶ **Customer/Client Satisfaction:** The more dissatisfied customers/clients appear to be with the existing business process, the greater the impact this score has and the higher the score it receives. Figure 2-19 reflects the scoring for this criterion.

Score	Description
1	Clients appear satisfied with how the business process works today.
2	Clients appear somewhat satisfied with how the business process works today.
3	Clients complain about how the business process works today.

Figure 2-19 Scores for Customer/Client Satisfaction

▶ **Pain Level:** Figure 2-20 shows that the higher the pain level for the department responsible for delivering the process results, the greater the need to increase efficiency and therefore the higher the score.

▶ **Process Exists?** This criterion simply states whether a formal process already exists, and Figure 2-21 defines this criterion.

Score	Description
1	The business process seems easy to implement and not cumbersome for the department to manage.
2	The business process requires an intermediate level of work.
3	The business process requires a significant effort because of the manual nature of the work.

Figure 2-20 Scores for Pain Level

Score	Description
0	A business process exists.
1	No documented business process exists.

Figure 2-21 Scores for Process Exists?

Figure 2-22 shows the scale and scores from the *Current State* category added to the process prioritization table, which continues to suggest that the budgeting process is the highest priority, since it has a total score of 20.

A review of the scores in the *Current State* category, shown in Figure 2-22, reveals that:

➤ The budgeting process has lower *Customer/Client Satisfaction*.

➤ The *Pain Level* appears the same for both business processes.

➤ Because the budget process does not have a formal process in place today, it receives a higher score. One can assume that this fact probably contributed to the poor *Customer/Client Satisfaction* score.

Scaling for Category 4: Value

The final category, *Value*, refers to economic, personal, or cultural value, and Figure 2-23 shows the relevant scale.

Process	Impact		Implementation			Current State			Value	
	Number Affected	Client Level	Time to Market	Funding	Timing of Next Cycle	Customer/ Client Satisfaction	Pain Level	Process Exists?	Benefit/ Return	Total Score
	3 = large number 2 = average number 1 = small number	3 = senior 2 = management 1 = other	3 = short 2 = average 1 = long	3 = small 2 = medium 1 = large	3 = close/ongoing 2 = intermediate 1 = far	3 = low 2 = medium 1 = high	3 = high 2 = medium 1 = low	1 = no 0 = yes	3 = high 2 = average 1 = low	
Salary Planning	3	2	1	1	1	2	3	0		13
Budget	1	3	3	3	3	3	3	1		20

Figure 2-22 Process Prioritization Table

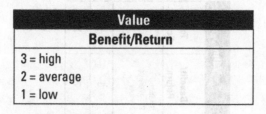

Value
Benefit/Return
3 = high
2 = average
1 = low

Figure 2-23 Value Category

▶ **Benefit/Return:** The more perceived value that the organization expects to obtain from an improvement effort, the higher the score. Figure 2-24 shows the explanation for this criterion.

Score	Description
1	The business process will deliver little expected value once improved.
2	The business process will deliver an average expected value once improved.
3	The business process will deliver a high expected value once improved.

Figure 2-24 Scores for Benefit/Return

Figure 2-25 shows the scale and scores for the *Value* category added to the process prioritization table. The scores listed for *Value* presume that the organization gains a higher value from improving the salary planning process because streamlining the process saves labor.

Figure 2-25 also shows the total score for each business process. After adding all the criteria scores together, we can see that the budgeting process has a higher *Total Score* (22) than the salary planning process (16). Once you complete this analysis on your process inventory, you immediately know where to focus your improvement efforts. In our example, completing this analysis shows that the budgeting process should come first, for the following reasons:

Process	Impact		Implementation			Current State			Value	
	Number Affected	Client Level	Time to Market	Funding	Timing of Next Cycle	Customer/ Client Satisfaction	Pain Level	Process Exists?	Benefit/ Return	Total Score
	3 = large number 2 = average number 1 = small number	3 = senior 2 = management 1 = other	3 = short 2 = average 1 = long	3 = small 2 = medium 1 = large	3 = close/ongoing 2 = intermediate 1 = far	3 = low 2 = medium 1 = high	3 = high 2 = medium 1 = low	1 = no 0 = yes	3 = high 2 = average 1 = low	
Salary Planning	3	2	1	1	1	2	3	0	3	16
Budget	1	3	3	3	3	3	3	1	2	22

Figure 2-25 Process Prioritization Table

▶ The budgeting process affects the senior level of employees in the company (*Client Level*).

▶ The improvement appears simple to design and implement (*Time to Market*).

▶ It requires minimal investment (*Funding*).

▶ The process is used throughout the year (*Timing of Next Cycle*).

▶ Both the clients (*Customer/Client Satisfaction*) and the department (*Pain Level*) do not appear happy with the process at the existing time.

▶ No formal process exists (*Process Exists?*).

Notice that much of the differentiation between the two processes comes from the Implementation category, suggesting that the budgeting process is more feasible to begin with than the salary planning process. The salary planning process received more significant scores than the budgeting process on only two criteria: *Number Affected* and *Benefit/Return*.

At this point, we have created the process inventory, developed prioritization categories, and defined how to measure the categories by introducing criteria and a scale. What happens now if your colleagues or sponsors criticize your approach because they feel that the return on investment should receive a higher weight than some of the other categories? In such a case, simply apply weighting to the prioritization categories.

Applying Weighting

To apply a weight to a category in the process prioritization table, start by deciding the importance of the category to the final result. Apply more weight to a category that you feel has a greater impact than another category. For example, make the score for the *Impact* category contribute more to the *Total Score* by giving it a higher weight than one of the other categories.

If you decide to apply weighting, assign a weight to each category on a scale of 1 to 100. Decide which is the most valuable category, then decide where each of the other categories falls with respect to that most valuable one: half as valuable, a third, and so forth. Assign weights so that the total of all categories equal 100. For example, if we decided to apply a weight to the four general categories, we might use the following weights:

▶ 35 percent for the Impact category

▶ 30 percent for the Implementation category

▶ 20 percent for the Current State category

▶ 15 percent for the Value category

In this example, I defined the *Impact* category as the most important, giving it 35 percent out of a possible 100 percent. Using these percentages, Figure 2-26 shows the addition of a *Subtotal* column for each category in the process prioritization table and a new *Total Weighted Score* column at the far right. (You will find it easier to calculate the weights if you use a spreadsheet application like Microsoft Excel.) To modify Figure 2-26, I created a formula in the *Total Weighted Score* column that applied the appropriate weights for each subtotal column and that added all the subtotals together to determine the total weighted score for each business process. Figure 2-27 shows the calculation for the salary planning process.

You can choose to show the weighted score for each category in the table by adding another column after each subtotal column or just include the formula as part of the spreadsheet cell, as I did in this example. Figure 2-28 shows the formula if you use Microsoft Excel. Cell O5 in this figure shows the formula as:

$$= (D5*(35\%)) + (H5*(30\%)) + (L5*(20\%)) + (N5*(15\%))$$

Notice that, even after applying weighting, the budgeting process still surfaces as the most important business process to address first.

You can also decide to spread the weight further across the criteria in a category. For example, I could have split the 30 percent weighting for the *Implementation* category as follows:

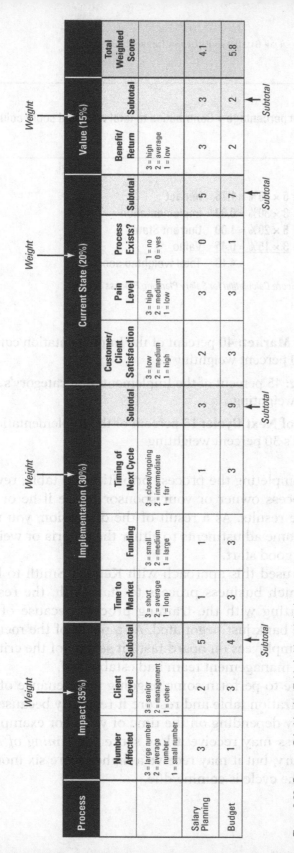

Process	Impact (35%)			Implementation (30%)				Current State (20%)				Value (15%)		Total Weighted Score
	Number Affected (3 = large number, 2 = average number, 1 = small number)	Client Level (3 = senior, 2 = management, 1 = other)	Subtotal	Time to Market (3 = short, 2 = average, 1 = long)	Funding (3 = small, 2 = medium, 1 = large)	Timing of Next Cycle (3 = close/ongoing, 2 = intermediate, 1 = far)	Subtotal	Customer/Client Satisfaction (3 = low, 2 = medium, 1 = high)	Pain Level (3 = high, 2 = medium, 1 = low)	Process Exists? (1 = no, 0 = yes)	Subtotal	Benefit/Return (3 = high, 2 = average, 1 = low)	Subtotal	
Salary Planning	3	2	5	1	1	1	3	2	3	0	5	3	3	4.1
Budget	1	3	4	3	1	3	9	3	3	1	7	2	2	5.8

Figure 2-26 Process Prioritization Table (with weights)

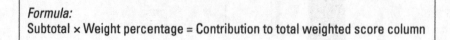

Formula:
Subtotal × Weight percentage = Contribution to total weighted score column

Example:

$$5 \times 35\% = 1.75 \quad \text{Impact}$$
$$3 \times 30\% = 0.90 \quad \text{Implementation}$$
$$5 \times 20\% = 1.00 \quad \text{Current State}$$
$$\underline{3 \times 15\% = 0.45} \quad \text{Value}$$
$$4.10 \quad \text{Total weighted score}$$

Figure 2-27 Weighted Score Calculation for Salary Planning Process

► **Time to Market:** 40 percent of the Implementation category's 30 percent weighting

► **Funding:** 45 percent of the Implementation category's 30 percent weighting

► **Timing of Next Cycle:** 15 percent of the Implementation category's 30 percent weighting

After completing the process prioritization table, review it with the process owner or your sponsor to see if he or she agrees with the results. As a result of the discussion, you may have to make some adjustments to either the criteria or weight, but you have a good start.

When I used this approach with Kendall Smith to help him decide which business process to start with, the results pointed to starting with the training process because of the acquisition the bank just negotiated. As a result of the merger, bringing new employees on board fast hit several of the criteria that he and his management team had established.

You have to perform some ongoing maintenance of the process prioritization table and rescore it regularly because the scores may vary depending on the time of year. For example, a business process may receive a low score for *Timing of Next Cycle* in February, but it may receive a higher score six months later because the cycle is coming due.

O5 f_x = (D5*(35%))+(H5*(30%))+(L5*(20%))+(N5*(15%))

A	B	C	D	E	F	G	H	I	J	K	L	M	N	O
	Impact (35%)			Implementation (30%)				Current State (20%)				Value (15%)		
	Number Affected	Client Level	Sub-total	Time to Market	Funding	Timing of Next Cycle	Sub-total	Customer/Client Satisf.	Pain Level	Process Exists?	Sub-total	Benefit/Return	Sub-total	Total Score
	3=large # 2=average # 1=small #	3=senior 2=mgmt 1=other		3=short 2=average 1=long	3=small 2=medium 1=large	3=close/ongoing 2=interm. 1=far		3=low 2=medium 1=high	3=high 2=medium 1=low	1=no 0=yes		3=high 1=low		
Salary Planning	3	2	5	1	1	3	3	3	3	0	5	3	3	4.1
Budgeting	1	3	4	3	3	3	9	3	3	1	7	2	2	5.3

Figure 2-28 Formula Example for Weighting

Chapter Summary: Step 1

Building the process inventory organizes the business process work and demonstrates to the process owner or your sponsor that you understand the business. The process owner and sponsor may or may not be the same person. I use *sponsor* to simplify the discussion. The process inventory assists you in assessing how big a job you have on your hands, and it provides a tool to discuss the overall breadth of business processes. Your sponsor will probably add or subtract from the process inventory; so think of the inventory as a vehicle to encourage discussion between you and your sponsor.

After developing the business process inventory, identifying the prioritization categories, establishing criteria, developing a scale, and applying these items to each business process, you now have clear direction on where to start your improvement efforts. You can add more prioritization criteria to the four general categories of Impact, Implementation, Current State, and Value to meet your needs.

After applying the prioritization criteria to the process inventory, you have another occasion to discuss a meaningful topic with your sponsor. If the results do not reflect what the sponsor considers of utmost importance, determine why your work and the sponsor's viewpoint seem disconnected, and decide whether you have to change the criteria, scale, or weighting. Validate that you and your sponsor agree on the priorities before beginning any process improvement work.

Time Estimate

To help plan the time that it takes to work through this step, Figure 2-29 summarizes the time you should allow to complete the process inventory and process prioritization table.

Build the Business Process Inventory

Start by listing any business processes identified either from your own knowledge or from your sponsor's knowledge.

Event	Time	Purpose
Build the business process inventory.	90 minutes	■ List business processes.
Sponsor meeting.	15 minutes	■ Gain approval on the list of business processes and how you grouped them. ■ Obtain preliminary insight on prioritization criteria.
Establish categories, criteria, scale, weighting.	90 minutes	■ Identify categories and criteria. ■ Determine the scale for each criterion. ■ Determine weighting, if appropriate.
Complete process prioritization table.	4 hours	■ Apply criteria, scale, and weight to each process listed in the process inventory.
Sponsor meeting.	45 minutes	■ Gain approval on the process prioritization table results.

Figure 2-29   Time Estimate—Step 1: Develop Process Inventory

Then talk to other employees in the department or area about what they do, and translate their work into business processes. You can discover a lot of information by looking at an organization chart. If you work as an internal consultant in a company, talk to your colleagues instead of asking for job descriptions. Job descriptions can make the work seem more formal to people, and, at this point, all you want to do is build the process inventory.

Sponsor Meeting

Meet briefly with the sponsor to verify that he or she agrees with the business processes listed. If you grouped the processes around themes, validate that the sponsor agrees with the themes. You should also gain a sense at this point as to whether the sponsor has any ideas about the prioritization criteria. Share the criteria you plan to include, and get a sense as to whether the sponsor feels you are on track. This helps with the next step and shows the sponsor what to expect next.

Establish Categories, Criteria, Scale, Weighting

Think about the Impact, Implementation, Current State, and Value categories. Then, after your discussion with the spon-

sor, decide whether you want to add categories or change existing categories. Adjust the criteria under each category, add new
criteria, or delete some. Decide how your scale should work and
what weights to assign if you choose to use weighting.

Complete the Process Prioritization Table

During this time, build the table and score each business
process listed in the left-hand column of the table.

A Second Sponsor Meeting

Review the results of the prioritization with the sponsor
and ask whether he or she expected the results shown. Have a
thorough discussion to ensure that you both agree on the priorities of the work.

What You Have Achieved

In this chapter, you have achieved the following:

▶ An understanding of the business because you see the business processes that a company or department is responsible
for delivering

▶ A grasp of what the organization deems important because
you identified and applied criteria to determine priorities

▶ Buy-in from the sponsor on the business processes to work
on first, second, and third

▶ And most important, the *power* to know where to focus your
time

KNOWLEDGE CHECK

Use this knowledge check to validate your understanding of the
material covered in step 1.

Match the correct answer to the statement by placing the
appropriate letter on the blank line.

_____1. How you to build a process inventory

A. Volume or number affected

_____2. A criterion under the Impact category

B. Scale

_____3. Time required to move through the ten steps

C. To set priorities and know where to start with BPI

_____4. Efficiency of the existing process according to the business

D. Talk to colleagues, read job descriptions, review department work

_____5. Measurement scheme used to quantify (or evaluate) criteria

E. To identify and organize business processes

_____6. Importance of a criterion

F. Value

_____7. The reason to create a process inventory

G. Weight

_____8. The reason to build a prioritization table

H. Time to market

_____9. Benefit delivered by a business process

I. Current state

1-D, 2-A, 3-H, 4-I, 5-B, 6-G, 7-E, 8-C, 9-F

Answers

CHAPTER 3

Step 2: Establish the Foundation

Avoiding Scope Creep

Pete Hodges, regional sales manager for a computer parts distributor, expressed concern that his company's sales process did not generate enough new customers and that the overall process took too long. When I spoke with Pete and his sales team, each defined the problem a little differently. Pete identified the problem as closing the sale, one district sales manager cited identifying the customer needs as the issue, and the sales representatives said they did not have enough leads.

How do you decide whom to believe? Pete asked me to look at their sales process from beginning to end, but how would an outsider begin to determine where their sales process starts and ends? I knew that I had to start by identifying the boundaries because the sales process may vary with every company. I also felt that I had to understand how they measure success, or, put another way, how would they know if their sales process is successful? They could define success as the number of new clients, as achieving a certain sales volume, or as something else entirely. I needed to establish a foundation that Pete and I could agree on so that we would start out on the same page.

As an analogy, think about building a house. What do you do first? Most people either hire an architect to help with the design or find an existing house plan they like. By starting with the design, you know the size of the house and have some idea of how much it will cost to build. A blueprint provides your contractor with step-by-step specifications to follow throughout the building process.

The *scope definition document* guides you through the exercise of establishing the foundation for a business process. It becomes your blueprint. Once you develop the process inventory described in Chapter 2, and once you decide on the business process to focus on first, this document provides the baseline information you need about that particular business process. It guides you throughout your business process improvement effort. Step 2 is the most important of the ten steps, and you should never skip it.

In an ideal world, you would start out by creating a contract to establish a clear definition of what *is* and *is not* included in a BPI effort. Because we do not live in an ideal world, the scope definition document provides you with the next best way to keep the work on track. It serves the same purpose as a contract because it establishes boundaries, but it does so in a manner that appears far less intimidating to your colleagues, an important point when working as an internal consultant in your company. When you work with an external customer, as I did with Pete Hodges, it clarifies the scope of work similar to a statement of work, a common tool used by customers and vendors.

Taking the time to set the foundation helps to prevent *scope creep*, a risk in many projects. Scope creep is veering away from the original purpose of the work without an increase in time, resources, or money. If you have ever built a house, then you have probably experienced scope creep. It occurs when you make changes after the contractor has started construction. Any change, such as adding an additional light fixture or changing the location of the stove, increases the cost of the house beyond what you originally agreed to pay.

Scope creep appears as a common problem in many areas of business. A software development company that I did work for shared a concern that their product development process took too long. It quickly became obvious that the continual addition of new functionality added throughout the design and development process was the root cause of the problem. Although the new, additional functionality added to the value of the software product, it also increased the time and resources required to develop the product, thereby adding to the cost of the end product and increasing the time to market.

In business process work, scope creep weaves its way in because new ideas, demands, and needs surface as you get into the work, and the temptation is to continually expand the scope of a business process. Let me share an example.

At one company where I worked and acted as an internal consultant, a simple human error led to an embarrassing predicament at the company's executive level. After senior management chastised and embarrassed the department responsible for the error, I came in to work with them over the next six weeks to examine their business processes in order to ensure that internal controls existed. Internal controls, as we will see in Chapter 7, help minimize human errors.

I started by compiling the process inventory, described in Chapter 2, and discovered that the department had 22 business processes, far too many to evaluate in a six-week period. After convincing senior management that we should concentrate on one business process per week, we agreed that we would focus our attention on six key business processes. I started by working with the project team to develop the scope definition document for the union negotiation process, one of the business processes we would examine over the ensuing six weeks. After completing the document, I reviewed it with the sponsor and gained her agreement on the content.

Partway through the work, a project team member identified a missing subprocess and wanted to go back and include it in the scope definition. My evaluation showed that doing so would introduce a major increase in scope and add at least another 40 hours of work, placing my commitment to the six-week schedule at risk. My evaluation convinced me that the subprocess did not represent an important element and did not warrant further expense or delay—but now I had to persuade the sponsor of my assessment.

I asked the sponsor if she felt the subprocess was important enough to:

1. Eliminate one of the remaining business processes that I had committed to complete in the six-week time frame.
2. Note the omission but remain on track to complete the remaining business processes on time.
3. Or extend the six-week timeframe to seven weeks.

The sponsor made the decision to stay on schedule because she agreed with my assessment that the subprocess's impact did not add significant risk and that the important consideration was to complete the remaining business processes.

As you can see, the sponsor owned making the decision, not me. I easily moved the responsibility for the decision to the sponsor for several reasons: We had clearly defined the process boundaries and responsibilities when we developed the foundation, the scope did not include the subprocess, and we had just determined that the subprocess did not introduce major risk. If the sponsor had not approved the scope definition document, we could have had a different situation, with scope creep rearing its ugly head.

In building the scope definition document, I find it emerges as a combination of the current and future state. For example, what the process does today and tomorrow is most likely the same, but the "customer needs" you define should focus on the future, especially if you have not validated them in over a year. The measurements of success should also focus on the future because you want to know how you will define success in the future state.

The Eight Sections of the Scope Definition Document

Now let us take a look at a completed scope definition document for the human resource processes of a computer company I worked with, a company I will call Alistar Corporation (because of the proprietary nature of the work). Figure 3-1 shows the completed scope definition for their compensation department's budget process. I will discuss each of the eight sections of the scope definition document in detail.

Process Name :   Budget Process

Process Owner :   Samantha Jones

Client :   President's Direct Reports

Description (purpose):

To develop and manage the compensation budget, which is based on a fiscal year (July through June). The process covers the funding and ongoing spending of the following compensation programs:

- Executive compensation
- Manager and professional compensation
- Office hourly compensation
- Variable pay awards
- Open positions

Scope (boundaries):

Start   Creating the business case for the annual budget

End   Year-end summary to corporate headquarters

Hourly compensation for plant workers is specifically *excluded* from the budget process.

Customer/client needs:

- "On demand" status of budget balances (including amounts spent, planned, and remaining)
- Ability to plan additional compensation in order to support pay-related needs throughout the year

Key stakeholders and interests:

Corporate headquarters	Accurate record of spending; compelling business case for budget proposal
Other executives (beyond president's direct reports)	Appropriate salary increases for their employees

Measurements of success:

1. "On demand" knowledge for the president's direct reports of their budget balances (the right information at the right time)
2. A process viewed as a reliable tool for use in employee-related activities like planning promotions and developing succession plans
3. Accurate tracking of spending
4. The ability to make better decisions on allocating funds

Process responsibilities:

1. Develop the business case for the annual budget.
2. Allocate the funds for each of the individual compensation programs.
3. Manage the budget balances.
4. Report ongoing spending to executives.
5. Ensure data integrity.

Figure 3-1 Scope Definition Document

Section 1: Process Name

This is the name of the business process, such as the hiring process, the sales process, the *budget process*, the software development process. For the Alistar Corporation it is the budget process, shown in Figure 3-2.

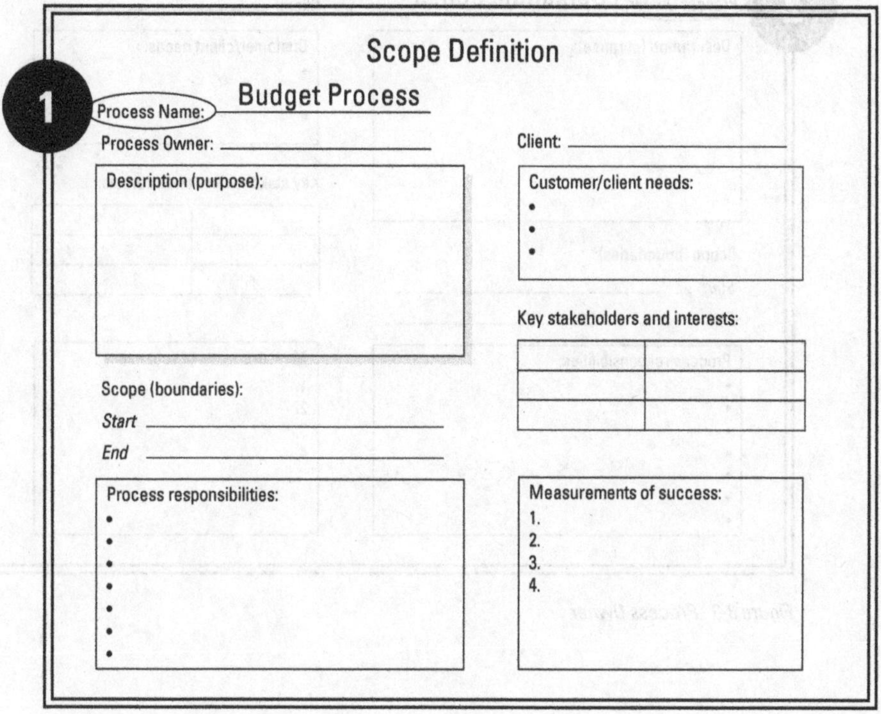

Figure 3-2 Process Name

Section 2: Process Owner

This is the person responsible for the overall process, no matter where he or she sits in the company. Many business processes cut across multiple departments, and you have to identify the *one* person who has ultimate responsibility for the process. The process owner has the authority to review and agree to your scope definition. This person may often be your sponsor, but not always. As shown in Figure 3-3, the process owner for the Alistar Corporation example is *Samantha Jones*.

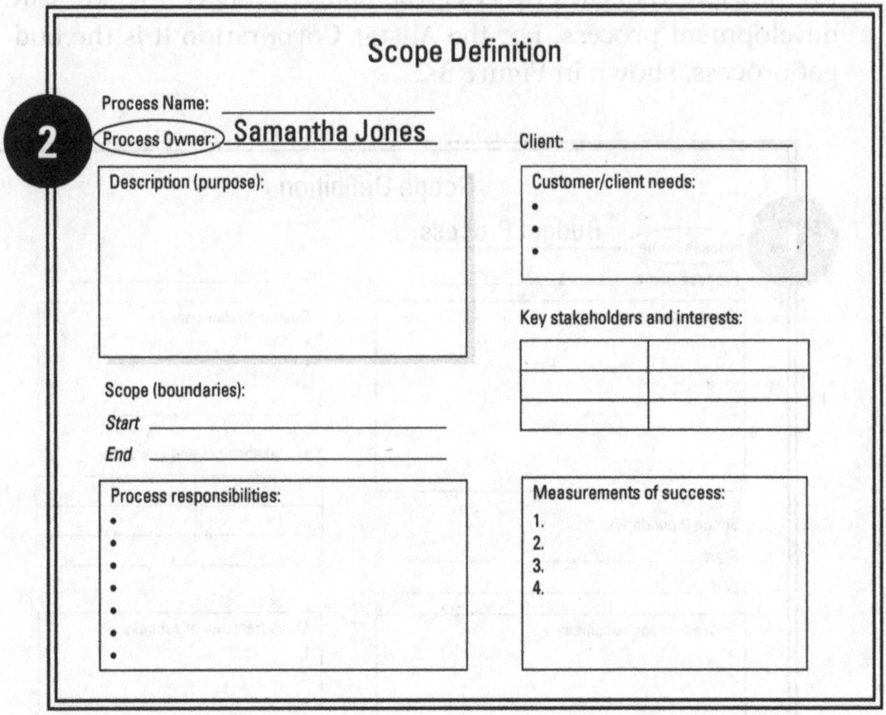

Scope Definition

Process Name: _____

② Process Owner: **Samantha Jones**   Client: _____

Description (purpose):

Customer/client needs:
-
-
-

Key stakeholders and interests:

Scope (boundaries):

Start _____

End _____

Process responsibilities:
-
-
-
-
-
-
-

Measurements of success:
1.
2.
3.
4.

Figure 3-3 Process Owner

Section 3: Description

This is the definition or purpose of the process. Think of how to explain the process to a person new or unfamiliar with it.

This third section may seem simple, but my experience says that you will spend considerable time defining the business process in Figure 3-4. While you will define the scope in the fourth section, you should identify anything specifically out of scope as you write the process description in the third section.

Figure 3-5 shows an example of a description for Alistar Corporation's compensation budget process. You can see that

```
┌─────────────────────────────────────────────────────────────┐
│ ┌───────────────────────────────────────────────────────────┐ │
│ │                    Scope Definition                        │ │
│ │  Process Name: _____                         │ │
│ │  Process Owner: _____    Client: _____  │ │
│ │  ┌──────────────────────────┐   ┌──────────────────────┐   │ │
│ │  │ Description (purpose):    │   │ Customer/client needs:│   │ │
│ │  │                           │   │ •                    │   │ │
│ │  │         (3)               │   │ •                    │   │ │
│ │  │                           │   │ •                    │   │ │
│ │  │                           │   └──────────────────────┘   │ │
│ │  │                           │   Key stakeholders and interests: │ │
│ │  └──────────────────────────┘   ┌──────────────────────┐   │ │
│ │  Scope (boundaries):            │                      │   │ │
│ │  Start _____     │                      │   │ │
│ │  End   _____     │                      │   │ │
│ │  ┌──────────────────────────┐   ┌──────────────────────┐   │ │
│ │  │ Process responsibilities: │   │ Measurements of success:│ │
│ │  │ •                         │   │ 1.                   │   │ │
│ │  │ •                         │   │ 2.                   │   │ │
│ │  │ •                         │   │ 3.                   │   │ │
│ │  │ •                         │   │ 4.                   │   │ │
│ │  │ •                         │   │                      │   │ │
│ │  │ •                         │   │                      │   │ │
│ │  └──────────────────────────┘   └──────────────────────┘   │ │
│ └───────────────────────────────────────────────────────────┘ │
└─────────────────────────────────────────────────────────────┘
```

Figure 3-4 Description

the scope *includes* five types of compensation programs and *excludes* one program (plant worker compensation). You can also see that the budget process includes two key areas:

1. The *funding* of compensation programs (how much money goes to each program). For example, if an 8 percent budget is received from headquarters, what percentage of that amount goes to each of the compensation programs (e.g., the executive compensation fund versus the office hourly compensation fund).
2. The tracking of *ongoing spending* throughout the calendar year.

One employee group intentionally omitted from this process consists of the hourly employees who work in the company's plant locations. The reasons they are excluded can vary,

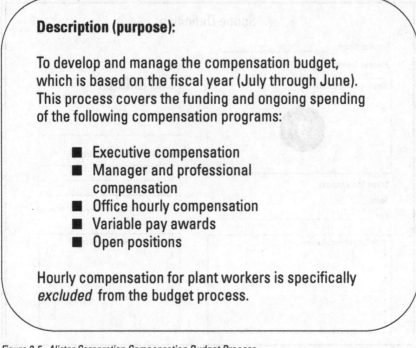

Description (purpose):

To develop and manage the compensation budget,
which is based on the fiscal year (July through June).
This process covers the funding and ongoing spending
of the following compensation programs:

- Executive compensation
- Manager and professional compensation
- Office hourly compensation
- Variable pay awards
- Open positions

Hourly compensation for plant workers is specifically
excluded from the budget process.

Figure 3-5   Alistar Corporation Compensation Budget Process

possibly because the funding comes from a different source or
because a union contract or labor law drives their pay increases.

The importance of getting the process description correct will become clear as the work progresses because you will
find yourself and others referring to this definition time and
time again as you create the process map. You may find it a
challenging exercise to write the description, especially if the
project team members have never done this kind of work. Like
most people, they may instinctively know about a process but
have a difficult time explaining it to someone else.

When writing process descriptions, you may need to:

- ▶ Use unusual or technical terms in your description.
- ▶ Emphasize areas that are out of scope.
- ▶ Further define a term by giving examples.

The following scenarios cover these three situations, and these examples should help you to write clear and easy-to-understand process descriptions.

Scenario 1: Unusual or Technical Terms

Figure 3-6 shows a process description that contains one unfamiliar term (development promotions) and one unusual application of another term (client requests), so the description includes a further explanation of these terms. The first footnote in the figure defines a *development promotion* because it is different from a regular promotion. A development promotion means movement within the same job family. For example, the financial analyst job family is a typical job family in a company's finance department. It may consist of three levels:

1. Financial analyst 1
2. Financial analyst 2
3. Financial analyst 3

Description (purpose):

This process covers:

Planned development promotions[1]
Unplanned salary adjustments based on client requests[2]

1   Development promotions are movements within a job family. There are typically two or more levels of the same type of job in a job family, with each level having increasing scope and responsibilities. Examples include:

- Financial analyst
- Human resource managers
- Engineers
- Programmers

2   Client requests, in this context, include only the following situations: retention adjustments, counteroffers, and unplanned projects.

Figure 3-6 Salary Adjustment Process

A financial analyst at each of these levels performs the same basic job, but the overall responsibility or scope and the pay range increase with each level. An employee moves from one level to the next through a series of development promotions without moving to a new job. The definition has to include an explanation of development promotions because they are paid for from a different budget than that used for regular promotions, which occur when an employee moves to a totally new job.

Defining terminology such as *development promotion* becomes important if the words seem technical in nature or if they can have different meanings to different people. When a 9-year-old says her blouse is cool, she probably means she will wear it; when a 90-year-old says her blouse is cool, she probably means that she is freezing. To minimize confusion, you should continually listen for such words and clarify them when appropriate.

How often have you found yourself thinking a word meant one thing, while someone else had a totally opposite understanding of it? This becomes more of a problem when you work for a global company whose employees reside in different countries.

At the Entertainment Park Group, another company I consulted with (the case study in Chapter 14), I worked on their hiring process. The global project team quickly became confused by the following terms: job seeker, applicant, qualified person, and candidate. To the members of the U.S.-based project team, the terms meant the same thing and could be used interchangeably. To the non-U.S. project team members, the terms had very different meanings, with each term denoting a change in the status of a person applying for a job.

From the non-U.S. team's perspective:

► A job seeker *may* turn into an applicant.
► An applicant *may* turn into a qualified person.
► A qualified person *may* turn into a candidate.

From that point on, each term had the same meaning to everyone. You want to ensure that everyone understands the terminology in use before moving to step 3, mapping the process, to minimize confusion and keep the work moving smoothly.

So spend some time defining the terminology that you use while developing the process description. Gaining agreement on what a word means can be more important than whether it is technically accurate. You do not want someone months later saying, "Well, that's not what I meant when I said 'candidate.'" That kind of comment only places your work in question.

Scenario 2: Areas Out of Scope

If you feel that people need to understand that certain aspects of a process are out of scope, you should explicitly say so in the description. Figure 3-7 shows an example of a process description that intentionally excludes four types of employees. In this example, everyone may not understand the term *downgrade*, and you may have to further define it, as we did in scenario 1 for the term *development promotion*.

Scenario 3: Providing Examples

If confusion occurs around a term, Figure 3-8 shows another option to clarify what you mean by providing examples. In this figure, you can see that I clarified the employees *eligible* for a recognition bonus award.

You can use either footnotes or an asterisk to define specific terms. If you need to define only one term, as in Figure 3-8, an asterisk works fine. If more than one term requires defining, as in Figure 3-6, footnotes are more appropriate for distinguishing between multiple terms.

Section 4: Scope

Scope is the breadth or area covered by a process. It sets the boundaries for the entire process and establishes the start and end points for the business process, as shown in Figure 3-9.

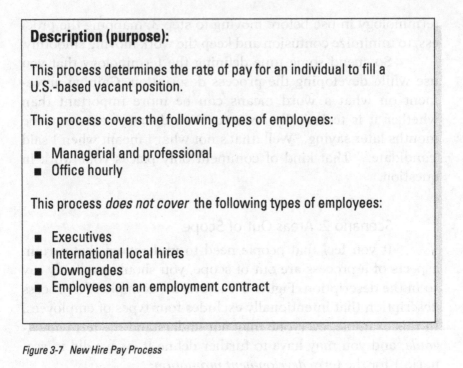

Description (purpose):

This process determines the rate of pay for an individual to fill a U.S.-based vacant position.

This process covers the following types of employees:

- Managerial and professional
- Office hourly

This process *does not cover* the following types of employees:

- Executives
- International local hires
- Downgrades
- Employees on an employment contract

Figure 3-7 New Hire Pay Process

Description (purpose):

This process is a cash reward program to recognize outstanding contributions beyond an eligible* employee's regular responsibilities.

*Eligible employees include:

- All managerial and professional employees *not* eligible for any other bonus program.
- All office hourly employees.

Figure 3-8 Recognition Bonus Award Process

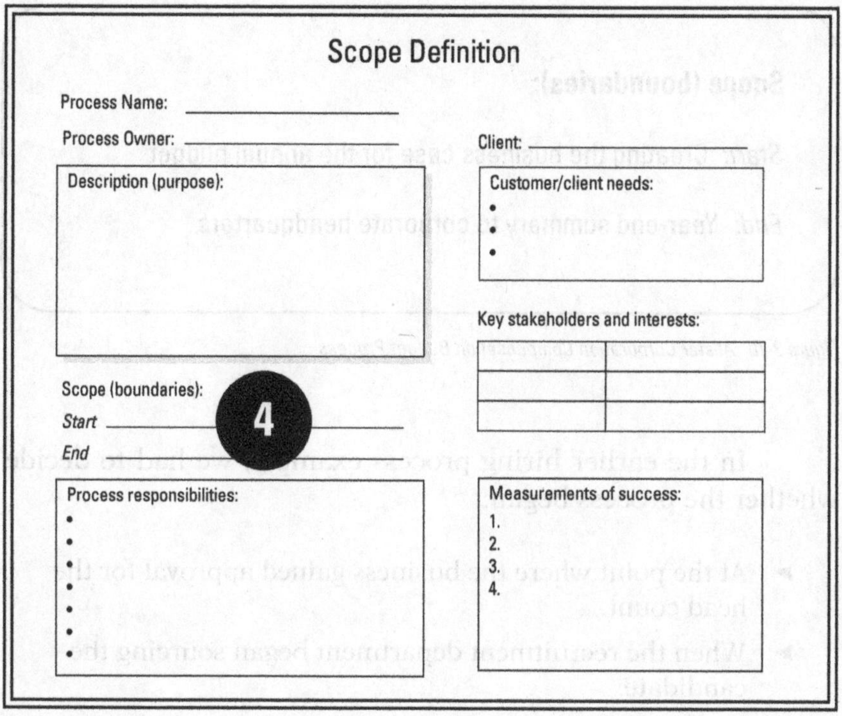

Scope Definition

Process Name: _____

Process Owner: _____   Client: _____

Description (purpose):

Customer/client needs:
-
-
-

Key stakeholders and interests:

Scope (boundaries):

Start _____

End _____

Process responsibilities:
-
-
-
-
-
-

Measurements of success:
1.
2.
3.
4.

Figure 3-9 Scope

Starting Point

In the Pete Hodges case, we defined the starting point as generating leads. We could have made the start of the process establishing sale quotas, but after some discussion we decided to leave quotas as a separate process. We decided to keep the sales process focused on activities that the sales rep had control over.

In our Alistar compensation budget process example in Figure 3-10, the process starts with creating the business case to justify a specific budget from corporate headquarters, because headquarters has the responsibility for making the budgeting (or funding) decisions. This means that the process starts long before any money is spent or tracked. The decision to start the business process at this point makes the process a bit more complicated than simply tracking spending.

Scope (boundaries):

Start: Creating the business case for the annual budget

End: Year-end summary to corporate headquarters

Figure 3-10 Alistar Corporation Compensation Budget Process

In the earlier hiring process example, we had to decide whether the process began:

► At the point where the business gained approval for the head count.
► When the recruitment department began sourcing the candidate.
► When the hiring manager selected the candidate.
► Or when the company hired the employee.

By simply reading the name of the process, the hiring process, you might say "when the company hires the employee." In our case, we began the process at the second point, when the recruitment department sourced the candidate.

Ending Point

In our compensation budget process example, the process ends after the compensation department completes a report at the end of the fiscal year for corporate headquarters that shows the total dollars spent over the past year and where spending occurred by the compensation program.

There is no right or wrong answer to where a business process begins and ends. It all depends on the project team's discussion and the sponsor's approval of the process boundaries, so you can stay on track. The importance of setting boundaries will become evident when we move to step 3, mapping the process.

Section 5: Process Responsibilities

Figure 3-11 shows space for a list of the major tasks the business process must deliver, and it constitutes another opportunity to validate the scope of the process.

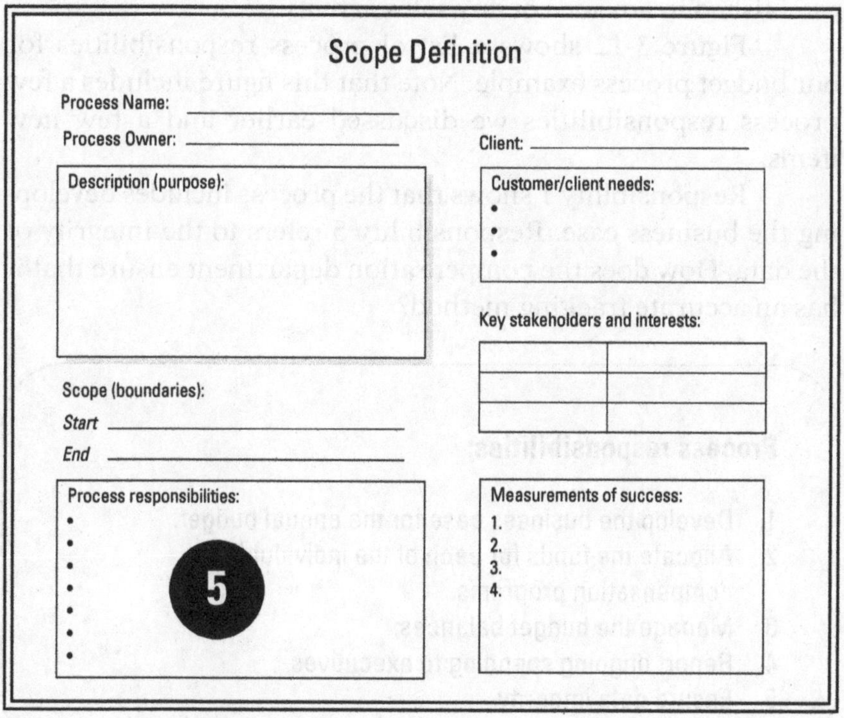

Scope Definition

Process Name: _____

Process Owner: _____

Client: _____

Description (purpose):

Customer/client needs:
•
•
•

Key stakeholders and interests:

Scope (boundaries):

Start _____

End _____

Process responsibilities:
•
•
•
•
•
•

5

Measurements of success:
1.
2.
3.
4.

Figure 3-11 Process Responsibilities

While the description section provides a narrative to explain the overall purpose of why the process exists, this section lists the major tasks taking place in the business process. The discussion of this section with the project team may cause you to go back and change either the description or scope that you already developed, and you should gladly make the changes. As people discuss the responsibilities of the business process, they naturally uncover new thoughts and ideas that you have to incorporate into the foundation so team members become more engaged and buy into the scope definition. You want to document any changes now rather than after you begin step 3.

In the sales process example, establishing sales quotas came up at this point. If Pete and I decided to include this as a process responsibility, we would have had to go back and change the starting point of the business process from generating leads to establishing sales quotas because sales quotas are established in advance of any sales activity.

Figure 3-12 shows a list of process responsibilities for our budget process example. Note that this figure includes a few process responsibilities we discussed earlier and a few new items.

Responsibility 1 shows that the process includes developing the business case. Responsibility 5 refers to the integrity of the data: How does the compensation department ensure that it has an accurate tracking method?

Process responsibilities:

1. Develop the business case for the annual budget.
2. Allocate the funds for each of the individual compensation programs.
3. Manage the budget balances.
4. Report ongoing spending to executives.
5. Ensure data integrity.

Figure 3-12 Alistar Corporation Compensation Budget Process

The process responsibilities section identifies everything included in a business process. For our budget process example, it is not just about managing the budget; it is much more. The process includes developing the business case, determining the budget allocation, defining the method to generate reports to keep executives apprised of ongoing spending, and a method to double-check the accuracy of the compensation department's work.

Section 6: Client and Client Needs

These two sections in Figure 3-13 identify the recipients of the outcome of the business process (the customers/clients) and what is important to them from the process (customer/client needs).

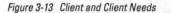

Scope Definition

Process Name: _____

Process Owner: _____   Client: _____   **6**

Description (purpose):   Customer/client needs:
                                               •
                                               •
                                               •

                                               Key stakeholders and interests:

Scope (boundaries):

Start _____

End _____

Process responsibilities: Measurements of success:
•   1.
•   2.
•   3.
•   4.
•
•

Figure 3-13 Client and Client Needs

When working as an internal consultant in your company, identifying the real client will challenge the project team members, who may incorrectly think of their boss or the sponsor as clients. Because the boss evaluates your performance and has the authority to give you a raise and because the sponsor has responsibility for the successful implementation of the business process improvement project, you naturally want to keep them both happy. Do not confuse them, however, with the client, and remember to define the value of the business process from the customer's or client's perspective and no one else's.

In our compensation budget process example, the clients are the half dozen senior-level executives who report directly to the president. As Figure 3-14 shows, they want to know at any point in time how much money they have spent on salary increases and how much they have remaining to spend. They also want assurance that sufficient money exists to reward employees throughout the year, especially when they want to promote an employee.

Client: President's direct reports

Client needs:

- On-demand status of budget balances (including amounts spent, planned, and remaining)
- Ability to plan additional compensation in order to support pay-related needs throughout the year

Figure 3-14 Alistar Corporation Compensation Budget Process

Section 7: Key Stakeholders and Interests

Although the customer/client is the main focus of business process improvement work, other areas or departments in a company can either affect a business process or receive the downstream effect of a business process. Figure 3-15 refers to the people in this group as *stakeholders*.

In addition to listing the groups affected by the business process, you should also identify what the stakeholders care about or where their interests in the business process lies. Figure 3-16 shows the stakeholders and what they care about in our compensation budget process example.

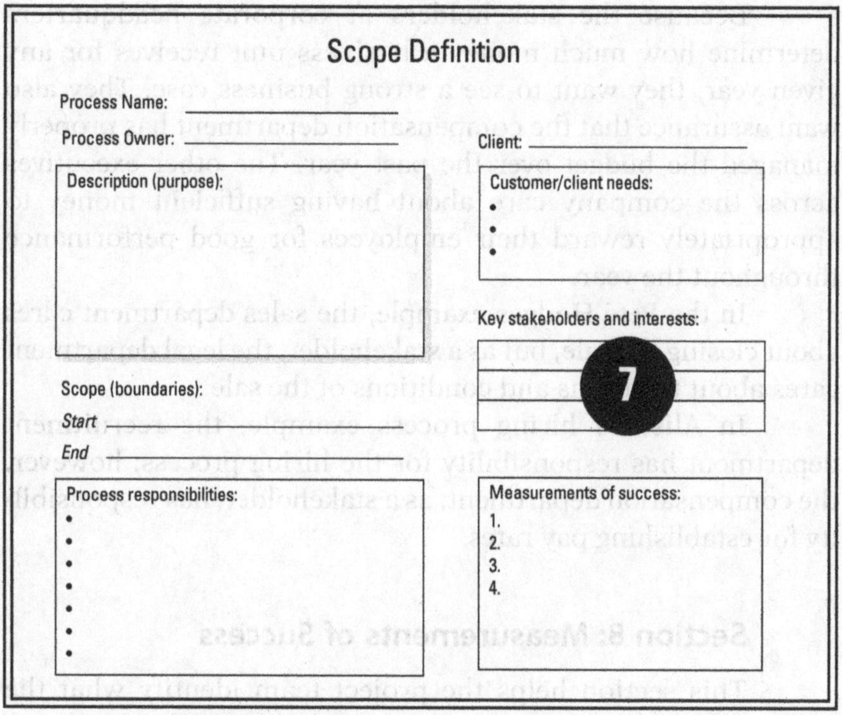

Scope Definition

Process Name: _____

Process Owner: _____   Client: _____

Description (purpose):

Customer/client needs:
-
-
-

Key stakeholders and interests:

7

Scope (boundaries):

Start _____

End _____

Process responsibilities:
-
-
-
-
-
-

Measurements of success:
1.
2.
3.
4.

Figure 3-15   Key Stakeholders and Interests

Key stakeholders and interests:

Corporate headquarters	Accurate record of spending; compelling business case for budget proposal.
Other executives (beyond president's direct reports)	Appropriate salary increases for their employees.

Figure 3-16   Alistar Corporation Compensation Budget Process

Because the stakeholders at corporate headquarters determine how much money a business unit receives for any given year, they want to see a strong business case. They also want assurance that the compensation department has properly managed the budget over the past year. The other executives across the company care about having sufficient money to appropriately reward their employees for good performance throughout the year.

In the Pete Hodges example, the sales department cares about closing the sale, but as a stakeholder, the legal department cares about the terms and conditions of the sale.

In Alistar's hiring process example, the recruitment department has responsibility for the hiring process; however, the compensation department, as a stakeholder, has responsibility for establishing pay rates.

Section 8: Measurements of Success

This section helps the project team identify what the organization should measure. The measurements of success, identified in Figure 3-17, should support the customer/client and stakeholder needs the project team defined as important.

You can also include internal requirements that a department may have for the business process. At this point, you do not have to worry about *how* to conduct the measurement; you just have to identify *what* you want to measure. Chapter 7 discusses how to develop the metrics.

As you can see from Figure 3-18, the first two measurements for our compensation budget process example relate back to the client needs, the third measurement supports both the client and stakeholder needs, and the fourth defines an internal metric for the compensation department.

Chapter Summary: Step 2

Discussing baseline information with the project team at the start of the first meeting allows everyone to have input and

Scope Definition

Process Name: _____

Process Owner: _____   Client: _____

Description (purpose):   Customer/client needs:
                                              •
                                              •
                                              •

                                              Key stakeholders and interests:

Scope (boundaries):

Start _____

End _____

Process responsibilities: Measurements of success:
•   1.
•   2.
•   3.
•   4.
•
•

8

Figure 3-17   Measurements of Success

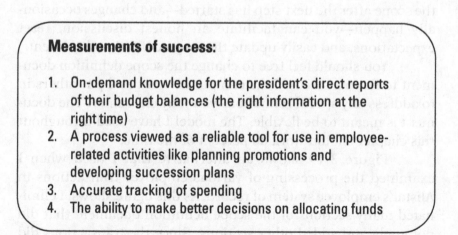

Measurements of success:

1. On-demand knowledge for the president's direct reports of their budget balances (the right information at the right time)
2. A process viewed as a reliable tool for use in employee-related activities like planning promotions and developing succession plans
3. Accurate tracking of spending
4. The ability to make better decisions on allocating funds

Figure 3-18   Alistar Corporation Compensation Budget Process assists the team in coming to a common understanding of the business process and any associated terminology. As you develop the scope definition document, remain flexible so that in the end you feel comfortable that everyone has had a chance to provide input to the scope of the work and that everyone understands what is and is not included in the business process. In my experience, involving people in developing or approving scope causes them to better respect and honor the agreements made. Never skip this step.

Once the project team has agreed on the content of the scope definition document, you have to review it with the sponsor and gain approval. The sponsor will appreciate the conciseness of the document, so keep it to a single piece of paper. You should view the scope definition as an easy read and a quick reference tool. The sponsor may want to make changes to the document after reviewing it or join your next meeting to discuss it with the project team. Either scenario works as long as the project team agrees with the proposed changes.

After everyone has reviewed and agreed to the scope definition document, you have a tool that works like a contract, one that you can revisit, as needed, to reinforce the agreements made. You should consider it "locked" to a certain extent. If you spent sufficient time developing the content in the document, you should expect minimal changes. If you do need to change the scope after the next step has started—and changes occasionally happen—you can facilitate an honest discussion, reset expectations, and easily update the scope definition document.

You should feel free to change the scope definition document to fit your needs. Take components out and put others in to address any specific situations you may encounter. The document is meant to be flexible. The model I have used throughout this chapter should work 80 percent of the time.

Figure 3-19 shows an alternative that I used when I examined the processing of various employee transactions in Alistar's employee system of record. As this figure shows, I eliminated many sections of the scope definition document that did not apply and added other sections. Since the transactions did not belong to a single business process, I deleted the process

Scope Definition
Employee Change Transactions

Key Stakeholders & Interests

Recruitment	Quick, accurate information. Filling the requisition in a timely manner. Processing the hire in a timely manner.
Compensation	Ensure the employee is paid correctly and is in the correct job. Ensure funding is available. Ensure that policy, if applicable, is followed.
Central Services	Completeness, timeliness, and accuracy of data.
Operations	Quick turnaround. Accurate information from compensation and central services.
Support Functions	Quick turnaround. Accurate information from compensation and central services.

Description (Purpose):

To ensure that the following key transactions are accurately processed in a timely manner for all employees:

• Hires	• Relevels
• Transfers	• Downgrades
• Promotions	• Status changes

Scope (Boundaries):

Start A candidate has accepted an offer.

End Employee system of record is updated.

Within Scope:
- Hiring an employee
- Transferring an employee
- Promoting an employee
- Releveling an employee
- Downgrading an employee
- Changing an employee's status (e.g., full time, part time)

Outside Scope:
- Approval for creating a position
- Candidate selection
- Executive pay
- Third-party employees
- Union negotiations

Figure 3-19 Alternative Scope Definition Document

name, process owner, process responsibilities, and the measurements of success sections of the template and adapted it for this specific case.

Time Estimate

To help plan the time that it takes to work through this step, Figure 3-20 summarizes the amount of time you should allow to complete the scope definition document.

Event	Time	Purpose
First project team meeting	90 minutes	■ Walk through roadmap (Chapter 1). ■ Complete scope definition document.
Sponsor meeting	30 minutes	■ Gain agreement on scope definition document.

Figure 3-20 Time Estimate—Step 2: Establish Foundation

First Project Team Meeting

The first project team meeting should allow sufficient time to walk through the roadmap, introduced in Chapter 1, so that the team can see how the journey will unfold. At this meeting you also lead the team through a thorough discussion of all the sections of the scope definition document.

Give the project team a blank copy of the scope definition document at the first meeting and facilitate a discussion to complete the document together as a team. You should keep track of the discussion during the meeting on a dry-erase board or electronic board, or use your laptop and project the content onto a screen to allow the participants to "see" the discussion as it unfolds and to keep them involved and interested in the work.

My preference is to use a dry-erase board because you do not have a barrier (your laptop) between you and the participants. I like to minimize the use of technology during a process meeting because it seems to put a filter between you and the team. You should stand during the creation of the scope definition document and visually write and edit the description on the board to engage the entire team. I like to use an electronic dry-erase board because it has the capability to either print a copy of the board contents by hitting a button or send the board contents to a computer. If you do not have an electronic dry-erase board, take a picture with your phone when done.

Sponsor Meeting

Before the initial project team meeting, you should have already scheduled time for a meeting with the sponsor for a date after the first meeting, where you will review the document and discuss any potential changes.

What You Have Achieved

In this chapter, you have achieved the following:

▶ A clear understanding of the business process you will start examining in step 3, mapping the process

▶ A common understanding of unusual terminology

▶ Buy-in from the sponsor on scope

▶ A pseudo contract—a document everyone believes in

▶ Most important, the *power* to keep scope creep at bay

KNOWLEDGE CHECK

Use this knowledge check to validate your understanding of the material covered in step 2. Answer True or False to the following questions.

1. The scope definition document is your blueprint or foundation to guide you through improving a business process.   True False
2. The process owner and sponsor is always the same person.   True False

3. Individual process responsibilities belong in the description section of the scope definition document. True False
4. Establishing the process boundaries helps to prevent scope creep. True False
5. In the Alistar example, "managing the budget balances" is an example of a process responsibility. True False
6. Stakeholders can affect a business process or receive the downstream effect of a business process. True False
7. Developing the scope definition document alone and reviewing it later with the project team is the most effective development method. True False
8. In section 8 you develop the actual metrics you plan to use to measure the business process. True False
9. The scope definition document is similar to a contract. True False
10. Step 2 is the most important of the ten steps and should never be skipped. True False

CHAPTER 4

Step 3: Draw the Process Map

Flowcharting and Documenting

Ed Seinfeld, the manager of HRIS (human resource information systems) for Alistar Corporation, wanted to understand how technology projects secured funding and how system expenses hit Alistar's financial planning processes like the five-year capital plan, annual operating plan, and monthly forecasts.

While trying to collect the system costs charged to the human resources and information technology departments, Ed discovered that no clear process existed, causing him to ask for my help in understanding what he called the technology funding process. When someone comes to me with this type of problem, I like to start by defining the process as we did in Chapter 3 and then draw a process map.

Drawing a process map is one of the best ways to help people understand any business process. It helps everyone involved in creating the process map learn how the process works, what activities constitute most of the work, where the handoffs occur between departments, and where the opportunities for improvement exist.

There are two schools of thought on how to approach this step, depending on the technique that someone subscribes to: total quality management (TQM) or reengineering. Both techniques are well-known process improvement methods:

▶ Reengineering focuses on the future state, driven by customer needs, and does not focus on the current process.

▶ TQM, also concerned with customer needs, examines the current process.

I have experience working with reengineering and understand why it became popular in the mid-1990s, but I find that most people have a difficult time becoming engaged in process work if you do not discuss how things work today. The technique I share in this chapter focuses on process-mapping the current process, although you can use the techniques for any process-mapping exercise. The training and development case study in Chapter 13 demonstrates a shift from the TQM approach to more of a reengineering approach.

Business process management (BPM), discussed in Chapter 12, can use the same concepts covered in this chapter; BPM simply focuses on an enterprise view of business processes instead of a functional view. Chapter 12 also provides an overview of notation standards associated with BPM.

Let us start at the beginning with a simple definition of a process map and the introduction of some basic components used to draw a map.

Process Map Overview

A *process map* is a visual representation of a series of connected activities that, when strung together, deliver a meaningful outcome to the customer/client. To lead into the mechanics of building a process map, let me start by sharing a simple example.

Figure 4-1 shows the basic components of a process map. Each rectangle in Figure 4-1 represents an *activity* in a process that adds value to the next step in the process.

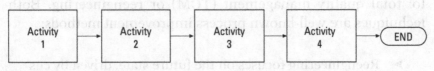

Figure 4-1 Process Map Components

Each activity consists of a series of *tasks*, and each activity should start with an action verb that demonstrates doing or performing something. Examples of action verbs include words like *develop*, *approve*, *update*, *run*, and *communicate*.

An action verb is the first word in the activity box, followed by the action itself. Figure 4-2 shows an example using each of the five sample action verbs.

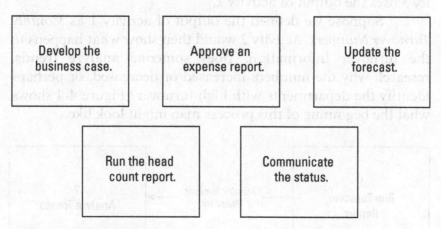

Figure 4-2 Action Verb Examples

You should have noticed the arrows in Figure 4-1 going from one box to the next. These arrows are known as *inputs* and *outputs*. Figure 4-3 shows an arrow leaving the first activity box and going to the second activity box. This arrow represents the *output* of the first box (activity 1) and the *input* to the next box (activity 2). As the figure shows, the text on the arrow reads *Output from activity 1* and *Input to activity 2*.

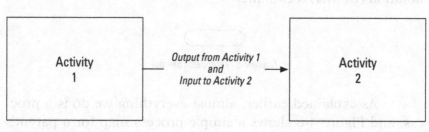

Figure 4-3 Output and Input

Whatever you write on the arrow must result from the actions taken in activity 1, and that output must then be used by activity 2 to accomplish its task. For example, if activity 1 states "Run a report," the output should identify what information results from running the report. Activity 2 would then state what to do with that information. When you add the next activity (activity 3), you follow this same logic and make sure that activity 3 uses the output of activity 2.

Suppose we defined the output of activity 1 as *Monthly Turnover Numbers*. Activity 2 would then show what happens to the turnover information. Does someone analyze trends, research why the numbers increased or decreased, or perhaps identify the departments with high turnover? Figure 4-4 shows what the beginning of this process map might look like.

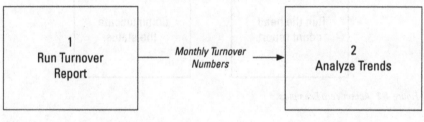

Figure 4-4   Start of Process Map

Now if you look back at Figure 4-1, you see the terminator symbol (depicted in Figure 4-5) at the end of the string of boxes to show that the process ends at that point. Process mapping includes numerous symbols, and I introduce them as I use them throughout this chapter. Chapter 12 covers some of the process map symbols used by the business process model and notation (BPMN) technique.

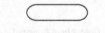

Figure 4-5   Terminator Symbol

As explained earlier, almost everything we do is a process, and Figure 4-6 shows a simple process map for a parent's routine in the morning. As you can imagine, a number of tasks occur within each of the four main activities shown. In this simple example, the parent seems to want to make sure that he or she showers and gets dressed before waking up the children. The parent also wants breakfast made before waking the children, suggesting that the parent wants a little quiet time, perhaps to enjoy a cup of coffee before the commotion begins. Eventually, we see that the parent drops the children off at school and then drives to work.

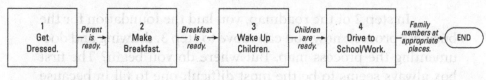

Figure 4-6 Morning Routine

As this example shows, you can draw either a high-level process map without a great deal of detail or an extremely detailed process map. We could have included many more activities in Figure 4-6 if we wanted to develop a detailed process map to show the parent's entire morning process. You have to decide on the level of detail required to achieve your goals. If you cannot decide how detailed a process map to draw, use the criteria in Figure 4-7 to help with your decision to draw a process map at a high level, detailed level, or somewhere in between.

Detailed Level	High Level
Draw a detailed-level process map if the process:	Draw a high-level process map if the process:
■ Is used often by many people. ■ Experiences high turnover among process workers. ■ Is a subprocess of another business process.	■ Is undefined and little shared understanding exists in the organization of the end-to-end business process. ■ Is a complex process. ■ Is a highly variable process. ■ Has many subprocesses.

Figure 4-7 Level of Detail for a Process Map

Even if you start at a high level, you can always add additional details if the need surfaces. The amount of time you spend drawing a process map varies depending on the goals. Think about what level of detail you need to accomplish your goals, and do not go any deeper.

Drawing the Process Map

In step 2 of the roadmap, you laid the foundation for the business process; now you can move to step 3, drawing and documenting the process map. But where do you begin? The first box always seems to be the most difficult one to fill in because you have to decide where to start.

To get started, use the scope definition document created in step 2, and reference the boundaries defined at that time. Look at where you said the process begins and ends, and use that information as the starting point.

Let us use Alistar Corporation's simple recognition bonus award process from Chapter 3 (Figure 3-8) to demonstrate the building of a process map. Since this process is about rewarding employees for good performance, our scope definition document lists the boundaries, as shown in Figure 4-8.

■ *Start:* Recommend employee for an award.

■ *End:* System of record is updated.

Figure 4-8 Boundaries

The entry point into the business process becomes the first data point to draw on the process map. In our example, we already identified the initial entry point when we established the boundaries in Figure 4-8. So we would write *Recommend employee for an award* on the process map and place an arrow going from this phrase to the first box. Figure 4-9 shows what the process map looks like at this point.

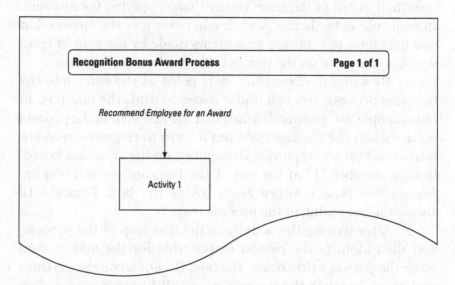

Figure 4-9 Recognition Bonus Award Process Map

The next step is to decide what to write inside the first box on the process map.

Box 1

Once we defined *Recommend employee for an award* as the entry into the process, we start by asking the project team questions to get them talking and thinking about the process. In this example, the team consists of individuals from the human resource compensation department. To start the conversation, you might say things like:

OK, an employee was recommended for a recognition
bonus award. What happens now?

Or . . .

Who recommends an employee for a recognition bonus award?

Or . . .

You've gotten a call from a manager who wants to give an
employee a recognition bonus award. What do you do?

You can ask whatever question(s) you feel will get the project team talking. As the facilitator, you have to draw the information out of the team rather than supplying the answers. In your role as facilitator, you should never give the answer, but you may have to rephrase statements made by the project team so what you write on the process map is clear and concise.

By using the boundary start point as the entry into the business process, you will find it easier to draw the first box. In our example, we eventually learn that the first step in the process occurs when the manager fills out a form to request a recognition award for an employee. Draw a box on the dry-erase board, write a number "1" at the top of the box, and write *Complete Recognition Bonus Award Form* inside the box. Figure 4-10 shows the beginning of the process map.

After writing the activity in the first step in the process, you then identify the person responsible for the activity and write the person's title below the box. Do not write the person's real name because the process map will become outdated as employees change jobs. Use their titles instead of their names because titles give the process map shelf life. For example, write *Manager* instead of "Bill Nguyen."

Does this seem too simple? Perhaps, but as we continue adding to the process map, you will see that, no matter how simple or complex your situation, the approach to drawing a process map is the same. I almost said the *process* to drawing a process map is the same, and there is that word *process* again!

As you look at Figure 4-10, notice several other items:

► The first activity starts with the word *Complete*, which denotes an action—a task the manager must do. Always start each activity with an action verb.

► Use an icon to depict any tools used to accomplish the activity. In this case, the icon stands for a hardcopy form, as shown by the document symbol in Figure 4-11. All the symbols used in this chapter are available in Microsoft Visio and most process mapping software.

► Type the form name, if desired, either inside or outside the document symbol. Figure 4-12 shows the two alternatives.

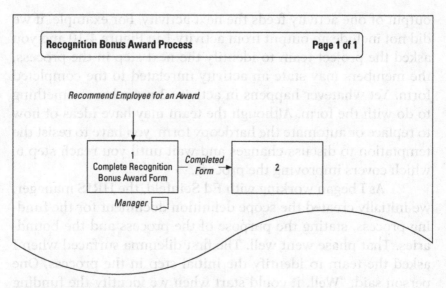

Figure 4-10   Recognition Bonus Award Process Map

Figure 4-11   Document Symbol

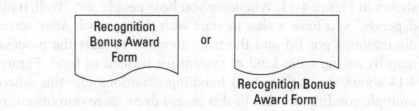

Figure 4-12   Document Symbol Examples

If you include numerous documents throughout the process map, it helps to identify each one.

In Figure 4-10, notice that the arrow leaving activity 1 shows the output of that activity as a completed form. Sometimes process maps omit text on the input and output lines, but leaving out such information can cause confusion because the output of one activity feeds the next activity. For example, if we did not include an output from activity 1 in Figure 4-10 and you asked the project team to identify the next step in the process, the members may state an activity unrelated to the completed form. Yet whatever happens in activity 2 must have something to do with the form. Although the team may have ideas of how to replace or automate the hardcopy form, you have to resist the temptation to discuss changes and wait until you reach step 6, which covers improving the process.

As I began working with Ed Seinfeld, the HRIS manager, we initially created the scope definition document for the funding process, stating the purpose of the process and the boundaries. That phase went well. The first dilemma surfaced when I asked the team to identify the initial step in the process. One person said, "Well, it could start when we identify the funding source." Another said, "I think the process starts when we determine whether it is capitalized or expensed." Yet a third person claimed we had to identify the type of system because of the different paths used to obtain funding for each system type. As the facilitator in this type of situation, how would you know where to begin drawing the process map?

I started the process map with a decision symbol, as shown in Figure 4-13. Whenever you hear people say, "Well, it all depends," you have a clue to start with this symbol. After some discussion, I got Ed and the team to agree to start the process map by asking what kind of system we wanted to fund. Figure 4-14 shows the approach to handling situations like this when multiple conditions exist. In this case, I drew three outputs coming from the first activity to show one route for an enterprise system, another for a business group system solution, and a third that addresses a solution for a single strategic business unit.

Figure 4-13 Decision Symbol

Another problem you may encounter when starting to draw a process map occurs when the business process has never

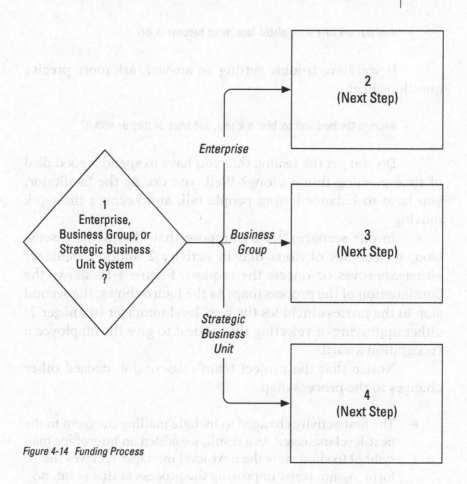

Figure 4-14 Funding Process

been documented before or no one on the project team has familiarity with the process. In either case, you might find yourself drawing a mix of the current process and a desired future state process. If you find yourself in this predicament, go with the momentum, while keeping track of the changes that have to occur to enable the new process to work. These changes become part of an impact analysis, which I discuss in Chapter 6.

Box 2

For the next box in the recognition bonus award process, we need to understand what happens to the form. Start by asking questions like:

Now that we have a completed form, what happens to it?

If you have trouble getting an answer, ask more precise questions like:

Whom is the form sent to, how is it sent, and what do they do with it?

Do you get the feeling that you have to spend a good deal of time pushing things along? Well, you do. As the facilitator, you have to balance letting people talk and keeping the work moving.

In our scenario, let us suppose that after some discussion, it becomes obvious that in activity 2 another manager either approves or rejects the request. Figure 4-15 shows the continuation of the process map. As the figure shows, the second step in the process includes the next-level manager (manager 2) either approving or rejecting the request to give the employee a recognition award.

Notice that the project team's discussion caused other changes to the process map.

▶ The first activity changed to include mailing the form to the next-level manager. As a result, we added an interoffice mail symbol to show how the next-level manager receives the form. Again, resist improving the process at this point, no matter how archaic the activity may seem.

▶ Activity 2 can have two possible outputs. The next-level manager can either approve or reject the proposed bonus award:

- If manager 2 approves the award recommendation, the process moves on to activity 3, and *Approval* appears as one output from activity 2 to activity 3.
- If manager 2 does not approve the award recommendation, *Rejection* appears as the second output from activity 2, and the terminator symbol denotes the end of the process. Writing the word *END* inside the terminator symbol clearly communicates the end of the process and makes a process map easier to read. The addition of the phone symbol indicates manager 2 calls

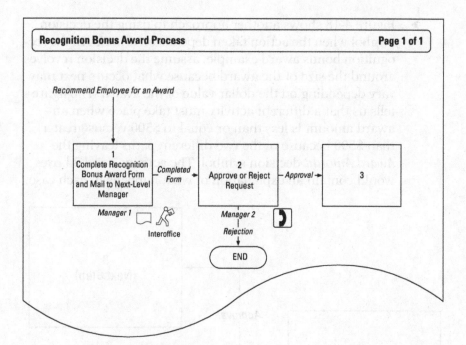

Figure 4-15   Recognition Bonus Award Process Map

manager 1 to explain the reason for rejecting the request.

You will find many different ways to draw multiple outputs from one activity, and the next few figures show some of the variations. Pick the one that works best for your situation.

▶ The alternative shown in Figure 4-16 requires additional real estate, or space, on a process map. So I do not use this approach when one output (e.g., *Rejection*) simply depicts the end of the process.

▶ Figure 4-17 shows another way to handle multiple outputs using the decision symbol. When using the decision symbol, the outputs can include *Yes/No* or anything else appropriate to the situation. You will find the decision symbol approach most useful when the two outputs denote obvious next steps instead of simply an end to the process.

▶ Figure 4-18 shows another approach to using the decision symbol when the action taken depends on criteria. In the recognition bonus award example, assume the decision revolves around the size of the award because what occurs next may vary depending on the dollar value of the award. The figure tells us that a different activity must take place when an award amount is less than or equal to $500 versus greater than $500 because of the two different paths leaving the *Award Amount* decision symbol. The activity 1 and 2 boxes would contain an explanation of what happens in each case.

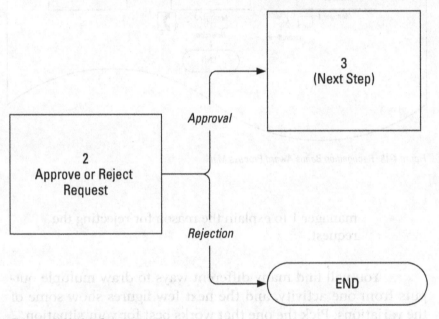

Figure 4-16 Multiple Outputs #1

Now, let us go back to the recognition bonus award process.

Box 3

After activity 2 in the recognition bonus award process, we understand that the second manager either approved or rejected the award request. Let us assume that the next-level manager (manager 2) approved the award recommendation and that we must decide what to write in box 3. Ask questions like:

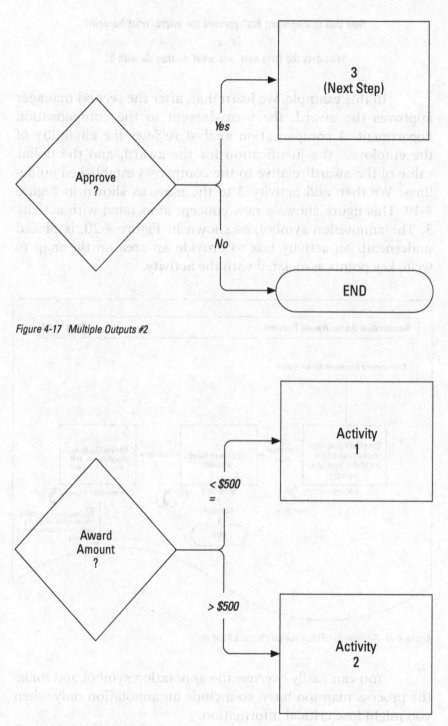

Figure 4-17 Multiple Outputs #2

Figure 4-18 Multiple Outputs #3

Now that management has approved the award, what happens?
Or . . .
Who gets the form next, and what do they do with it?

In this example, we learn that, after the second manager approves the award, the form is sent to the compensation department. A compensation analyst reviews the eligibility of the employee, the justification for the award, and the dollar value of the award relative to the company's established guidelines. We then add activity 3 to the map, as shown in Figure 4-19. This figure shows a new concept associated with activity 3. The annotation symbol, as shown in Figure 4-20, is placed underneath an activity box to provide an area on the map to write key points associated with the activity.

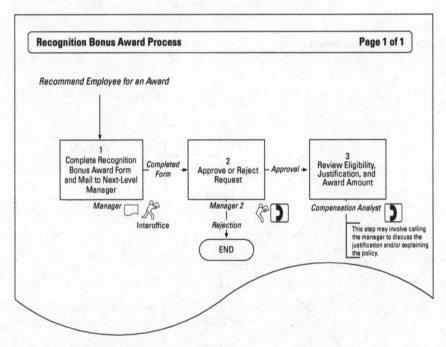

Figure 4-19 Recognition Bonus Award Process Map

You can easily overuse the annotation symbol and make the process map too busy, so include an annotation only when you might lose critical information.

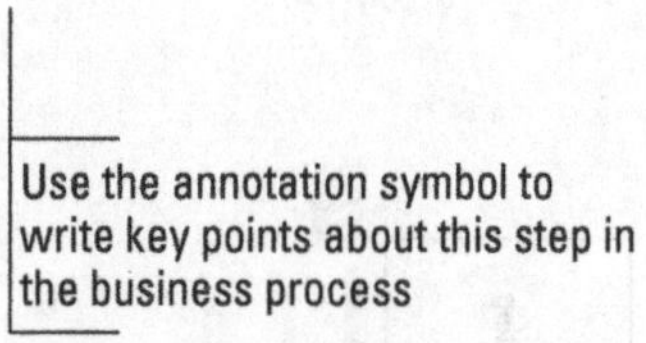

Use the annotation symbol to
write key points about this step in
the business process

Figure 4-20 Annotation Symbol

Boxes 4–8

Figure 4-21 shows the final recognition bonus award process map. Notice that the *Final Approval* output from activity 6 causes two simultaneous things to happen: the manager communicating the award to the employee face to face (activity 7) and compensation's updating the system of record with the award amount and effective date (activity 8). In this scenario, I drew the two activities resulting from activity 6 as one box on top of the other because they happen at the same time by different people.

Also, notice in Figure 4-21 that I keep describing the tools used to perform activities by adding icons because this will help with the improvement step. I included icons for using the phone, Outlook email, face-to-face communications, and the system of record (SOR).

The process map becomes more interesting and easier for someone to read by the addition of icons. The process map in Figure 4-21 shows the standard way to draw a process map, but you may find other types of process maps useful.

The Cross-Functional Process Map

Figure 4-22 shows the two different groups of people responsible for the activities in the recognition bonus award process: managers and compensation. Compensation resides in a different department from the managers who request and approve the awards. When a process includes different groups, you may find it helpful to create a cross-functional process map. This kind of map, shown in Figure 4-22, draws its name from the cross-functional bands, or horizontal rows, used to show the

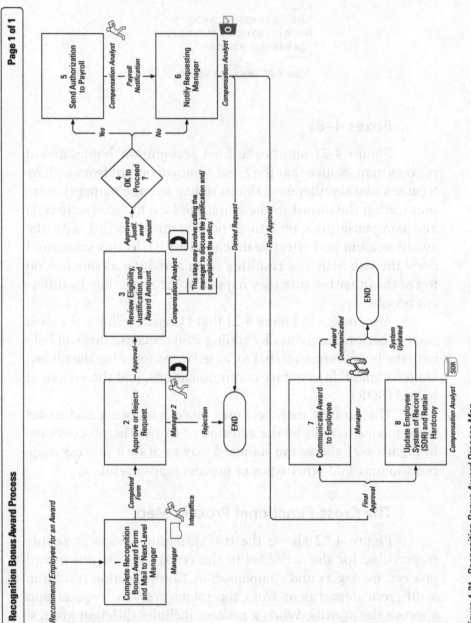

Recognition Bonus Award Process

Recommend Employee for an Award

1 — Complete Recognition Bonus Award Form and Mail to Next-Level Manager
Manager — Interoffice

Completed Form →

2 — Approve or Reject Request
Manager 2

Rejection → END

Approval →

3 — Review Eligibility, Justification, and Award Amount
Compensation Analyst

This step may involve calling the manager to discuss the justification and/or explaining the policy.

Approved Justification and Amount →

4 — OK to Proceed?

Yes → 5 — Send Authorization to Payroll
Compensation Analyst — Payroll Notification →

No → Denied Request

6 — Notify Requesting Manager
Compensation Analyst

Final Approval →

Final Approval →

7 — Communicate Award to Employee
Manager

Award Communicated →

8 — Update Employee System of Record (SOR) and Retain Hardcopy
Compensation Analyst — SOR

System Updated → END

Figure 4-21 *Recognition Bonus Award Process Map*

departments involved in the process. You may hear the bands in this type of a process map referred to as swim lanes.

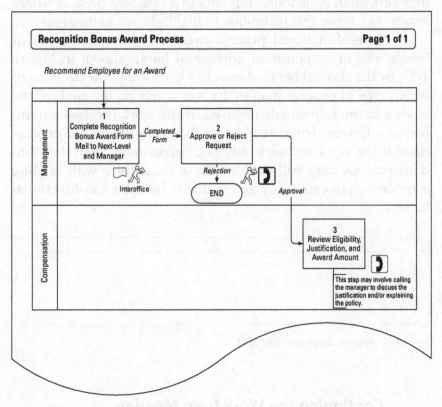

Figure 4-22 Cross-Functional Process Map

The cross-functional bands can represent as many groups as required. In Figure 4-22, the process map has two horizontal cross-functional bands: one for management and another for the compensation department. When using this style, include a new functional band, or swim lane, for each department or group involved in the process, and place activities in the appropriate bands depending on the department or group responsible for the activity. In Figure 4-22, activities 1 and 2 fall within the management band because managers perform these activities, whereas activity 3 falls within the compensation band for similar reasons.

Using a cross-functional process map makes it easy to

see when responsibility for a step in a process moves from one department to another, something known as a *handoff*. Because handoffs often contribute to points in a business process where issues occur, use this technique to highlight such situations.

Cross-functional process maps can have two types of bands: the more common horizontal band, shown in Figure 4-23, or the vertical band, shown in Figure 4-24. The decision of which type of process map to draw depends on the goals of the work and the individuals involved. If the work involves a number of different departments, use the cross-functional process map; if the work includes only one department, then the standard process map will suffice. Those unfamiliar with reading a process map can easily get confused by the cross-functional bands.

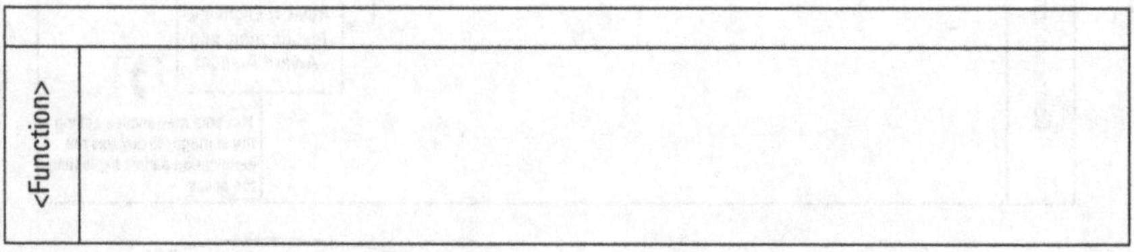

Figure 4-23 Horizontal Cross-Functional Band

Continuing the Work from Meeting to Meeting

More often than not, you will find it difficult to complete a process map in one meeting unless the work encompasses a simple business process or you plan a long meeting. Because everyone involved in helping to draw the process map returns to their normal jobs once the meeting ends, you will find that no one remembers the details of the process map you started creating when they come back together at the next meeting. As a result, to jump-start their memories at the next meeting, you have to accomplish several tasks between meetings.

▶ First, after each process mapping meeting, convert your hand drawing into a formal document using a software

Figure 4-24 Vertical Cross-Functional Band

application like Microsoft Visio, SmartDraw, or another process mapping tool you have available. If the project team does not finish drawing the process map in one meeting, document the work done to date so the team members start the next meeting with a precise picture of where they left off. It helps to use an electronic dry-erase board so you leave the meeting with a copy of the project team's work. If you do not have an electronic board available, take a picture using your phone or copy the drawing onto paper before leaving the meeting room. Another alternative that works well, if you have the available resources, is to have someone assist you who can draw the process map during the meeting using a laptop and the appropriate software application. If you have assistance, you should still use the dry-erase board so everyone can "see" the creation of the process map because doing so keeps the team engaged.

▶ Second, once you convert the process map from the first meeting to a software application, print it and enlarge it to a poster size. If an enlarging machine is not available, locate a copy center, like FedEx/Kinko, which charges a moderate fee for black-and-white enlargements.

▶ Third, bring copies of the process map to the next meeting for the project team.

At the next meeting, hang the enlarged process map on the wall and begin the meeting by walking the team members through the partially completed process map to remind them of what they accomplished at the first meeting. You should walk them through the process map box by box, highlighting what occurs at each step, naming the responsible party, identifying the tools used, and explaining annotations. Physically point to different sections on the enlarged process map, explain the output of each box, and describe how the output is used in the next step of the process.

Let us step through this process using the recognition bonus award process map from Figure 4-21.

Figure 4-25 shows sample dialogue we might use to start the second meeting. Continue this type of dialogue until you reach the point where the project team left off at the last meeting. By physically pointing to the enlarged process map and walking the team through how they created the map, you engage the participants and enable them to picture the result of their work thus far. Think of this step as telling a story, reinforcing the salient points from the team's prior discussions.

You should allow and encourage the project team to stop and change the process map as you walk through it because it is

Pointing to "Recommend employee for an award"

"We said in our last meeting that the process starts when an employee is recommended for an award and this leads to our first box. In box 1, we have the employee's manager completing a hardcopy form and justifying why the employee should receive an award. When the form is complete, the manager sends the form via interoffice mail to the next-level manager. So coming out of box 1, we have a completed form.

Pointing to box 1

Pointing to the output line

Pointing to box 2

In box 2, the next-level manager reviews the information on the form and, if they have additional questions, they call the requesting manager. Eventually, they either approve or reject the request. If they reject the award, then the process ends. If they approve the award, then the process moves to box 3.

Pointing to box 3

Pointing to the "Rejection" output from box 2

Figure 4-25 Sample Dialogue

the first time that they see the map in its clean state. Stop every time someone has a question and discuss the issue. If anyone has a question, it may mean that something on the process map needs to change. In addition, proactively watch the team members as you walk through the map to validate they can follow along and encourage the team to discuss any unclear points. Physically write any changes directly on the enlarged process map using a thick marker so everyone can see the map changing. As mentioned, you can also use a laptop and projector to display the process map on a screen, but you may find, as I have, that this is not as engaging or as flexible in a team setting. You should spend all your time facilitating the discussion, not looking at a laptop.

After reviewing the enlarged process map hanging on the wall, switch back to the dry-erase board and continue drawing the next steps in the process. When you leave the second meeting, you now have marked-up poster pages and new hand-drawn pages. After the second meeting, update the electronic version of the process map with the changes and incorporate them to prepare for the next meeting. Again, make copies for the project team, enlarge the updated process map, and walk the team through the updated map at the next meeting starting at activity 1. Go through these steps every time the team meets, regardless of the number of meetings, and always start back at activity 1.

In my experience, not many process maps result in a one-page document. Often, a single business process requires multiple 8½ × 11–inch pages. As you add new pages to the process map, you will find yourself breaking up the flow, either on the same page or on another page. Use the connector symbols, shown in Figures 4-26 and 4-27, to designate movement on the process map:

Figure 4-26   On-Page Connector Symbol

Figure 4-27   Off-Page Connector Symbol

▶ Use the on-page connector, shown in Figure 4-26, when moving to another, nonsequential box on the *same* page of the process map. Inside the symbol, include the activity number that the reader should go to next.

▶ Use the off-page connector, shown in Figure 4-27, when moving to another box on a *different* page of a process map. Inside the symbol, include the page number and activity number that the reader should go to next.

When you have a multiple-page process map, hang the enlarged process map pages around the conference room, moving from left to right.

Documenting the Process

Imagine that a new person joins your department and has to learn about one of the business processes. Do you just hand him or her a process map and walk the new person through the steps? You could, but a better way includes documenting the discussion that occurred during the drawing of the process map, thereby creating a business tool that the organization can use as a standard operating procedure for training new employees.

I call this tool the *detail document*, a narrative description of the process map, which should accompany the map. Because people have different learning styles, having both graphical and text representations of the business process provides everyone with a choice on how to reference the process materials. Figure 4-28 shows the beginning section of the detail document for the recognition bonus award process, which begins when an employee is recommended for an award.

Write the design document after each meeting at the same time you update the process map. Do not put off writing the design document until the process map is complete because waiting will cause you to forget some of the project team's discussion.

The detail document, combined with the process map, provides employees unfamiliar with the business process the information they require to understand the process, and it gives the process workers the information they need to do their jobs.

This documentation becomes important for step 6, when you move to improving the process, saving time as the project team attempts to recall the details of the process discussed weeks earlier.

Also start thinking about how to package the entire business process for future reference. In addition to storing the materials on a collaboration site, network drive, or storage media, I like to create a binder because some people find it easier to read process information in hardcopy format. Up to this point, you have completed three pieces of process information that can comprise a binder:

No.	Activity Description	Responsible Party	Tools	Output
1	**Complete the recognition bonus award form, and mail it to the next-level manager.** When a manager wants to recommend an employee for a recognition bonus award, he or she completes the recognition bonus award form. While completing the form, the manager has to look up the employee's record in the company's system of record to obtain their employee ID and other information required on the form. The manager also reviews the guidelines for recognition awards to determine the size of the award to propose. The guidelines show the minimum award amounts, based on the employee's annual salary as follows: ■ $100 if <$30,000 annual salary ■ $250 if between $30,000 and $50,000 annual salary ■ $500 if > $50,001 annual salary Having completed the form, the manager forwards it via interoffice mail to the next-level manager for approval.	Manager 1	Hardcopy form	**Completed form** A completed form is mailed to the next-level manager.
2	**Approve or reject request.** The next-level manager reviews the recognition bonus award form and decides either to: ■ Agree with the recommendation as presented. ■ Ask several questions about information on the form. ■ Or absolutely not agree that the employee should receive a recognition award. The approving manager refers to the guidelines for award amounts and reasons for giving a recognition award to make a decision whether to approve or reject the request. The approving manager may call the requesting manager to discuss either the dollar value of the award or justification. If the approving manager agrees, he or she forwards the signed form to the compensation department.	Manager 2 (approving manager)	Phone, interoffice mail	There are two possible outputs: *Approval:* The approving manager approves the request for an award. *Rejection:* The approving manager does *not* approve the request for an award and notifies the requesting manager of the decision.
3				

Figure 4-28 Recognition Bonus Award Process Detail Document

1. Overview (scope definition document)
2. Process map and legend
3. Detail document

The legend referenced under number 2, "Process map and legend," provides an explanation of symbols used throughout the process map. Two important symbols I have not used so far include the internal control and cyclical/recurring symbols, shown in Figures 4-29 and 4-30.

Figure 4-29   Internal Control Symbol

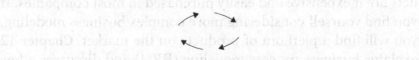

Figure 4-30   Cyclical/Recurring Symbol

▶ Use the internal control symbol (Figure 4-29) to denote that the activity constitutes a potential problem requiring additional attention. Chapter 7 covers internal controls.

▶ Use the cyclical/recurring symbol (Figure 4-30, also called the workflow loop symbol in Microsoft Visio), which originates from total quality management, when an activity repeatedly occurs throughout the year or because of its cyclical nature.

Figure 4-31 shows the cyclical/recurring symbol placed around an activity box to denote that the activity occurs on a cyclical or recurring basis.

Process Mapping Tools

In this chapter I mention using Microsoft Visio and SmartDraw to create process maps. Both of these software prod-

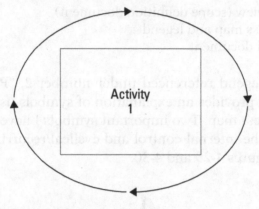

Figure 4-31 Cyclical Activity Sample

ucts are inexpensive and easily purchased in most companies. If you find yourself considering more complex business modeling, you will find a plethora of products on the market. Chapter 12 explains business process modeling (BPM) and discusses a few of the BPM software tools. For the business individual who wants to document his or her company's business processes, though, Visio and SmartDraw remain the easiest to use and the least expensive.

Microsoft Visio

Since Microsoft bought out this product, it has been continuously improved. I like Visio because of the ease of creating a process map from scratch or adapting an existing template. Visio is inexpensive, and the newest version includes BPM symbols.

To share your Visio process map, you can save it as an Adobe PDF file, or, if you work in an enterprise environment, you can share the process map with colleagues who do not use Visio through SharePoint. You can also save it as another file format that you can paste into one of the Microsoft Office Suite products. It takes a few extra steps to save it this way, so it is not as quick as SmartDraw's one-click export.

SmartDraw

This software allows you to build flowcharts and other types of charts and diagrams. It is easy to use and offers many templates, including BPM templates, which helps you to start quicker. Things I like about SmartDraw include the ability to:

▶ Build a high-level process map and add subprocesses. You can hide or show the subprocesses with one click. You will find this helpful for a complex process map.

▶ You can convert a file to Microsoft Office Suite products (Word, Excel, PowerPoint, and Outlook) and Adobe PDF with a single click.

▶ Add notes and hover over one. However, once you convert the process map, the notes appear as end notes on a separate page.

SmartDraw, like Visio, is inexpensive, and the technical support is wonderful.

Chapter Summary: Step 3

Drawing the process map helps everyone involved better understand how the business process works, where handoffs occur between departments, and the background needed to apply the improvement techniques described in Chapter 6.

Decide on the type of process map to draw depending on your requirements: either a high-level or detail-level process map, and either the standard or cross-functional process map. You have great flexibility deciding how to flowchart and embellish the process map and document the process. Select the process mapping tool that works best for your scenario. Microsoft Visio and SmartDraw are two inexpensive software tools you can use to draw a process map. Creating the process map and detail document provides the organization with a tool that can be used as a standard operating procedure to train new employees.

Keep the project team involved from meeting to meeting

by updating the process map and detail document between the meetings. Start each meeting by walking the team through the work done to date. As questions surface, stop and make changes with a thick marker on the enlarged process map.

The sample dialogue shared throughout this chapter should help you develop confidence in leading this type of work. The techniques presented in this chapter work, even if you work alone, to increase your understanding of a business process or to lead a business process improvement effort with others. When you work alone, the blank template in Figure 4-32 provides some structure.

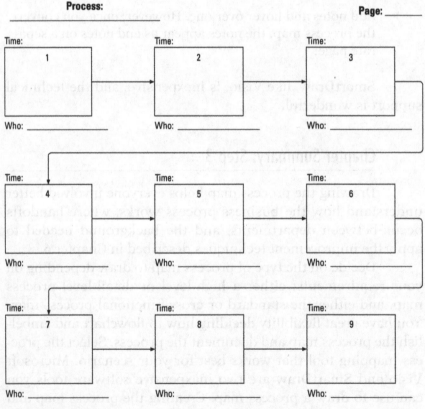

Figure 4-32 Blank Template

I often use this template as I talk one-on-one with someone about a business process because it keeps me focused on my goal. If the person you talk to veers off on a tangent, having this template in front of you (either physically or mentally) helps you to remember to redirect the conversation back to the main topic.

Time Estimate

To help in planning the time that it takes to work through this step, Figure 4-33 summarizes the amount of time required to complete the process map and detail document.

Event	Time	Purpose
Second project team meeting	3 hours	■ Review scope definition document and share sponsor feedback. ■ Begin mapping the process.
Postmeeting work	2 hours	■ Draw process map using Microsoft Visio or similar tool. ■ Create the detail document.
Follow-on project team meetings (until map is complete)	3–4 hours	■ Review enlarged process map to date (15–30 minutes depending on how far into the process map the team got at the last meeting). ■ Continue mapping the process.

Figure 4-33 Time Estimate—Step 3: Map Process

Second Project Team Meeting

This is the second time that the project team meets and the first time that you review the final scope definition document. Spend the first 20 minutes reviewing the scope definition document to help all members recall what they said the last time they met and to share the sponsor's feedback on the document. Because the project team will not have seen the scope definition document formatted before, it will appear more formal, and the team members may want to make adjustments. Once everyone agrees with the final version of the scope definition document, move to building the process map, following the techniques outlined in this chapter.

Postmeeting Work

During this personal time, draw the process map and document the discussion about each activity. Write the detail document as you progress through the work instead of putting it off until the end because you may well forget portions of the rich discussion.

Follow-On Project Team Meetings

The first part of each future meeting should begin with a walkthrough of the enlarged version of the process map, moving activity by activity through the entire map. The greater the number of meetings you have, the longer this exercise takes. Although it may seem repetitive, this exercise is critical because it keeps the project team engaged, and it enables you to pick up where the team left off the last time they met. Remember that, even though you have worked on the process map and know it by heart, everyone else went back to their normal jobs and probably have not even thought about the business process.

As you walk through the process map, remain flexible and ready to make changes. Your flexibility ensures the ongoing improvement of the process map and keeps the team involved. Remember to draw the changes directly on the enlarged copy of the process map using a marker so that everyone can see the changes.

Once you finish walking through the enlarged process map, switch to the dry-erase board and use it to continue drawing the process map from the point where the team left off the last time you met. You will find yourself referring to the wall hangings throughout the process mapping session as the project team discusses new topics, so leave the enlarged copies hanging up throughout the meeting.

You may find yourself in a predicament when the sponsor wants to do the work fast and suggests all-day work sessions. Unless you have a pressing reason, I recommend that the meetings on process work not last longer than three or four hours. It gets harder to sustain the level of involvement required when meetings extend beyond this timeframe because of the mental strain of the work. In general, I find two hours too short and longer than four hours too tiring for everyone involved.

What You Have Achieved

In this chapter, you have achieved the following:

► Agreement by the project team on the process definition and scope

► An understanding of when to draw a high-level or detail-level process map

► The importance of inputs and outputs

► A grasp of how to create a standard and cross-functional process map

► Knowledge of many of the standard flowcharting shapes

► Insight into how to lead a team through the work and keep them interested

► Most important, the *power* to uncover the opportunities for improvements

KNOWLEDGE CHECK

Use this knowledge check to validate your understanding of the material covered in step 3. Fill in the blanks with the correct answer.

1. A process map is a visual representation of a series of connected _____ that deliver a meaningful outcome to the _____.

2. The _____ of one activity must be used as the _____ to the next activity.

3. One reason to use a high-level process map (instead of a detailed one) is when the process is _____ (four possible answers).

4. You should refer to the _____ section of the scope

definition document when starting to draw the process map.

5. Use the _____ symbol when a step in the process has more than one output based on a specific question.

6. Use a _____ process map when you want to clearly show the responsibility of different departments and the handoffs between departments.

7. Use a(n) _____ connector to designate movement to another page of a process map.

8. Create a _____ to accompany a process map to narratively describe the business process.

9. To denote when an activity constitutes a potential problem, add the _____ symbol next to the activity on the process map.

10. Creating a current state process map helps you to uncover opportunities for _____.

CHAPTER 5

Steps 4–5: Estimate Time and Cost and Verify the Process Map

Introducing Process and Cycle Time and Gaining Buy-In

Alistar Corporation's compensation department understood its business process for granting recognition bonus awards to employees, but Stuart Wang, the director of compensation, wanted to know what it cost to administer the business process. This step identifies what a single business process costs an organization. Throughout this chapter, you will see how I answer Stuart's question using simple formulas that you can use.

The process map you drew in step 3 provides you with the information required to accomplish this step. At the end of this step, you will know how long the process takes and how much it costs.

Business Process Timing

You often hear two types of time related to business processes: process time and cycle time.

▶ **Process time** is the time required to complete a single activity in a process. For example, in the morning routine process covered in Chapter 4 (Figure 4-6), this means how long it takes for activity 1, getting dressed, to be completed.

▶ **Cycle time** is the time required to complete an entire process, from its first to its last step. You may also hear this referred to as elapsed time. In the morning routine example, it is the measure of time from when the parent began getting dressed in activity 1 until everyone arrived at work or school. You cannot calculate the cycle time by just adding up the process times for each activity because cycle time includes waiting time, which adds considerably more time to the total.

So let us start our discussion by focusing on process time.

Process Time

To establish a time-based improvement target, you first have to define how long the process takes today. You do this by going through the process map and identifying how long each activity takes. This is your baseline time. Without a baseline, you cannot establish an improvement target.

Project team members may feel uncomfortable starting off with this step because they do not like estimating and prefer using a more formal technique to measure process time. You can use one of the formal quality control methods, like a time study, where you observe and measure the time it takes an employee to complete each activity in a process. Although a time study and other techniques provide a definitive analysis of time, you will find that most formal techniques are extremely structured and time-consuming, and they often require a skilled person to effectively apply them. Sometimes you require this level of detail, but it is often not necessary with business processes. You can also look at historical data or test a sample in lieu of a full-blown analysis.

An effective alternative to the formal methods is simply to ask the project team how long each activity takes. Generally, estimating works well for the administrative type of processes used as examples throughout this book. This timing provides useful directional information, and you can always supplement it with a formal technique if you find the need for more statistical data at a later date. I experimented with both approaches for a business process I worked on to see whether any significant difference in the numbers would surface. First, I estimated the process timing with the project team and then conducted a time study. I found the results so close that it suggested the time study was not worth the extra time required. When working with a manufacturing process, however, you may find that you have to use one of the more formal quality control tools.

Most people have a fairly good idea of how long it takes to complete the tasks that comprise a business activity. Although some may have trouble initially with this exercise, it gets easier with time, and participants will become more comfortable with estimating. To identify the process time estimates, proceed box by box on the completed process map, adding the information to the process map above each activity box in the upper left-hand corner.

To demonstrate how to complete this step, let us use Stuart Wang's recognition bonus award process map from Chapter 4, Figure 4-21. To get started, I said:

> In activity 1, we said that the manager completes the recognition bonus award form and mails it to the next-level manager. How long do you think it typically takes a manager to complete the form?

Of course, the project team felt uncomfortable giving an estimate because they said the managers perform this step, not them. So I rephrased the question:

> How long do you think it would take you to complete the form?

If I still had trouble getting a time estimate, I would have asked one of the team members to fill out the form. Your main goal at this point is to keep the work progressing.

If the project team members want to confirm the time estimates after the meeting, let them do that. I generally find very little change between the estimates a team gives me and the later confirmation. If the team simply cannot give you an estimate because the first step in the process does not involve them, you can always come back to activity 1 later. Just move on to an activity where the team owns responsibility and can provide an answer. Return to the earlier activity at a future date with accurate information. Eventually, you will get answers, and sometimes the team may give you a range instead of a single time. For example, the team may feel more comfortable saying that it takes 10–15 minutes instead of a single number, and you should simply accept a range. Rest assured that, after the first answer, the process does move more quickly.

Record the time estimate above each activity on the process map. Keep moving through the map, adding process time estimates until you have walked through the entire process. When I update the process map, I use a white clock symbol to denote process time. I do not draw clocks during the meeting; instead, I simply write the time as, say, *20 minutes* above the activity on the left-hand side of the activity box.

Cycle Time

Cycle time is the measure of the overall time it takes for the entire process, or, in our example, how long it takes from the time the first manager initiates the request for a bonus award through the time that he or she can communicate the award to the employee.

To estimate the current cycle time for Stuart's case, I included waiting, or delay, time. After the manager in activity 1 completed the form, we had to determine the time lapse before manager 2 would approve or reject it in activity 2. The timing between activities 1 and 2 varies depending on the managers involved, and we uncovered a variety of reasons for the delay in completing activity 2.

To help the project team state cycle time, you have to lead them through another discussion by saying something like:

> We know that it takes the manager in activity 1 about 20 minutes to complete the form and send it to the next-level manager, but I want you to think now about interruptions that the manager may have or additional tasks, unrelated to completing the form, that the manager may have to handle before finishing the form. The phone may ring, a colleague may

walk into the office, or their boss may request something unexpectedly. With all these interruptions, how long do you estimate it takes to finish the form and send it on its way?

In Stuart's case, we estimated a one-hour cycle time for activity 1, so I recorded the cycle time estimate on the process map above activity 1 on the right-hand side of the activity box. I use a dark clock symbol to denote cycle time when I update a process map.

Figure 5-1 shows the recognition bonus award process map with process and cycle times added above each of the activities. Figure 5-1 also shows that three of the activities (2, 3, and 8) state a range of process time because the project team had a difficult time providing a single number.

When you add up the process activity times, as depicted in Figure 5-2, it becomes clear that the entire business process requires between 70 and 87 minutes, roughly between 1 and 1½ hours, assuming that compensation approves the award in activity 4. I derived this estimate by totaling the minutes in the low end and high end of the range.

After completing the process time summary, you have an estimate of the time employees spend performing the activities that comprise the recognition bonus award process.

Figure 5-1 also shows that the team suggested a modest 1-hour cycle time for activity 1, but look at activity 2, where the process map suggests that approving or rejecting the award may take five days. Include notes around the cycle time in the detail document so you have that information available when you move to the improvement step.

Figure 5-3 shows the overall cycle time estimate for this business process at 11 days (or 92 hours), assuming that compensation approved the award in activity 4. Since I wanted to work with days when discussing cycle time, I translated the project team's hours into number of days in Figure 5-3 by dividing the hours by 8, the normal number of working hours in one day.

Figure 5-4 shows the formula used to translate hours to days for activity 1.

When you compare the process and cycle times for this

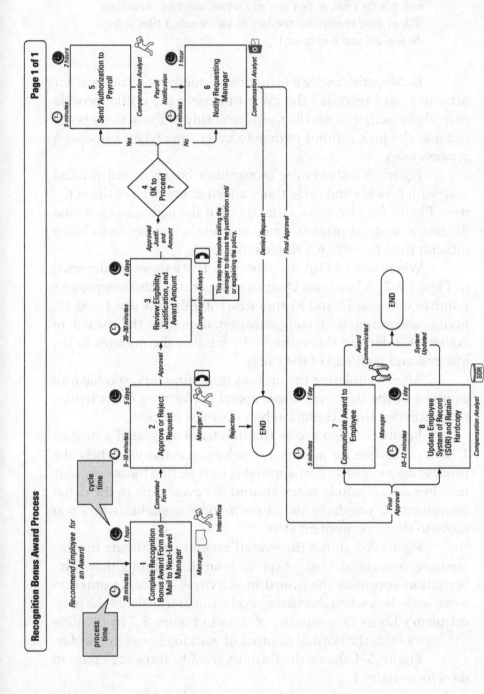

Figure 5-1 Recognition Bonus Award Process (with Process and Cycle Time)

Activity Number	Low End	High End
1	20 minutes	20 minutes
2	5 minutes	10 minutes
3	20 minutes	30 minutes
4	n/a	n/a
5	5 minutes	5 minutes
6	5 minutes	5 minutes
7	5 minutes	5 minutes
8	10 minutes	12 minutes
Total	**70 minutes**	**87 minutes**

Figure 5-2 Process Time Summary: Recognition Bonus Award Process

Activity Number	Number of Hours	Number of Days
1	1 hour	0.125 day
2	40 hours	5 days
3	32 hours	4 days
4	n/a	n/a
5	2 hours	0.25 day
6	1 hour	0.125 day
7	8 hours	1 day
8	8 hours	1 day
Total	**92 hours**	**11.5 days**

Figure 5-3 Cycle Time Summary: Recognition Bonus Award Process

business process, you can see a significant variance between the numbers. Although the physical work involved in this business process requires only 1 to 1½ hours, the time it takes to complete the entire process from beginning to end can take as long as 11 days. From this comparison, it became apparent that the greatest opportunity for improvement lies with the cycle time, not with the process time. Generally, customers and clients see only cycle time because they cannot see the steps involved in a

Formula:

$$\frac{\text{Number of hours}}{8 \text{ hours}} = \text{Number of days}$$

Example:

$$\frac{1 \text{ hour}}{8 \text{ hours}} = 0.125 \text{ day}$$

Figure 5-4 Hours-to-Day Translation

department's internal processes. When a customer/client complains about the turnaround time of a business process, it usually points to a problem with the cycle time.

I suggest that you do not collect and add the process and cycle times to the process map until *after* you have finished drawing the map in its entirety, for two reasons:

1. The project team has gone through the process map multiple times, and they will feel comfortable with the steps involved in the process.
2. If you attempt to collect time information as you draw the process map, the project team will begin thinking about how long an activity takes instead of getting the activities correct. The team should initially focus on getting the steps accurate and not worry about the timing.

Process Cost

Now that we know how long it takes to complete each activity in the process, we can determine how much the process costs the business. Stuart Wang recognized that it took his staff 1 to 1½ hours to process a single bonus award, but he still did not know the cost of the process. At this point, we have all the information we need to calculate the cost. Figure 5-5 shows the three components that comprise the total cost:

1. The cost of the people who do the work
2. The cost of technology tools used in the process

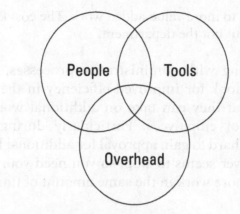

Figure 5-5 Process Cost Components

3. The cost of overhead such as space, air conditioning, and the like

People Costs

The first component consists of employee costs. Any improvement in process time generates an employee-related cost savings because the employees spend less time on the process. You can define cost savings as either *hard* cost savings or *soft* cost savings:

▶ **Hard cost savings** equate to a reduction in head count, or the number of employees that support the business process, thus lowering the labor cost. This quantitative measure means that, for example, you reduce your employees from a number like 20 to perhaps 18 in a department. The reduction may result in a layoff or reassigning employees to another department, but the overall number of employees supporting the business process declines and thereby lowers the cost of the business process.

▶ **Soft cost savings** signify a reduction in the number of employees who support the business process, but in this case the affected employees do not leave their current department. Instead of laying them off or moving the employees to different jobs, managers shift the employee's workload to more value-added work. The cost leaves the process but not the department.

In working with administrative processes, I find that sponsors often look for improved efficiency in their business processes so that they can take on additional work with the same number of employees. Particularly during economic downturns, it is hard to gain approval for additional head count, yet the work never seems to stop; so you need your employees to accomplish more work in the same amount of time.

Determining the People Costs

Estimating the labor cost of a business process requires four steps:

1. List process activities and times in a spreadsheet.
2. Identify the annual volume.
3. Determine the FTE (full-time equivalent) number to use.
4. Determine the salary and employee benefit rate to use for the employees or process workers.

Now let us take a look at how I identified the costs associated with the employees involved in the recognition bonus award process.

Step 1: Process Activities and Time

Figure 5-6 shows the first step, creating a spreadsheet that includes all the activities listed on the process map. The activity number and description appear in the first two columns of the spreadsheet, the total process time required by all employees appears in column three, and only the compensation department's process time appears in column four. This figure shows that each recognition bonus award takes 78.5 minutes, or 1.3 hours, of process time to complete and that compensation has responsibility for 46 of those minutes. The figure also shows how to handle a process time range. When the project team gave me a range of 5–10 minutes for activity 2, I used the midpoint of the range (7.5 minutes) in the spreadsheet.

Activity Number	Description	Total Time	Compensation Department Time
1	Complete recognition bonus award form and mail to next-level manager.	20.0	—
2	Approve or reject request.	7.5	—
3	Review eligibility, justification, and award amount.	25.0	25.0
4	n/a		
5	Send authorization to payroll.	5.0	5.0
6	Notify requesting manager.	5.0	5.0
7	Communicate award to employee.	5.0	—
8	Update employee system of record and retain hardcopy.	11.0	11.0
	Total minutes/award **(Total hours/award)**	78.5 (1.3 hours)	46.0 (.8 hours)

Figure 5-6 Recognition Bonus Award Process: Process Timing

If multiple departments are involved in the work, you can add more columns to Figure 5-6 to accommodate as many departments as necessary.

Step 2: Annual Volume

The second part of the formula includes the volume of recognition bonus awards. How many recognition bonus awards does the compensation department process in a year? Let us assume that compensation processes 1,500 awards annually.

To calculate the total labor hours spent on this process, multiply the number of awards per year (annual volume) by the process time required for each award. Assuming we are interested only in the compensation department's labor, Figure 5-7 shows how to calculate the department's total time dedicated to the process.

To calculate the number of hours that the compensation department spends administering the recognition bonus award process annually, simply divide the total annual minutes from Figure 5-7 by 60 minutes.

This calculation shows that the compensation department spends 1,150 hours a year administering the recognition bonus award process. The next step includes translating the

Formula:
Annual volume × Minutes per award = Total annual minutes

Example:
1,500 awards × 46 minutes = 69,000 total annual minutes

Figure 5-7 Annual Process Time (in minutes)

1,150 hours into the number of employees, or head count, that those hours represent.

Step 3: FTE Formula

Use of the term FTE (full-time equivalent) varies from one business to another, but it usually describes the total number of hours that an employee can be paid for in a work year. Assuming that an employee works 40 hours in a week, one FTE equates to 2,080 hours in a year (40 hours × 52 weeks).

Using the FTE concept, the third step translates the 1,150 hours spent on the recognition bonus award process into the number of employees those hours represent. Without the FTE concept, you might wonder whether 1,150 hours constitute one employee, two employees, or more employees. If we use the FTE concept, though, we can see that one FTE may mean:

► One employee working 2,080 hours a year.

► Or two employees working part time at 1,040 hours each.

Using the FTE concept enables you to account for percentages of an employee's time spent on a business process.

You normally never use the standard 2,080 hours as your baseline because employees take vacations and earn holidays. Talk to your sponsor to identify what baseline you should use in your labor calculation. With Stuart's input, I used 1,880 annual hours as the baseline for the recognition bonus award process. Figure 5-8 shows how I calculated this number.

As Figure 5-8 shows, I subtracted vacation, sick, and holi-

Labor Calculation Used: 1,880

Annual hours	2,080*
Less 2 weeks vacation	80
Less 1 week sick	40
Less 10 days paid holidays	80
Total	**1,880**

*40 hours per week × 52 weeks in a year

Figure 5-8 Calculating the Baseline

day hours from the standard 2,080 hours to arrive at my baseline of 1,880. If the group you work with has many employees with a lot of seniority, you may have to increase the hours subtracted for vacation to three or four weeks. Likewise, if your company has more or fewer holidays, you may have to adjust the paid holiday number.

The next task is to divide the total hours spent on the business process by the baseline so you can determine the number of employees required to support the process. Figure 5-9 shows this calculation. As the figure shows, the recognition bonus award process requires 0.611 of an employee, which equates to slightly more than half an FTE, or half a person, annually. Any improvements you introduce to the process that decreases the process time also decreases the FTE, or number of employees, required to support the business process.

Formula:

$$\frac{\text{Total process hours}}{\text{Baseline hours}} = \text{Total number of FTEs required to support the business process}$$

Example:

$$\frac{1{,}150 \text{ hours}}{1{,}880 \text{ hours}} = 0.611 \text{ FTE}$$

Figure 5-9 Calculating the Number of FTEs

Step 4: Employee Salary and Benefit Costs

The fourth step involves calculating the cost of the 0.611 FTE. First, identify the employees to include in the cost estimate by looking at who performed each activity on the process map. If your client is a single department, as in Stuart's case, the sponsor may only want to understand what the process costs that particular department. In this case, identify the employees who work in the compensation department, even though the other departments may have some responsibility for the process.

The only compensation department employee on the process map is the compensation analyst. Assuming that this level of employee earns $70,000 per year, Figure 5-10 shows the formula to identify how much of this employee's salary to apply to the recognition bonus award process. The figure shows that $42,770 of the employee's $70,000 annual salary is charged to the recognition bonus award process.

Formula:
Annual salary × FTE = Employee labor cost dedicated to business process

Example:
$70,000 × 0.611= $42,770 labor-only employee cost

Figure 5-10 Employee Labor Cost

But we have not finished the employee labor cost calculation. Next, we add the employee benefit rate to the employee's salary because employees cost a company more than just their salaries. You may have heard the employee benefit rate referred to as the EB rate. This rate adds the cost of company-sponsored benefits to the employee's salary to come up with a total employee cost. Use your company's standard EB rate to perform this calculation. In Figure 5-11, we use a 30 percent EB rate to show the formula for calculating the labor plus EB cost.

At this point, we have determined that it costs Stuart Wang 0.611 of an employee, at an employee cost of $55,601, to support the 1,500 annual volume of recognition bonus awards.

Formula:
Employee labor cost × (100% + 30% EB rate) = Total employee cost dedicated to business process

Example:
$42,770 × 130% = $55,601 total employee cost dedicated to business process

Figure 5-11 Calculating the Total Employee Cost

In summary, the four components of people cost for Stuart Wang are:

1. Process activity time: 46 minutes
2. Annual volume of awards: 1,500 awards
3. FTE: 0.611
4. Labor cost: $55,601

To explain how to calculate the labor cost for a business process, I used a simple example on purpose. You would use the same method to calculate the labor when a process includes many different types of employees whose rates of pay vary. In the recognition bonus award process, for example, the process could have included a compensation manager, compensation consultant, and compensation analyst, all with different rates of pay. The same formulas work, but you would have to include more columns in the spreadsheet. The case study in Chapter 13 shows an example that includes multiple types of employees performing process activities.

Tool Costs

The second cost component includes the tools used by the business process. This category may include technology tools, like software applications, or internally developed tools, such as a reference guide.

Determining Tool Costs

To estimate the tool costs, identify the tools used by employees who support the business process. This list can become extensive and vary depending on the complexity of the process. To capture this information, you can either create a separate spreadsheet that includes the details for the tools used or just add columns to the process timing table in Figure 5-6. Figure 5-12 shows an updated table with two additional columns to include the tools used and their cost.

Activity Number	Description	Total Time	Compensation Department Time	Tools Used	Tool Cost
1	Complete recognition bonus award form and mail to next-level manager	20.0 minutes	—		
2	Approve or reject request	7.5 minutes	—		
3	Review eligibility, justification, and award amount	25.0 minutes	25.0 minutes		
4	OK to proceed?	—	—		
5	Send authorization to payroll	5.0 minutes	5.0 minutes		
6	Notify requesting manager	5.0 minutes	5.0 minutes	Outlook	$75
7	Communicate award to employee	5.0 minutes	—		
8	Update employee system of record and retain hardcopy	11.0 minutes	11.0 minutes	System of Record	$350
	Totals	**78.5** minutes (1.3 hours)	**46.0** minutes		**$425**

Figure 5-12   Recognition Bonus Award Process: Process Timing and Tool Cost

The current recognition bonus award process appears extremely manual because it uses hardcopy forms and inter-office mail. The only technology-related tools include Microsoft Outlook, the company's email system used to notify the requesting manager of the award status, and the company's employee system of record to document the award amount. The software license costs for the two applications become the only tool costs to include in the spreadsheet and, with volume license discounts, totaled $425. This, however, is not the actual cost because the employee uses the software applications to perform other tasks not associated with this business process. As a result, we have to multiply the $425 by the 0.611 FTE to apply the portion of the license fees attributable to supporting this one business process. You may decide not to even include this figure since it is so small and only a portion of the business process uses it. Figure 5-13 shows the formula to perform the calculation.

Formula:
Tool costs × FTE = Total tool cost dedicated to business process

Example:
$425 × 0.611 = $260 tool cost dedicated to business process

Figure 5-13 Calculating the Tool Cost

Once you improve a business process, you will probably use additional technology, and this component of cost often increases. So far, though, we have identified the following costs for the recognition bonus award program:

1. Labor (salary + EB): $55,601
2. Tools: 260
3. Total: $55,861

Overhead Costs

The third component of cost includes overhead, which refers to the ongoing expenses associated with running a business. It includes things like the physical office space an employee occupies, utilities, supplies, taxes, insurance, and computer equipment.

Calculating overhead varies by company. You may find that your company considers all administrative processes as overhead costs because they do not deliver a product sold to external customers.

Determining Overhead Costs

Companies generally use a standard overhead rate, so use that number for your calculation. For example, a 150 percent overhead rate means that for each $1.00 of direct labor, an additional $1.50 is added for overhead costs. To calculate overhead rates, divide overhead costs by direct (e.g., labor) costs.

You should not have to calculate the rate if you use your company's standard overhead percentage.

Figure 5-14 applies Stuart Wang's standard overhead rate of 110 percent to the process-related employee cost.

Formula:
Employee labor cost × Overhead rate = Process overhead cost

Example:
$55,601 × 110% = $61,161 process overhead cost

Figure 5-14 *Calculating the Overhead Cost Formula*

Putting It All Together

The administration of the recognition bonus award process costs Stuart Wang $117,022 a year, calculated by adding the three cost components together:

1. Labor (salary + EB): $55,601
2. Tools: 260
3. Overhead: 61,161
   Total: $117,022

You may also hear the term *fully loaded* with reference to the total employee-related costs that include employee benefits and overhead.

In the recognition bonus award process example, if we included employees outside the compensation department, we would realize a higher overall process cost because we would have to add the labor and overhead costs associated with managers.

Alternative Cuts of the Data

You may want to break down the cost summary into additional detail, depending on your situation. For example, you may want to know the cost for administering a single bonus award. To calculate the cost for each recognition bonus award, simply divide either the labor cost or total cost by the 1,500 annual volume number. Figure 5-15 shows the calculation used to determine that a single bonus award costs Stuart $37.07 when he looks only at labor.

When Stuart looks at the total cost per award, Figure 5-16 shows that a single bonus award costs $78.01 when you consider all costs.

Formula:

$$\frac{\text{Employee labor cost}}{\text{Volume}} = \text{Individual award cost}$$

Example:

$$\frac{\$55,601}{1,500 \text{ awards}} = \$37.07 \text{ per award (labor only)}$$

Figure 5-15 Cost per Award (using labor costs only)

Formula:

$$\frac{\text{Total process cost}}{\text{Volume}} = \text{Individual award cost}$$

Example:

$$\frac{\$117,022}{1,500 \text{ awards}} = \$78.01 \text{ cost per award}$$

Figure 5-16 Cost per Award (using total costs)

To further analyze the data, you may find it helpful to summarize the process information in a single spreadsheet like the one shown in Figure 5-17. This table combines the time and cost estimates for the compensation department and provides summary information in one place. Activities performed by employees outside the compensation department (i.e., managers) are grayed out. If you wanted to include costs for the entire company, you would then have to identify a standard salary for managers and apply the same formulas introduced in this chapter to determine the people, tool, and overhead costs for the managers.

Activity Number	Description	Time Estimate		Cost Estimate			
		Process Time (Minutes)	Cycle Time (Days)	Labor ($)	Tools ($)	Overhead ($)	Total ($)
1	Complete form/mail						
2	Approve/reject request						
3	Review form	25.0	4.0	20.15		22.25	42.40
4	n/a						
5	Send authorization	5.0	0.25	4.03		4.45	8.48
6	Notify manager	5.0	0.125	4.03	.00	4.45	8.48
7	Communicate award						
8	Update employee system of record	11.0	1.0	8.86	.00	9.79	18.65
	Totals	46.0	5.4	$37.07	$.00	$40.94	$78.01

Figure 5-17 Recognition Bonus Award Process Summary

In looking at Figure 5-17, we see that:

➤ It takes 46 minutes for compensation to process one award.

➤ It takes 5.4 days to complete the overall cycle.

➤ Each award costs $37.07 in labor costs, $0.00 in tool costs, and $40.94 in overhead costs, for a total cost of $78.01.

You should be familiar with the time estimates in Figure 5-17 because they come from our earlier work in Figures 5-2 (process time) and 5-3 (cycle time).

Analyzing the Cost Estimate Columns

Now let us take a closer look at the cost estimate columns in Figure 5-17. Under Cost Estimate, you see four columns for

Labor, Tools, Overhead, and Total. The next section explains how to break down these cost estimates by individual process activities because this helps you easily notice where an opportunity may exist to reduce the process time. For example, just looking quickly at the total column in Figure 5-17, we can tell that the most expensive step in the process is activity 3, reviewing the form, because it costs $42.40 each time compensation processes an award.

Now let us look at each of the cost estimate columns.

Labor Cost Estimate

Two components that contribute to the labor cost are process time and the employee's labor cost. Because we show process time in minutes in Figure 5-17, we have to convert the employee's annual salary into minutes, so that we know what each activity costs. The next two figures show how this is done.

Figure 5-18 shows how we converted the compensation analyst's annual hours to minutes. Once we know the annual minutes worked, we apply a simple formula to calculate the cost per minute. Figure 5-19 shows the formula to use to calculate the employee's rate of pay per minute.

Formula:
Annual hours worked × 60 minutes/hour = Annual minutes worked × FTE rate = Annual minutes worked on business process

Example:
1,880 hours × 60 minutes/hour = 112,800 minutes × 0.611 = 68,921 annual process minutes

Figure 5-18 Annual Minute Calculation (Labor Cost)

So, what does it cost for the compensation analyst, who earns $0.806 per minute, to review the form in activity 3? By simply multiplying the $0.806 rate of pay by the 25 minutes it takes to review the form, we find it costs $20.15 in labor cost. Figure 5-20 shows the formula to calculate the cost per process activity.

In this example, I added the $20.15 to the labor column

Formula:

$$\frac{\text{Employee labor cost}}{\text{Process-related annual minutes}} = \text{Pay per minute}$$

Example:

$$\frac{\$55,601}{68,921 \text{ minutes}} = \$0.806 \text{ per minute}$$

Figure 5-19 Employee's Rate of Pay per Minute

Formula:

Process time × Pay per minute = Cost per process activity

Example:

25 minutes × $0.806 = $20.15 per form

Figure 5-20 Process Cost by Activity (Labor Cost)

in Figure 5-17 for activity 3. Apply this same formula to the other process activities listed in Figure 5-17 to determine the labor cost for each step in the process, and you see that sending the authorization and notifying the manager (activities 5 and 6) cost $4.03 each, and updating the employee system of record (activity 8) costs $8.86.

Tool Cost Estimate

To calculate the tool cost for each process activity, divide the tool cost for the entire process ($260) by the annual minutes spent on the process (68,921 minutes from Figure 5-18) to arrive at the tool cost per minute for the process. Because of the negligible amount, I did not add a cost in the tools column for activity 6 or activity 8.

Overhead Cost Estimate

To calculate the overhead cost, apply the overhead rate to the employee's pay per minute. In Figure 5-21 we add Stuart's 110 percent overhead rate to the employee's salary.

Formula:
Pay per minute × Overhead rate = Overhead cost
per activity

Example:
$0.806 × 110% = $0.89 overhead cost per activity

Figure 5-21 Overhead Cost per Activity

Now that we know that each activity adds $0.89 in over-head expense, Figure 5-22 shows applying the per-minute over-head cost to the reviewing-the-form activity to show that activity 3 costs $22.25 on top of the labor cost.

Formula:
Minutes × Overhead cost per minute = Overhead cost per process activity

Example:
25 minutes × $0.89 = $22.25 overhead cost per form

Figure 5-22 Process Cost by Activity (Overhead Cost)

Apply this same formula to the other process activities listed in Figure 5-17 to determine the overhead cost for each step in the process, and you see that sending the authorization and notifying the manager (activities 5 and 6) cost $4.45 each, and updating the employee system of record (activity 8) costs $9.79 in overhead costs.

You should now understand how to calculate each number in Figure 5-17, and you can tell from this analysis that the most costly activity in the business process is reviewing the form, followed by updating the employee system of record, and, finally, notifying the manager and sending the authorization.

By the end of this step, you have completed the process map and added the process and cycle times to it. Before moving on to the improvement stage, there is one more step.

Verify the Process Map

After you complete the process map, review it with interested parties to confirm that it accurately reflects the existing process. This step helps you prevent someone's claiming, to downplay your improvements, that you started with a flawed process.

This step may happen fast, or it may take weeks depending on the knowledge of your project team and the number of people who have to review the process map. You may want to validate the accuracy of the process map with three groups of employees:

▶ Process workers

▶ Stakeholders

▶ Sponsor

Process Workers

Process workers are the employees who perform the activities depicted in the process map, such as the compensation analyst in the recognition bonus award process. If you had a compensation analyst on the project team, then this step is easy. If not, then this step takes longer to complete.

Although the recognition bonus award process is an intentionally simple example that consists of only two groups of process workers (managers and compensation analysts), in a complex process you will probably have to incorporate a dozen different process workers in this step. You do not have to meet with all of them, just those most responsible for the process activities or others crucial to the business process. Review the scope definition document created in step 2 to help decide on whom to include. If an employee has ownership for delivering one of the process responsibilities you identified, include that individual in the process verification.

If you have a large number of process workers to interview, allow your project team to help. Delegation not only offloads a portion of the work from you, it also engages the team and strengthens the members' sense of ownership. Everyone involved in the validation should focus on the:

► Accuracy of the process map
► Points requiring clarification
► Accuracy of the time estimates

After finishing the verification, the project team should reconvene and decide whether to make changes to the process map.

Stakeholders

Depending on the foundation you established in step 2, you may or may not choose to walk your *stakeholders* through the completed process map. Take a look at what you said the stakeholders care about, and decide whether you believe that a stakeholder may not agree with something in the process map.

If you decide to meet with a stakeholder, schedule the meeting after completing the validation with the process workers and after incorporating any changes to the process map so you share an accurate, up-to-date version. You should perform the validation with the stakeholders yourself and not delegate the responsibility to another project team member because you have the best overall knowledge to correctly position the work. Meeting with the stakeholders also provides you with a good networking opportunity.

Sponsor

The sponsor should also validate the process map before you move to the next step. If you have a different sponsor from the process owner, include both of them in this step and try to do this with them at the same time. The sponsor and process owner may have a point of view that you have not considered. Before jumping in and walking the sponsor and/or process owner through the process map, go back and review the scope definition document you created in step 2 with them. Even though the sponsor approved the scope definition document, the review refreshes the memory and provides a transition tool. Highlight the boundaries from that document as a transition to the entry point into the process map.

Once you have completed the reviews and you have made the changes to the process map, you can move to step 6, applying improvement techniques.

Chapter Summary: Steps 4–5

In step 4, you learned the difference between process and cycle times. While process time helps you to summarize the labor required to deliver a business process, cycle time identifies how long the process takes from beginning to end, a key metric that customers/clients often list as a top concern.

Identifying the people, tool, and overhead costs associated with a business process brings a financial component to your work and positions you as a businessperson who understands how processes and costs relate to each other. The full-time equivalent (FTE) formula identifies the percentage of employee time spent supporting a business process. Learning to apply the overhead rate gives you a total employee cost perspective. Sometimes the sponsor cares only about a subset of numbers, such as the labor costs associated with a business process, in which case your job gets easier.

After completing the calculations described in this chapter, you can cut the data numerous ways to meet your needs, stating the cost for each step in the process, the cost per transaction, the time from beginning to end, where to focus your time in the improvement stage, or any other statistic that you want to share.

In step 5, you verified the accuracy of the process map with the process workers, stakeholders, sponsor, and process owner so when you move to step 6, improving the process, you feel comfortable that any improvement targets you set have the appropriate support from these groups.

In conducting the verification, focus on the accuracy of

the process flow and on the validation of the time estimates that the project team defined. Also identify any points of confusion or concern that surface, and address each one with the project team.

Time Estimate

To help plan the time that it takes to work through the two steps covered in this chapter, Figure 5-23 summarizes the amount of time you should expect to spend on steps 4 and 5 (estimating the process and cycle time, calculating the costs, and verifying the process map).

Event	Time	Purpose
Project team meeting: estimate process and cycle time	1–2 hours	■ Add process and cycle time to the process map in preparation for the improvement phase. ■ Identify volume.
Postmeeting work: calculate costs	16 hours	■ Identify the people, tool, and overhead costs associated with the business process.
Sponsor meeting	1 hour	■ Review the process summary.
Verify process map	5 hours (over 2 weeks)	■ Verify the accuracy of the process map before moving to the improvement phase.
Postvalidation work: update process map	4 hours	■ Make changes to the process map and documentation based on feedback.

Figure 5-23   Time Estimate—Steps 4–5: Estimate Time and Cost and Verify Process Map

Project Team Meeting

This meeting is a continuation of the project team meetings. I like to start this task as part of an existing meeting because doing so makes the work look like a natural continuation of the process mapping work. The time required for this step depends on the complexity of the process map. You may start off slow, but you will gain speed as the team becomes comfortable with this step.

Postmeeting Work

This time provides you with personal time to perform the calculations covered in this chapter and includes:

▶ Identifying the FTE number to use

▶ Calculating the FTEs required to support the business process

▶ Calculating the people costs, including the employee benefit rate

▶ Calculating the tool costs

▶ Calculating the overhead costs, using the overhead rate

▶ Determining the cost per transaction (in our example, per award)

▶ Summarizing the process times and costs

Sponsor Meeting

When you find yourself close to completing the analysis, schedule time with the sponsor to review the summary information you compiled. The sponsor will have a keen interest in your summary, and this meeting provides you with the chance for increased visibility.

Verify the Process Map

This time provides you with the occasion to meet with process workers, stakeholders, the sponsor, and the process owner to verify the accuracy of the process map you have drawn and make adjustments. For my example, I estimated five hours over a two-week period.

Postvalidation Work

This time provides you with personal time to make the appropriate changes to the process map and documentation.

What You Have Achieved

In this chapter, you have achieved the following:

▶ An estimate of how long the process takes to deliver the results

► An understanding of the labor required by the process

► Knowledge of the total cost for the business process

► An understanding of the cost of a single transaction

► Agreement on the validity of the process map

► Buy-in from the sponsor and/or process owner on the process map

► Recognition from your sponsor and/or process owner on your financial evaluation

► Most important, the *power* to know where to focus your efforts in the improvement stage

KNOWLEDGE CHECK

Use this knowledge check to validate your understanding of the material covered in steps 4–5.

Part 1: Select the best answer in the following multiple-choice questions by circling the correct choice.

1. What is the focus during process validation?
   a. Verify the accuracy of the process map.
   b. Validate the process and cycle time estimates.
   c. Identify areas requiring additional clarification.
   d. All of the above.

2. Which of the following is an example of hard cost savings?
   a. Qualitative savings.
   b. Deploying employees to more value-added work.
   c. Reducing head count.
   d. None of the above.

3. What are the categories that comprise process cost?
   a. Labor, software, and office space.
   b. People, tools, and overhead.
   c. Employee benefits, email system, and utilities.
   d. All of the above.

4. FTE, or full-time equivalent, is a method used to do what?
   a. Calculate employee benefits.

b. Calculate the number of employees required to support a business process.
c. Calculate the overhead expenses associated with running a business process.
d. All of the above.

5. Whom must you involve when verifying the process map?
a. The affected department.
b. The process owner and your manager.
c. Process workers, stakeholders, and sponsor.
d. All of the above.

Part 2: Identify whether the following statements refer to process or cycle time.

____1. The time required to complete a single activity in a process.   Process   Cycle

____2. The time required to complete an entire process.   Process   Cycle

____3. The time a customer or client can see.   Process   Cycle

____4. The elapsed time in a business process.   Process   Cycle

____5. The time that includes waiting time between steps in a business process.   Process   Cycle

____6. The time that incorporates the cost of the process workers.   Process   Cycle

____7. The type of time affected by annual volume.   Process   Cycle

Answers

Part 1: 1–d, 2–c, 3–b, 4–b, 5–c

Part 2: 1–process, 2–cycle, 3–cycle, 4–cycle, 5–cycle, 6–process, 7–process

CHAPTER 6

Step 6: Apply Improvement Techniques

Challenging Everything

On the basis of his prioritization results, Kendall Smith, the banking vice president from Chapter 2, picked where he wanted to start his process improvement effort. First, I helped him develop the scope definition document on the training process for newly hired employees; then we created the process map, including the time estimates. We validated the process map and set our improvement target as a 50 percent reduction in cycle time for the course development process.

As a result of drawing the process map for your current business process in step 3, you saw how the process works; then in step 4, you identified how long the process takes and how much it costs. Now we look at how to make the process more effective, efficient, and adaptable.

While listening to the project team talk about your process throughout the previous steps in the roadmap, you probably already have thoughts on how to improve the process. This knowledge, combined with the information in the scope definition document, prepares you for this step. If you think about the very manual recognition bonus award process we used as an example over the last several chapters, you undoubtedly have ideas on how to improve that process. Clearly, we can find ways to reduce the 11 days of cycle time.

The improvement technique wheel in Figure 6-1 shows the *Business Process* at the center of the wheel, the six techniques used to improve business processes wrapped around it in the middle circle, and the customer/client on the outer circle as a reminder of why we want to improve the business process in the first place. This chapter discusses each of the techniques and how to use them in business process improvement.

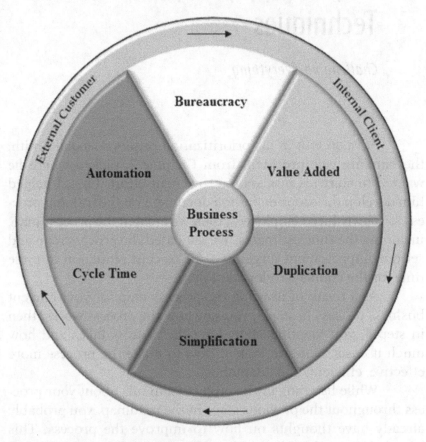

Figure 6-1 Improvement Technique Wheel

To use the improvement technique wheel, start at the top with *Bureaucracy*, the first improvement technique, and move clockwise around the spokes of the wheel, ending with *Automation*. The wheel depicts the automation technique last because we want to focus on automating an efficient rather than an inefficient business process. Applying the other five techniques first ensures that we remove the process inefficiencies before moving to automation.

Use each of the techniques one at a time during a project team meeting. I like to start this exercise at a new meeting, when the team has a fresh perspective, rather than at the middle or end of another team meeting. This work is difficult, and it helps to have an alert group.

The project team members should feel a bit uncomfortable during this step in the roadmap because your role is to challenge the status quo and push them to think strategically. Strategic thinking sounds complex, and some people feel that only a few people possess this skill, but it simply means an ability to conceptualize and see the big picture. Like anything else, you can improve the skill with practice.

To get started, introduce the improvement technique wheel, define each of the techniques, and explain how you will accomplish the work. Then walk through the process map that you created and focus on a single technique, applying it as thoroughly as possible before moving to the next technique. As you move along the improvement technique wheel, you will start to see the relationship of one technique to another. For example, in most cases, simplifying an activity or eliminating bureaucracy also reduces cycle time.

During this phase of the work, enlarge the completed process map to a poster size, as you did in step 3, so that everyone stays interested and can follow along as the team moves through the activities on the process map. Even with all the process mapping software tools available, I find that using paper and intentionally marking up a process map better engages a project team. I like to compare it to talking to someone in person or on the phone versus via email.

You can use the improvement technique wheel with any improvement method if your company subscribes to a particular standard.

Eliminate Bureaucracy

Tamara Chase, a buyer who specializes in purchasing merchandise for the home and garden line of a nationwide retailer, became frustrated when time after time her orders were not filled in a timely manner. Tamara works under pressure because of the competitive nature of her market, and she did not like having to wrestle with an internal process that negatively affected her ability to bring product into her stores.

The order processing cycle time, overburdened with multiple layers of approvals, seemed to be getting longer and longer. Tamara needed approval before she submitted an order for a new product to her central purchasing group, and then purchasing had to obtain additional approvals. The number of approvals required made it difficult for her to buy and distribute new products to her retail stores in time to beat the competition, and Tamara increasingly heard complaints from the store managers.

In a business process, bureaucracy requires following a series of activities that hinders an effective and efficient process. The process gets bogged down in red tape, sometimes for no apparent reason. Everyone knows bureaucracy when they see it. Red tape and inflexibility go hand in hand with bureaucracy.

You can normally trace the cause of bureaucracy to either the need for excess control, the fear of making a mistake, the desire to cover our backs in case something goes wrong, or simply a process that grew over time. You might wonder, because bureaucracy seems so counterproductive, how it can have any advocates. Even though no one outwardly admits to supporting bureaucracy, you will run into resistance as you work to eliminate it because of the fear of the unknown and the inclination of human nature to just carry on doing things in the same old way. In Tamara's case, I started by asking what would happen if the company eliminated some levels of approval. Would the world fall apart? Was Tamara incompetent? Would the next approval level not catch any possible errors? How often did the approval levels above Tamara disapprove her recommendation?

Jack Welch, former CEO of General Electric, is well-known for his dislike of bureaucracy. He calls it "productivity's enemy." Think about bureaucracy from this perspective: as the enemy.

It takes extra work to search for bureaucracy because it has become so commonplace, but the project team members will find countless steps in a business process that introduce bureaucracy—and they should strive to eliminate them. To accomplish this task, begin by walking through the process map box by box and challenge the project team to identify bureaucracy. Mark the activities identified as bureaucratic with a colored highlighter on the enlarged process map posted in the room. Use different-colored highlighters for the six improvement techniques. For example, use a green highlighter for bureaucracy, a pink highlighter for value added, and so forth.

In Alistar's recognition bonus award process, recall that activity 1 involved completing a form and sending it to the next-level manager. Do you see any potential bureaucracy in this step? You might ask:

Why is the form sent to the next-level manager?

This question helps the project team determine whether the requirement to gain another manager's signature adds value to the process or just adds a bureaucratic step. Who owns the budget? If manager 1 owns the budget, why does manager 2 have to approve an award? You may uncover other problems with the business process that do not relate to bureaucracy, but hold off on those issues and stay focused on bureaucracy to keep the team moving and on track.

Typically, you see a relationship between multiple approvals and bureaucracy, as in Tamara's case. If the reason for a second or third approval adds no value, eliminate the multiple approvals. The scope definition document you created in step 2 guides you through the exercise of eliminating bureaucracy. If an activity does not support the statements made in the scope definition, get rid of it.

In Tamara's case, the process required four approvals before purchasing sent the order to the vendor. After some discussion, we reduced the bureaucracy by keeping only two levels of approvals: central purchasing and finance. Although we focused on eliminating bureaucracy and reduced the number of approvals required, we also reduced the cycle time as a result. You can start to see the connection among the six techniques because reducing bureaucracy also reduces cycle time.

Another filter that you can use to eliminate bureaucracy is evaluating whether an activity supports a SALT requirement of a business process. SALT stands for:

Statutory
Audit
Legal
Tax

▶ **Statutory** denotes that the activity supports legislation or a government statute, such as imposing statutes of limitations, whether enacted by a national or state legislative governing body.

▶ **Audit** means examining records or transactions to check for accuracy or compliance with preestablished guidelines or rules.

▶ **Legal** signifies that the activity supports a law, like the labor laws that control minimum wage levels and overtime pay.

▶ **Tax** denotes a financial charge or fee paid to a government body, like a sales tax, income tax, or value-added tax.

If an activity supports SALT, it probably should remain, except perhaps for audits because we often audit too frequently. Validate the reason for an audit to determine whether it should continue. If an audit does remain, ask whether a spot audit can replace a normal audit to reduce the time required to conduct it. You run a spot audit on a subset of data or transactions. Spot audits do not cost as much as normal audits because they do not take as long to complete, yet they generally find the errors.

Tom Terez, well-known for his work on employee engagement (http://buildabetterworkplace.wordpress.com/), stated that the number one complaint employees had about their jobs was "too much workplace bureaucracy." He also found that employees spend about ten hours every week tangled in corporate red tape and cumbersome workplace rules.

Here are some questions you can ask the project team as you work to eliminate bureaucracy:

▶ How many approvals do we have in place? Why?

▶ Why must we approve an expenditure that has already been budgeted?

▶ Can we reduce the number of approvals required?

▶ Do we make decisions at the right point in the process?

▶ Do we generate unnecessary paperwork?

▶ How many copies of each document do we make?

▶ Why do we keep hardcopies?

▶ Do people receive information that they do not need?

▶ Do we understand what people do with the information or reports that we send them?

▶ Does one person check the work of another? Why?

▶ How do we use the information requested on a form in making decisions?

▶ Can we eliminate any forms? Do we absolutely need them?

▶ Does anyone read the weekly reports you produce?

▶ Do we have unnecessary rules?

▶ Does a policy or procedure get in the way?

▶ What will happen if an employee makes a mistake?

▶ Does the added scrutiny seem worth the expense?

Help the project team conceptualize the business process without bureaucracy. Ask them to show how an activity contributes to addressing the customer's/client's needs. If an activity does not contribute to customer/client satisfaction, if it negatively affects cycle time, or if it increases cost, then eliminate it.

Value Added

Tina Hernandez, marketing director for the consumer product division of a global company, felt that her company experienced an unusually long time to market. As Tina described the situation, time to market includes everything from idea conception through customer availability.

After I completed a value-added analysis, it became apparent that the problem lay with the distribution component of their marketing strategy. We identified activities in the distribution process that did not add value for the customer. Because every activity in a business process adds to the cost of the end product or service and because every step adds labor, overhead, or other expenses, you should spend time evaluating each activity to determine whether it adds value. Would customers willingly pay for a step in the business process if they were aware of the step?

The value-added analysis examines how each activity in a business process contributes value to the customer/client. Review the scope definition document from step 2 to understand what the customers/clients consider valuable, and ask whether each activity in the process contributes to delivering what you listed as customer/client needs. Then ask whether the customers/clients would agree that an activity adds value and whether they would pay for that step if you based your charges on a cost-per-activity fee.

In Alistar's recognition bonus award process, activity 3 had the compensation analyst reviewing the eligibility of the employee for a bonus award, ensuring that the manager provided appropriate justification, and validating that the award amount falls within the guidelines. Do you think that manager 1 would agree that these tasks add value to the process? You might ask questions like:

▶ Whose decision is it to determine when an employee deserves recognition?
▶ Why can't the manager be trusted to know whether an employee is eligible for an award?
▶ What happens if a manager exceeds the award guidelines?
▶ Do managers have a budget that they control?

These questions help determine whether the process should include the compensation department in this step. Why does the compensation analyst perform these tasks? Is the reason to check on the managers? Are the managers incompetent? If you look at the time that this step requires, you can see that it takes 20 to 30 minutes of process time and four days of cycle time. If the activity does not provide added value to the customer/client, you should try to eliminate it.

Notice again the close relationship between the improvement techniques—in this case, between the bureaucracy and value-added techniques. If we eliminate activity 3 from the recognition bonus award process because it does not add value for the customer/client, we also remove a degree of bureaucracy from the business process. However, we may have encountered resistance from the group if we tried to eliminate this activity when we discussed bureaucracy because the organization would defend the need for the step. Once the project team members discuss the same activity from the customer's/client's perspective as part of the value-added technique, they might have a harder time making the case that the step adds value to the customer/client.

With that said, what about the business or the operation? Should you always delete a step in the process just because it does not add value to the customer/client? The answer is yes, but now office politics comes into play. Even though activity 3 in the recognition bonus award process does not add value from the customer's/client's perspective, does it add value from the business's perspective—in this case, the compensation department? Even if a process step does not contribute to the customer's/client's value perspective, the step may still appear crucial to the organization. How would the compensation department feel about eliminating this step? It will probably claim that the step adds value; how else can they guarantee compliance or consistency across the company?

This may seem like a genuine concern because Alistar's compensation department owns responsibility for the consistent application of the company's pay programs. However, if you attribute the value of an activity to the business and not to the customer/client, then you should challenge the thinking and push for a candid answer to the question, "Why?" If you cannot eliminate the step, you can probably minimize it.

Just as we saw when we examined bureaucracy, numerous steps in a business process do not add any value to the final output; so you should eliminate these activities as well. Walk through the process map again box by box, this time challenging the value-added contribution of each activity. Mark the activities that have value to the customer/client in one color, those with value to the organization or business in another, and those with no value in a third color. Your process map should start looking like an artist's palette.

You can use the value-added analysis table shown in Figure 6-2 as an alternative to color coding the process map for value-added activities. If you choose to use the table, simply list the business process activities in the left column and add three additional columns for customer/client value added, business value added, and non–value added. Put an X in the appropriate column for each activity. Figure 6-2 shows what the analysis might look like for Alistar's recognition bonus award process.

Number	Activity	Customer/Client Value Added	Business Value Added	Nonvalue Added
1	Complete recognition bonus award form and mail to next level manager		X	
2	Approve or reject request			X
3	Review eligibility, justification, and award amount		X	
4	Send authorization to payroll	X		
5	Notify requesting manager		X	
6	Communicate award to employee	X		
7	Update employee system of record and retain hardcopy		X	

Figure 6-2 Recognition Bonus Award Process: Value-Added Analysis

Although color coding brings more visual clarity to the work and allows everyone to stay involved, the value-added analysis shows the same information and may work better for complex processes. Even if you color-code the map, use the value-added analysis as a way to summarize the project team's final decisions.

In my experience, the hardest activities to eliminate are those that the business considers valuable for its own reasons because the temptation to say an activity adds business value, instead of being a bureaucratic step, is far too easy. You have to show courage when talking about business-value-added activities. Remember to think strategically and keep the big picture in mind. Make the project team uncomfortable by challenging the status quo. The main question to ask when applying the value-added technique is, "Would the customer/client pay for this activity?"

Eliminate Duplication

Wendy Chan, manager of the workforce analysis group for a software company, has responsibility for running the company's monthly head count reports to track turnover and other employee-related statistics. Departments on the operational side of the business also track their own head count, instead of relying on Wendy's data, so that they have the information available to conduct additional analysis.

Duplication, or redundancy, occurs when multiple groups involved in a business process form silos with no integration between them. Each group or department maintains a separate set of data because they want to have all the information they require in order to tell their story as they want it heard. Sometimes the duplication appears innocent because one group or department simply does not understand what the other group is doing; at other times, one group may not believe in the other's competence, or, worse, the groups compete.

In Wendy's case, the workforce analysis group did not provide the level of detail that the operational groups wanted, and so operations duplicated the work instead of asking the workforce analysis group to change their report to meet the operation's business need. The workforce analysis group would have gladly changed the report if told about operations' dissatisfaction. This example demonstrates both a lack of awareness of client needs by the workforce analysis group and shows how easy it is for duplication to occur.

Each time a step in the business process moves from one department to another, a handoff occurs. Handoffs can easily lead to duplication of efforts, errors, and redundancy of information, so you should pay attention to any activity on the process map where a handoff occurs.

You can spot the duplication of efforts when you find multiple employees keeping copies of the same documents. Think of your own company, and you can probably identify cases where more than one person files a copy of a document for some reason. Look at Alistar Corporation's recognition bonus award process:

- ▶ Manager 1 retains a hardcopy of the completed form when the bonus award is requested.
- ▶ Manager 2 keeps a hardcopy of the signed form when approving the bonus award.
- ▶ Compensation files a hardcopy in its recognition bonus award file.
- ▶ Personnel retains a hardcopy in the employee's personnel file.

Does everyone need a copy of the document? When multiple employees maintain the same data, it increases the cost to the company. It takes time for an employee to copy and file a document, and a cost is associated with the employee's labor. Copies take up storage space, and a cost is associated with the increased storage requirements. Although the space required may seem small, think about it on a company-wide scale and imagine the cost multiplied across your entire company. Also consider the legal implications of maintaining documentation, and answer the question, "Where should the company's official documentation be stored?"

A challenge exists when a company does not define a single source of data. In Wendy's case, which head count report is correct? Do the operations and the workforce analysis groups calculate head count differently? Do the groups use different sources of data? Data errors can easily occur when different groups use different sources. As a result, you begin to doubt the integrity of the data. *Data integrity* means consistent, correct, and accessible data. Problems with data quality, or data integrity, cost companies billions of dollars a year. Working to confirm that you have a single source of data helps to reduce costs and errors.

When you completed step 5 and verified your process map with the process workers, stakeholders, and the process owner, the project team made the appropriate changes so that the map accurately reflected how the process works. During the validation meetings, confirm where handoffs and possible duplications occur. In addition to the steps in the process, look for duplication in data and reports generated from the process because employees often duplicate data or reports.

You may have to talk to other departments to uncover redundancy if your process map focuses on only one department. Find out what happens at the other end of an activity after you hand work off to another department. Look for occasions where you can:

▶ Establish a single source of data.
▶ Eliminate two employees doing the same work, like generating similar reports.
▶ Eliminate two people maintaining the same data.
▶ Eliminate the dual entry of information.
▶ Minimize document storage.

Simplification

The inefficient warehouse process uncovered by Tina Hernandez caused her company's marketing team to reevaluate their distribution strategy. Tina's colleague admitted that his marketing team spent more time developing the product, price, and promotion components of their overall strategy than they did the fourth "P" (placement). They did not think too long about distribution decisions and instead continued with business as usual. With Tina's concern about time to market, the marketing team reconsidered and agreed that they had to make a change. Marketing felt they could identify more streamlined distribution options to further improve the product's time to market.

Simplification, or streamlining the process, means reducing or eliminating the complexity of an activity in a business process so that the process becomes easier to understand and more efficient. When you keep a process simple, it becomes easier to sustain and more flexible in responding to customer/client needs. Keep one of the Dalai Lama's quotations in mind as you work to simplify a business process: "Simplicity is the key to happiness in the modern world." Albert Einstein came up with his own observation: "Simplicity means the achievement of maximum effect with minimum means."

Over time, our business processes become increasingly burdensome as we accommodate changes in the business. We cause our processes to become bloated by continually adding complexity. Looking at your process map, identifying where complexity exists, and simplifying the related activities become your main focus with this technique.

In the recognition bonus award process, we started by looking at the form used in activity 1. Since we decided we could not eliminate the form, we simplified and redesigned it to keep the information required to a minimum, while ensuring that managers could easily obtain the required data without having to go to a myriad of sources to obtain the information. To simplify the form, I asked the project team questions like:

▶ Is any unnecessary information requested on the form?
▶ Where does the manager obtain the information requested on the form?
▶ Is the information readily available?
▶ How often do managers call compensation with questions on how to complete the form, and what kinds of questions do they ask?

When you start looking at your company's forms, you will find most of them more complex than necessary and, as a result, take longer to complete. Streamline all your forms so they include only the information essential to making a decision. Look for chances to simplify all reports and documentation.

You can find countless examples of unnecessary complexity in business processes, so keep the old KISS engineering philosophy in mind: Keep it simple, stupid. (If you find *stupid* offensive, you can say, "Keep it simple, silly" or "Keep it short and sweet" or "Keep it sweet and simple." You get the idea.)

In activity 3 in the recognition bonus award process, how often does compensation have to call the manager, or vice versa, in completing the tasks associated with this step? Think about the number of times a phone call is made to ask a process question. Eliminate unnecessary calls by simplifying the language on forms and providing any required information directly on the form.

Here are other questions you can ask the project team as you work to simplify the process:

▶ Can we streamline any step in the process?

▶ Can we streamline or simplify any of the forms?

▶ How many emails are sent at any point in the process? A substantial number of emails signify that unnecessary complexity exists.

▶ Where do employees go to obtain information to complete any step in the process?

▶ Do you see any roadblocks?

▶ Do you see unnecessary handoffs?

▶ Can we standardize a step, a report, or a form to make it easier to understand?

▶ Do we know the number of errors we make and why?

▶ Can we eliminate or combine any steps in the process?

▶ Must process workers call other people to complete any step in the process?

> ► Does everyone understand the process?
> ► How do we use data and reports throughout the process?

You should consider redesigning the process to make it simple for the customer/client. When you applied the value-added technique, you retained activities that added value to the customer/client; now you focus on the ease of interaction.

As you apply the improvement techniques, you will start uncovering cultural changes that have to occur in the organization, and these types of changes are often difficult to implement. Nevertheless, keep track of them, even though they may take a long time to accomplish. Later in this chapter, I discuss the *impact analysis* as a tool to capture changes that have to occur to implement a new, improved business process. Do not exclude a change from your plans just because it appears challenging. Sometimes we exact the biggest gains from difficult changes.

You should continue to notice the similarity between several of the improvement techniques. When you simplify a business process, you also have the opportunity to eliminate bureaucracy. When you eliminate redundancy, you simplify the process. When you look at value-added activities, it leads to reducing bureaucracy. Although the distinctions among the techniques may seem blurry, I encourage you to work through them one at a time because you use slightly different mental filters for each technique. It does not matter what you call something, as long as you reach every nook and cranny in a business process.

Reduce Cycle Time

Kendall Smith wanted to reduce the cycle time required to develop new training by 50 percent. It normally took his training department six months to design and develop a new course, but Kendall wanted to reduce the development time to 90 days because of the upcoming bank merger.

Chapter 5 defined cycle time as the overall time it takes to complete an entire process—from the first step to the last, including waiting or elapsed time. Customers and clients care about cycle time because they feel it; they recognize how long it takes to receive the result. The business cares about reducing cycle time because doing so increases productivity and frees up resources.

In the recognition bonus award process, the cycle time summary in Figure 5-3 showed that one bonus award can take 11 days to process (cycle time), even though the activities involved in producing the award only take about one hour (the process time). Eleven days may or may not seem too long, but if your customers/clients say that they want a quick turnaround, then 11 days will feel too long to them. In this case, you should reduce the cycle time of the business process.

Look at each activity in the business process to identify where to reduce cycle time, so you can adapt to business changes and respond faster to your customers/clients. Look at activities that have long cycle times, and identify how to reduce the time required for those activities. In Figure 5-3, what activities contributed to the high cycle time? The two activities with the highest cycle time are:

- ▶ **Activity 2:** Approving or rejecting an award by manager 2 can take five days.
- ▶ **Activity 3:** Compensation's review of the information can add another four days.

If we can eliminate the second manager's approval, along with compensation's review of the data and the notification, we eliminate nine days.

At Alistar, we reduced the cycle time by eliminating activity 3. Compensation no longer reviewed the form. Instead, they delegated authority to the managers to make decisions on their own employees. Because compensation expressed concern about managers following the guidelines, compensation agreed to perform quarterly audits in order to validate that managers followed the company guidelines for bonus awards. This change reduced the bureaucracy and improved the client's perception of the process because the cycle time went down.

Look at how you can reduce the cycle time of any activity with a high number. Understand why a delay exists. Asking *why* will prove to be one of your best weapons in completing this work. For example:

➤ Why can't manager 1 use the budget as he or she sees fit?
➤ Why won't a spot (or occasional) audit work instead of reviewing every proposed award?

Even when the project team gives you an answer, you can ask why as a follow-up question to further fine-tune the process.

A cycle time analysis, shown in Figure 6-3, provides you with another tool to help with this technique. In this example, I adapted Figure 5-3 to include the potential reasons for a delay and possible ways to reduce the cycle time for the recognition bonus award process. I added two new columns: *Cause(s) of Delay* and *Possible Resolutions*. After building the table and entering the data in the first two columns, start by defining a threshold for the *Days* column, which assists you in deciding where to focus the project team's attention.

Activity Number	Days	Cause(s) of Delay	Possible Resolutions
1	0.125 day		
2	5 days	Cause 1 Cause 2 Cause 3	Resolution 1 Resolution 2
3	4 days	Cause 1 Cause 2 Cause 3	Resolution 1 Resolution 2
4	n/a		
5	0.25 days		
6	1 day		
7	1 day		
8	1 day		

Figure 6-3 Recognition Bonus Award Process: Cycle Time Analysis

In Alistar's case, the project team set the threshold at four days; that is, they decided to examine any activity that took four days or longer. As a result, we focused our analysis on activities 2 and 3, which appear in the white rows in Figure 6-3.

Once you define the threshold, discuss why these activities take so long, and list the potential causes for the delay in the table. After listing the possible causes, move through the causes one by one, identify alternatives that may eliminate or reduce the delay, and write the alternatives in the possible resolutions column.

As you work to reduce cycle time, focus on topics like:

- ▶ Reducing handoffs
- ▶ Optimizing activities that add value to the process
- ▶ Eliminating activities that do not add value
- ▶ Reducing the cycle time of high cycle time activities or, better still, eliminating them
- ▶ Performing activities in parallel instead of one at a time
- ▶ Combining activities
- ▶ Benchmarking the industry standard (benchmarking is discussed in Chapter 13)

In addition to making the business process effective for your customer/client, reducing cycle time also leads to an efficient process for the business, thus increasing productivity and freeing up resources to do more valuable work.

Automation

Now that you have squeezed every last bit of efficiency from the process using your analytical and mental skills, you can look at how technology can help the process become even more effective and efficient.

In this discussion of the use of technology to automate the process, I focus on technology that you probably have available to you or that you can purchase inexpensively. I do not talk about major system implementations because one employee trying to improve an everyday business process does not have the authority to spend a few million dollars on a new computer system. Even if you can purchase a new application, you probably have to suffer through a long procurement process. If you have implemented company-wide systems, you should still follow the techniques presented in this chapter to ensure that you have an efficient process that maximizes your technology investment.

You may hear different schools of thought about whether automation belongs at the beginning or the end of business process improvement. You may have heard this basic question:

Does the technology drive the process?
Or . . .
Does the process drive the technology?

If your background includes large system implementations, you have probably seen the technology drive the business process. A company buys a new enterprise resource planning system, and everyone gets busy defining new business processes on the basis of the system's available functionality.

You find technology at the end of the improvement technique wheel because I lean toward the second scenario; I like to see an efficient process drive the technology. We want to focus on automating an efficient, not an inefficient, process. Of course, you may not always have this choice.

If you think of technology right away during the improvement phase, you can too easily start thinking about building a spreadsheet or a database, when in reality you should probably eliminate the activity altogether because it provides no added value to the customer/client. Therefore, I like to apply the other five techniques first, *then* look at the new business process for points in the process where technology can increase efficiency.

Bill Gates is credited with saying, "The first principle for any technology you contemplate introducing into a business is that automation applied to an efficient operation will magnify the efficiency. The second is that automation applied to an inefficient operation will just magnify the inefficiency." I could not agree more.

Alistar Corporation's recruiting process provides an example of how automation can help improve a business process. The company has a volume-driven hiring process, which requires them to fill an unusually large number of hourly jobs that pay little more than the minimum wage. Recruitment departments, like Alistar's, often measure their success by a series of statistics such as time to fill, number of open requisitions, or number of hires. Alistar had cumbersome reporting techniques, so we redesigned a couple of their reports to take advantage of the data sitting in their recruiting system and combined that data with additional data in a Microsoft Access database to deliver reports that provided the appropriate statistics to senior managers.

Additionally, we used Microsoft's InfoPath software to build a form that allowed managers to submit approvals for open positions electronically, which used workflow to send requests to the recruitment department.

Spend time learning about the existing technologies in your company so you are aware of the tools you can use in the automation phase. Become familiar with the existing systems that support your company's business processes. In addition to existing systems, some of the common, inexpensive tools you probably have available are:

- ▶ Microsoft Office tools like Word, Excel, PowerPoint, and Access
- ▶ File-sharing and collaboration software like Microsoft SharePoint
- ▶ Business intelligence and warehouse tools
- ▶ Network drives or collaboration sites where you can store shared documents
- ▶ Email and the capability to design forms
- ▶ Text messaging
- ▶ Workflow
- ▶ Portals or intranets
- ▶ Other available options that work with your enterprise resource planning tool (e.g., Winshuttle functionality that integrates with SAP and allows for the automation of transactions and the mass upload of data)

All these simple, everyday tools can help automate your business processes.

In summary, Alistar's recognition bonus award process

shows how to use several of the improvement techniques. Figure 6-4 shows an updated version of the process map after we applied all the techniques. The figure shows that we made the following changes to the recognition bonus award process:

▶ We gained agreement on eliminating the second manager's approval and allowing the original manager to manage his or her own budget.

▶ Although we could not gain agreement to eliminate the form entirely, we simplified it and introduced technology in activity 1 by creating a Microsoft InfoPath form that would workflow to payroll instead of using interoffice mail to send the hardcopy.

▶ We eliminated the requirement for compensation to review every form. Instead, we instituted a new quarterly audit process, depicted at the bottom section of Figure 6-4. Compensation now audits 20 percent of awards submitted for the prior quarter by running a standard report from its system of record. This spot audit randomly selects the awards to review.

▶ Compensation agreed to permit the managers to determine the appropriate justification for an award, so the only items left to audit include the award amounts and the employee's eligibility.

▶ Compensation still felt the need to keep track of managers who did not follow the guidelines so that repeat offenders could receive constructive feedback through the performance management process.

As this walkthrough shows, we reduced the cycle time from 11 days to three, a meaningful improvement to the business process. Managers like the authority they now have, and Compensation feels that it can still hold managers accountable for following the guidelines.

Impact Analysis

As the project team works to improve the business process, they identify changes that have to occur in the organization

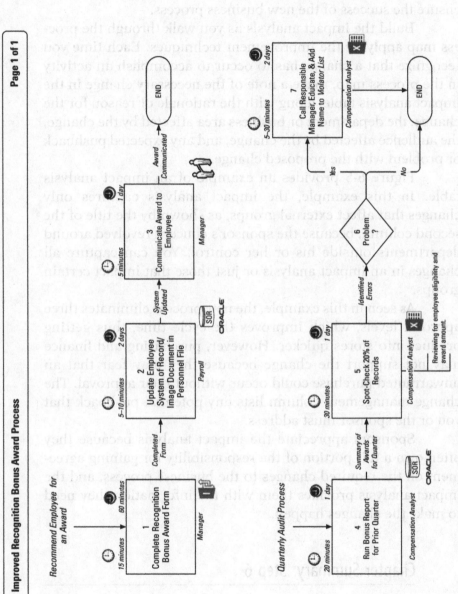

Figure 6-4 Alistar Corporation Improved Process Map

to obtain the expected degree of improvement. The impact analysis tool allows you to capture the changes that must occur to ensure the success of the new business process.

Build the impact analysis as you walk through the process map applying the improvement techniques. Each time you recognize that a change has to occur to accomplish an activity in the process map, make a note of the necessary change in the impact analysis table, along with the rationale or reason for the change, the department or business area affected by the change, the audience affected by the change, and any expected pushback or problem with the proposed change.

Figure 6-5 provides an example of an impact analysis table. In this example, the impact analysis captures only changes that affect external groups, as shown by the title of the second column, because the sponsor's concern revolved around departments outside his or her control. You can capture all changes in an impact analysis or just those that impact certain groups.

As seen in this example, the new process eliminates three approval levels, which improves the cycle time, thus getting product into stores quicker. However, purchasing and finance may not support the change because they may fear that an unwarranted purchase could occur without their approval. The change management column lists any potential pushback that you or the sponsor must address.

Sponsors appreciate the impact analysis because they often own a fair portion of the responsibility for gaining agreement on the required changes to the business process, and the impact analysis provides them with the information they need to make the changes happen.

Chapter Summary: Step 6

Applying the six improvement techniques one at a time assists you in evaluating your business processes in a thoughtful, planned approach. The improvement technique wheel guides you through eliminating bureaucracy, evaluating value-

Reference Number	Process Change(s) That Affect External Groups	Rationale	Area Impacted	Population/ Group Impacted	Change Management
1	<List the change that has to occur.>	<State why the change is important.>	<List the department (e.g., training) or business area (e.g., retail).>	<List the affected groups.>	<Identify the potential problems with the proposed change.>
2	Eliminate three of the approval levels required on purchases today.	Reduces cycle time by speeding up the approval process. Gets product into retail stores quicker, thus better positioning the business in a competitive environment.	Purchasing; finance	Senior buyer; purchasing manager; finance manager	Only one person in purchasing and finance will now approve buyer purchases. Because multiple levels of managers are accustomed to approving purchase orders over $10,000 today, the managers may not feel comfortable with the change.

Figure 6-5 Impact Analysis

added activities, eliminating duplication and redundancy, simplifying the process/reports/forms, reducing cycle time, and applying automation tools.

Although the differentiation among the techniques may appear blurry at times, you should use the techniques one at a time because the project team will use slightly different mental filters for each. Applying the techniques one at a time ensures that you squeeze every last drop out of each one.

Remember that:

► Bureaucracy is "productivity's enemy."

► Use **SALT** as a filter to eliminate bureaucracy.

▶ Keep it simple, silly.

▶ "Simplicity is the key to happiness in the modern world."

▶ "Automation applied to an efficient operation will magnify the efficiency."

▶ "Automation applied to an inefficient operation will magnify the inefficiency."

Use either color coding on your process map to highlight the six improvement techniques, or capture the data in a table like the value-added analysis in Figure 6-2 or the cycle time analysis in Figure 6-3.

Saving the automation technique until last guarantees that you apply technology to an efficient, not an inefficient, process.

Creating an impact analysis as you apply the improvement techniques helps you know whom you have to meet with to gain agreement for proposed changes.

Time Estimate

Figure 6-6 summarizes the time you should expect to spend applying the improvement techniques (step 6).

Event	Time	Purpose
Project team meeting: individual improvement techniques Develop impact analysis	1–2 hours per technique (depending on the size of the process map)	■ Identify points in the process to apply a technique, moving clockwise along the improvement technique wheel. ■ To identify the changes that have to occur to implement the new business process.
Postmeeting work	40 hours	■ Update the process map and documentation to incorporate changes made. ■ Gain approval, if required.

Figure 6-6 Time Estimate—Step 6: Apply Improvement Techniques

Project Team Meeting

During the project team meetings, spend at least one hour to apply each technique as thoroughly as possible. Create the impact analysis as you apply each technique. I like to start this meeting by introducing the improvement technique wheel and then going on to define one technique at a time. For example, define bureaucracy and ask the team to share an experience they have had with bureaucracy. This starts the conversation flowing. If you leave a technique too soon, you miss some of the opportunity for improvement, so demonstrate patience and hesitate if the project team seems ready to move to the next technique. Let everyone feel somewhat uncomfortable and squirm a bit before moving to the next technique.

Postmeeting Work

This time provides you with the chance to update the process map and the corresponding documentation on the basis of the changes the project team made. You may also have to gain approval for some of the changes that the process team has suggested, with either the sponsor, process owner, or a stakeholder.

What You Have Achieved

In this chapter, you have achieved the following:

- ▶ An awareness of six improvement techniques
- ▶ An understanding of how to create a value-added analysis
- ▶ A grasp of how to use SALT as a filter for bureaucracy
- ▶ An awareness of how to eliminate non–value-added work
- ▶ An insight into how to eliminate duplication or redundancy
- ▶ An understanding of how to simplify, or streamline, a business process
- ▶ A grasp of how to reduce cycle time
- ▶ An awareness of how to develop a cycle time analysis
- ▶ An insight into how to automate a business process
- ▶ An analysis of the changes that have to occur

▶ Most important, the *power* to understand how to look systematically for ways to improve a business process

KNOWLEDGE CHECK

Use this knowledge check to validate your understanding of the material covered in step 6. Match the correct answer to the statement by placing the appropriate letter on the blank line.

_____ 1. Multiple groups maintain the same data; redundancy.

_____ 2. Time required for the end-to-end process to be completed.

_____ 3. One improvement technique has no relationship to another technique (True/False).

_____ 4. Following a series of required activities hinders the process; red tape.

_____ 5. The order in which to apply the improvement techniques is important (True/False).

_____ 6. Technology is applied to improve the process.

_____ 7. Streamline the process and eliminate complexity.

_____ 8. A filter (like legal or tax requirements) is used to help eliminate bureaucracy.

_____ 9. Each activity in a process contributes value to the customer.

A. Bureaucracy; B. Value added; C. Duplication; D. Simplification; E. Cycle time; F. Automation; G. SALT; H. False; I. True

1-C, 2-E, 3-H, 4-A, 5-I, 6-F, 7-D, 8-G, 9-B

Answers

Step 7: Create Internal Controls, Tools, and Metrics

Making It Real

Establishing internal controls, developing tools to increase the effectiveness, efficiency, and adaptability of a business process, and developing metrics bring the process to life beyond just creating a process map:

▶ Internal controls help prevent errors.

▶ Tools help employees perform their job more easily.

▶ Metrics show whether the process works as planned.

Internal Controls

Imagine the level of embarrassment when an employee received congratulations from a colleague on her promotion to an executive-level position *before* her vice president had a chance to share the good news directly with her. This happened at a bank that brought me in after this occurrence to help them put internal controls in place for their key business processes. It seemed the colleague had viewed the employee's new title when they right-clicked on the colleague's name in their email system even though no update had occurred in the human resource information system.

Senior management had chastised and embarrassed the

department responsible for the error before I came in to work with the firm over the next six weeks. In this case, it was a simple human error that caused all the commotion. Yet the department ended up spending an unanticipated $150,000 in labor and travel costs to create appropriate internal controls for their business processes to prevent future mistakes.

Human errors or employee misunderstandings occur every day in business, costing billions of dollars nationally. Think about the debacles we face with businesses each day because proper processes, procedures, or controls simply do not exist. Human error in health care alone (as designated by *preventable adverse events*) leads to the death of 210,000–400,000 patients a year by those who seek care at a hospital, according to a study in the *Journal of Patient Safety*.

Balbir S. Dhillon, a professor at the University of Ottawa, has published many articles and books presenting statistics on reliability and safety. In his 2004 book, *Human Reliability and Error in Medical Systems*, he estimates the annual national cost between $17 billion and $37.6 billion. Although he does not have updated statistics, online research continues to put the cost well into the billions. This makes medical errors the third leading cause of death. (The Centers for Disease Control and Prevention statistics list heart disease and cancer as the leading causes of death.)

Internal controls ensure accuracy and reliability at crucial points in a business process and can help reduce the number of errors introduced in the process.

The Sarbanes-Oxley Act, introduced in 2002, resulted from corporate and accounting scandals, not necessarily human errors; however, this law requires a focus on internal controls. Section 302 pertains to financial reports and states, "The signing officers are responsible for internal controls and have evaluated these internal controls within the previous ninety days."

When you start looking at a business process to identify internal controls, you may be surprised that none exist. In my experience, this happens frequently. Employees more often than not try to do a good job, but mistakes happen and a systematic approach to preventing the same error from recurring is not always in place. To establish internal controls, identify the points in the business process where something can go wrong.

To begin, start by walking through the improved process map you created in step 6 and move through it box by box, asking the project team what can go wrong with each activity. If a mistake can happen, signify this likelihood with an icon to denote that an error might occur. I like to use a warning symbol, as shown in Figure 7-1, to denote that an internal control should exist because everyone recognizes what this cautionary sign means.

Figure 7-1 Warning Symbol

Move through the entire process map, and put warning symbols next to each activity that may cause an error. Do not discuss the details about the mistakes or how you can avoid the error until you have identified *all* the potential problem spots. If the project team members have trouble identifying potential problems, ask them, "What can go wrong at this point?" If an activity includes the use of spreadsheets or other tools, delve into those items and again ask what problems can occur. Think of what can go wrong with everyday tools, like formulas in spreadsheets, and look for ways to avoid the errors.

Once the project team identifies the potential problems, discuss how to avoid each one. I suggest listing all the problem spots *first* before discussing each one in detail because it takes quite a bit of time to adequately discuss what can go wrong and how to avoid the pitfalls for each activity marked with a warning symbol. If you stop and have a thorough discussion each time you put a warning symbol on the process map, human nature comes into play, and the team may get discouraged with the degree of work involved in error proofing. As a result, participants may fail to identify as many potential problem spots as they should.

Once you have gone through the entire process map and

added a warning symbol wherever a mistake can happen, lead the project team through a discussion of each potential error, and then agree on how to avoid them in the future.

Figure 7-2 shows a table you can use to list the internal controls on a dry-erase board to keep the conversation visible to the project team.

Activity Number	Activity Description	Possible Issue(s)	Internal Control(s)

Figure 7-2 Internal Controls

- ▶ **Activity Number:** This is the number you gave the activity on the process map.

- ▶ **Activity Description:** The text description comes from the activity box on the process map.

- ▶ **Possible Issue(s):** Identify the various mistakes that might occur with this activity. The project team may find more than one potential mistake because, once they start thinking about errors, they may uncover multiple opportunities for errors. Document each mistake in the possible issue column, using a new row for each potential mistake.

- ▶ **Internal Control(s):** Identify how to error-proof each of the potential mistakes that the project team identified. This column becomes the list of internal controls for the business process.

Figure 7-3 shows the recognition bonus award process from Chapter 6 (Figure 6-4) with two internal controls identified. Notice the addition of a warning symbol to activity 1, completing the recognition bonus award form and emailing it to payroll, and to activity 5, spot-checking 20 percent of the records in the quarterly audit process.

Once the project team identifies potential mistakes, discuss how to solve them. Figure 7-4 summarizes the potential errors that can occur with the recognition bonus award process and identifies the controls the compensation department put in

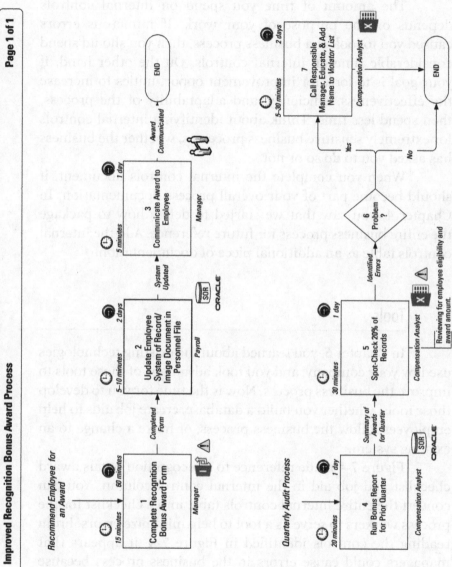

Figure 7-3 Alistar Corporation Improved Process Map: Sample Internal Control

place. This figure shows that more than one error may occur for a single activity.

The amount of time you spend on internal controls depends on the purpose of your work. If numerous errors caused you to look at a business process, then you should spend considerable time on internal controls. On the other hand, if your goal is to look for improvement opportunities to increase the effectiveness, efficiency, and adaptability of the process, then spend less time. Think about identifying internal controls for extremely sensitive business processes, whether the business has asked you to do so or not.

When you complete the internal controls document, it should become part of your overall process documentation. In Chapter 4, you saw that we started to define how to package the entire business process for future reference. Add the internal controls table as an additional piece of documentation.

Tools

In Chapter 6, you learned about the existing technologies used by your company, and you took advantage of those tools to improve the business process. Now is the time for you to develop those tools, whether you build a database, create job aids to help employees follow the business process, or make a change to an existing system.

Figure 7-4 made reference to a recognition bonus award checklist and job aid in the internal control column. You can convert the entire internal controls table into a checklist for the process workers to serve as a tool to help minimize errors. From reading the controls identified in Figure 7-4, it appears that managers could cause errors in the business process because the compensation department delegated them the authority to administer their own recognition bonus awards. It also seems that the compensation analysts may make additional errors in running the spot audits. So let us take a look at two job aids I developed to help the managers and compensation analysts.

Activity Number	Activity Description	Possible Issue(s)	Internal Control(s)
1	Complete recognition bonus award form and email to payroll	Employee may be bonus or incentive eligible. If so, then the employee is not eligible for a recognition bonus award.	When running the quarterly audit, the compensation analyst will: ■ Check the employee job numbers in the employee system of record to validate that they do not have "bonus" or "other bonus" checked as an attribute of the job. ■ Confirm the employee's eligibility following the criteria outlined in the recognition bonus award checklist.
		Managers across the company may not use the same criteria in determining the amount of money given to an employee.	■ Managers will use the justification criteria and award guidelines outlined in the recognition bonus award job aid created for them by the compensation department. ■ Compensation analyst will validate the award amounts in the quarterly audit. ■ Compensation analyst will provide feedback to managers who do not follow the guidelines and will regularly audit those managers.
2	Spot-check 20% of records	Compensation analyst may not agree with some of the justification reasons used by managers.	■ Compensation analyst will validate any questionable justifications with a compensation consultant.
		Compensation analyst may forget a step in the audit.	■ Compensation analyst will use the recognition bonus award checklist when conducting the audit.

Figure 7-4 Recognition Bonus Award Process: Internal Controls Document

Job Aids

Simple, quick job aids can provide easy step-by-step directions or guidelines to help drive consistency in a business process. They can help with complex tasks and provide reference information at employees' fingertips that they otherwise have to repeatedly look up. Try to keep job aids to a one-sheet document that is either single- or double-sided for ease of use. Figure 7-5 shows an example of a job aid that you can create for managers so they have the necessary information at their fingertips.

Figure 7-6 shows an example of a checklist you can create.

As these two examples demonstrate, you can create countless tools, depending on the complexity of your business process. You can create a tool to simplify a step in the process, to drive consistency across multiple departments, or to explain how to use a particular item like a Microsoft Access database. Job aids can help process workers and stakeholders more easily understand a complex business process.

Custom Email Forms

Figures 7-7 and 7-8 show that you can create custom forms in Microsoft Outlook by using the forms feature of the software. You can then use the normal capabilities of the email system to send the form to other employees. These two figures resulted from working with a client in the compensation department who expressed concern that his recruiters did not always provide the necessary information for the department to provide a salary rate quotation on a new employee; the client had to make multiple phone calls to collect the required information. The tool I created improved the workflow and eliminated the missing information because the recruiter could not send the form without filling in all the fields.

Use tools like this when you need to ensure that a requester supplies the required information for either making a decision or acting on a transaction and to avoid the need to call the requester and ask for the missing information.

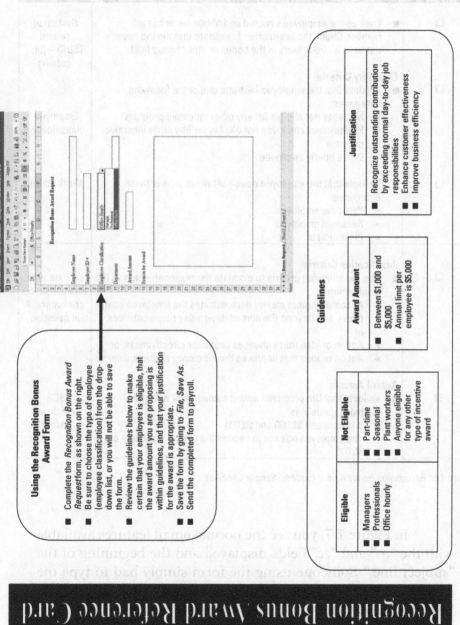

Figure 7-5 Sample Manager Job Aid

Recognition Bonus Award Reference Card

Using the Recognition Bonus Award Form

- Complete the *Recognition Bonus Award Request* form, as shown on the right.
- Be sure to choose the type of employee (employee classification) from the drop-down list, or you will not be able to save the form.
- Review the guidelines below to make certain that your employee is eligible, that the award amount you are proposing is within guidelines, and that your justification for the award is appropriate.
- Save the form by going to *File, Save As*.
- Send the completed form to payroll.

Recognition Bonus Award Request

	Eligible	Not Eligible
	- Managers - Professionals - Office hourly	- Part-time - Seasonal - Plant workers - Anyone eligible for any other type of incentive award

Guidelines

Award Amount

- Between $1,000 and $5,000
- Annual limit per employee is $5,000

Justification

- Recognize outstanding contribution by exceeding normal day-to-day job responsibilities
- Enhance customer effectiveness
- Improve business efficiency

Done	Action	Tool
❑	■ Look up the employee's record and obtain his or her job number. Check the job number to validate that the job does not have a check mark in the bonus or other bonus field.	System of record (SOR)—job catalog
❑	**Eligibility Criteria** ■ Validate that the employee falls into one of the following categories: ▶ Manager not eligible for any other incentive program ▶ Professional employee not eligible for any other incentive program ▶ Office hourly employee	Employee classification
❑	■ Validate that the employee does *not* fall into one of these categories: ▶ Part-time employee ▶ Seasonal employee ▶ Plant worker	Work status
❑	**Justification Criteria** ■ Use the following criteria to evaluate the reasonableness of the justification: ▶ Accomplishment clearly demonstrates the employee going above and beyond the normal day-to-day responsibilities; or ▶ Action or idea that enhances customer effectiveness; or ▶ Action or idea that improves the efficiency of the business.	Validate with compensation consultant, if in question
❑	**Award Amount** ■ Validate that the proposed award amount falls within the following guidelines: ▶ It is between $1,000 and $5,000. ▶ The employee has not exceeded the annual maximum of $5,000.	SOR (employee history)

Figure 7-6 Recognition Bonus Award Process: Sample Checklist

In Figure 7-7, you see the normal email features available with the "to" and "cc" fields displayed and the beginning of the "subject line." Someone using the form simply had to type the name of the candidate on the subject line and enter the message in the white text section.

In Figure 7-8, the second tab, internal candidate, is selected, and the recruiter now enters the current salary information when requesting a salary rate quotation. Compensation then fills in the percentage increase, which populates the new salary fields. When creating a custom Microsoft Outlook form,

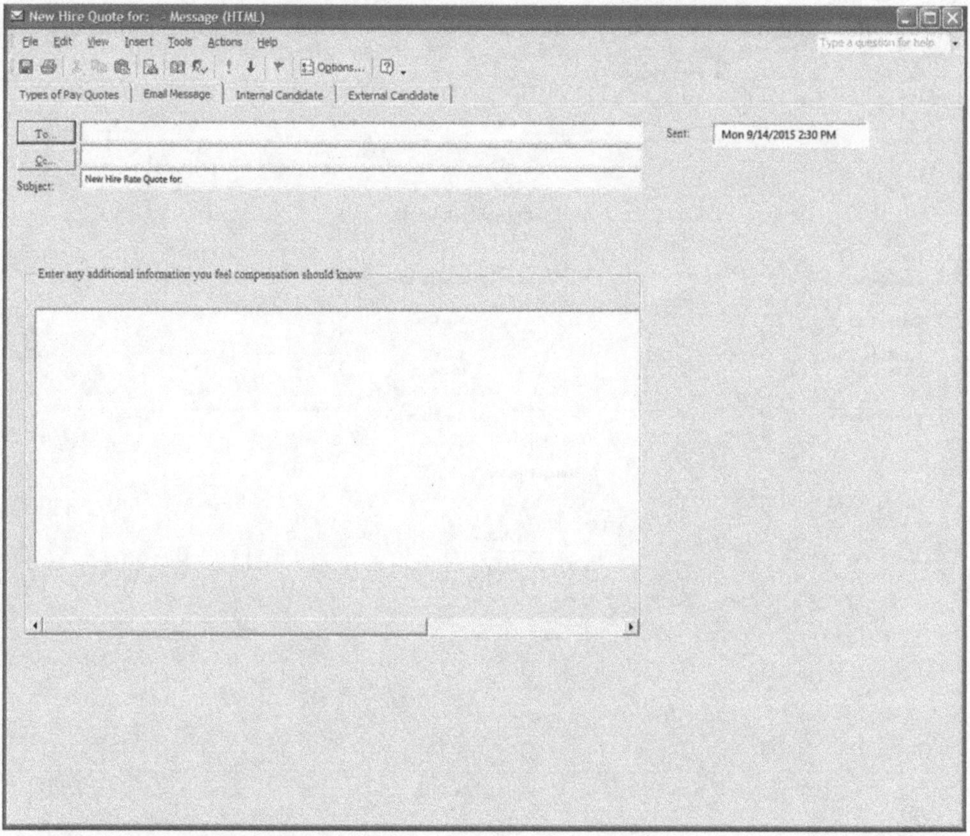

Figure 7-7   Custom Microsoft Outlook Form, Tab 1: Email Message

you can designate a data entry field as mandatory, or you can make one field populate another field. In Figure 7-8, once compensation enters a number in the percentage increase field and clicks the Calculate button, the new salary automatically appears in the hourly, weekly, and annual fields.

You can also add different tabs across the top of the form to separate the information. Figures 7-7 and 7-8 show four tabs created: Types of Pay Quotes, Email Message, Internal Candidate, and External Candidate. Creating tabs keeps the form uncluttered and makes it simple for users to pick the appropriate tab to complete.

Figure 7-9 shows another job aid I created to complement the custom Microsoft Outlook form.

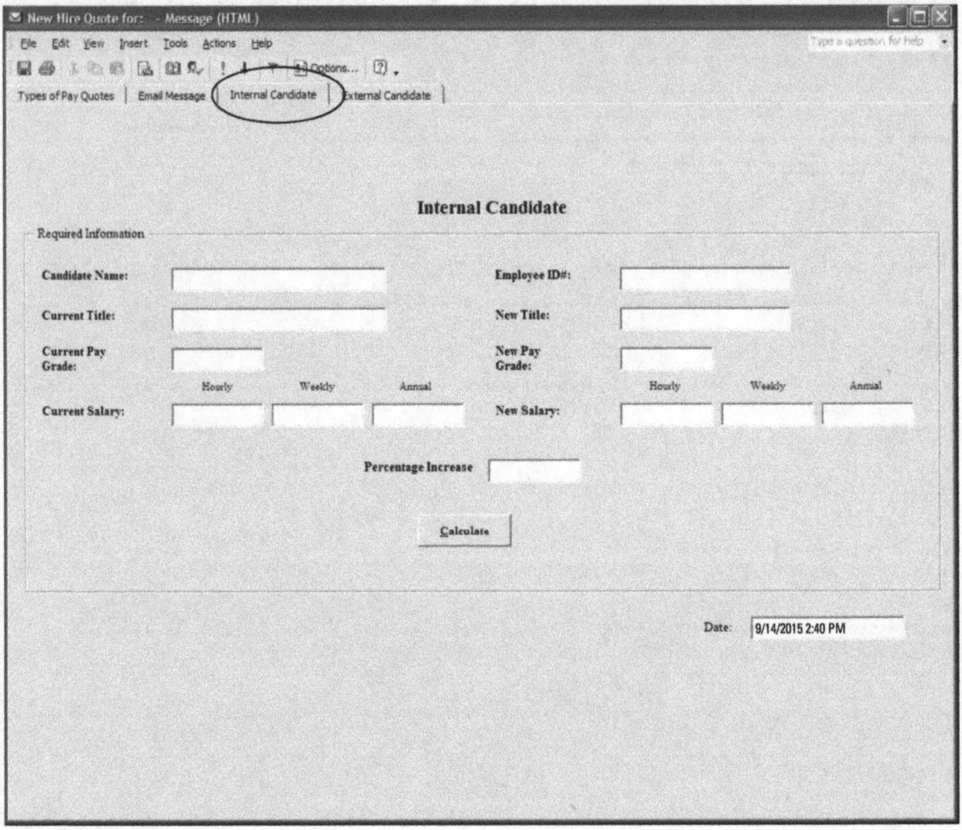

Figure 7-8   Custom Microsoft Outlook Form, Tab 2: Internal Candidate

Creating custom Microsoft Outlook forms is a simple way to standardize information required for a process while benefiting from tools already available in most companies. Figure 7-10 shows how simple it is for users to open the form you created by going to *Home, New Items, More Items,* and *Choose Form* in Microsoft Outlook (version 2010). To create a custom form, you have to show the *Developer* ribbon by placing a checkmark next to the Developer box (*Outlook Options, Customize Ribbon*). Several books on the market can provide additional detail on designing custom forms, which you might need if you want to develop complex ones.

You can create other types of forms using form-building

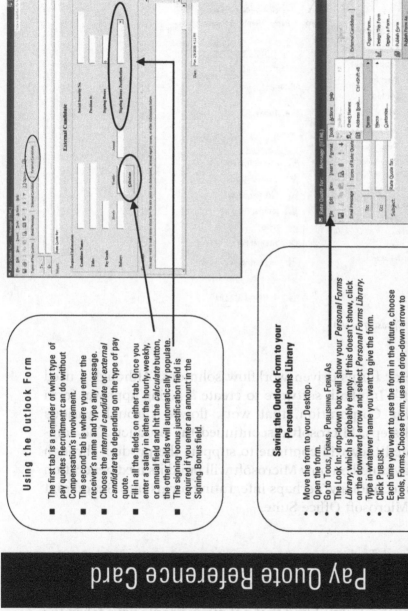

Figure 7-9 Sample Job Aid

Figure 7-10 Choosing a Form

software or forms-driven workflow solutions. Although I used Microsoft's InfoPath software to create a hiring approval form for Alistar Corporation, that work flowed through various approval steps, Microsoft discontinued the product. The company stated they will continue to support the product through 2023. Stay tuned on how Microsoft will build its next generation of forms technology, perhaps integrating forms into SharePoint and the Microsoft Office Suite.

Excel Tools

Everyone knows that Microsoft Excel allows you to create spreadsheets, but I find that not many people have taken the time to delve deeper into what they can accomplish with this application. Some employees (unless they come from finance) tend to shy away from using Excel because they do not have adequate knowledge on how to create formulas or pivot tables. Their reluctance presents you with an opportunity to make spreadsheets seem less intimidating and simple to use. To do so, you can create ones that do not look like spreadsheets at all. Figure 7-11 shows an example of a spreadsheet that does not look threatening.

This spreadsheet includes functionality behind each of the buttons that automatically calculates the appropriate pay range for a particular job. Although you may need an intermediate skill level with Microsoft Excel to create sophisticated spreadsheets, you can create many tools with a minimum of ability and effort. Think about how to simplify spreadsheets you use every day and make them more user-friendly. To streamline a business process, instead of waiting for a large system implementation, explore the additional capabilities of software applications already available to you.

Add the tools to your list of process documentation started in Chapter 4.

Metrics

Every day we deal with metrics, even though we do not always think of them as such. How quickly did you get out of the house this morning, and how does that time compare to last week's? How has your golf handicap changed over time? How many pounds have you lost or gained over the past year? How does your performance rating compare to last year's (if your company still uses ratings)?

Some people say, "If you can't measure it, you can't manage it." Albert Einstein says the opposite: "Everything that can be counted does not necessarily count; everything that counts cannot necessarily be counted." So this differentiation suggests we should show caution and strike a balance between the value of the metric and its cost. Nevertheless, organizations like metrics, and they should have metrics for their business processes. Just do not go overboard. Think about the metrics you and the

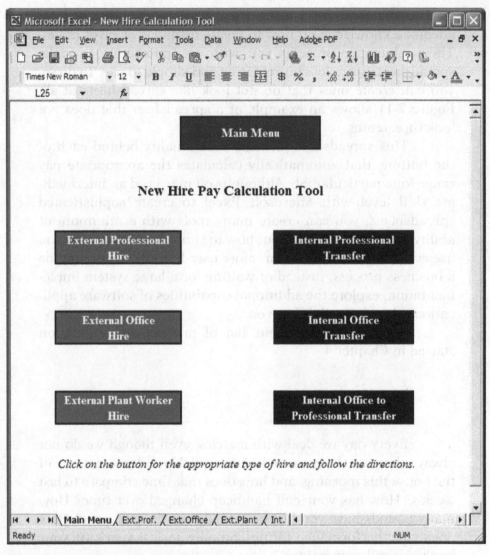

Figure 7-11 Sample Microsoft Excel Spreadsheet

project team propose, and balance their usefulness with the expense of capturing the data required for them.

If the project team members spent sufficient time thinking about the customer's/client's needs when they established the foundation in Chapter 3, the scope definition document helps them define the business process metrics. Look at the identified measurements of success, and think about them from three perspectives: effectiveness, efficiency, and adaptability. Remember from Chapter 1 that:

- ▶ **Effectiveness** denotes the quality of the process. Does the process produce the desired results and meet the customer/client needs?
- ▶ **Efficiency** signifies the productivity of the process. Does the process minimize the use of resources, improve cycle time, and eliminate bureaucracy?
- ▶ **Adaptability** denotes the flexibility of the process. Does the process remain flexible in the face of changing needs?

You often find that the measurements of success identified in the scope definition document are heavily weighted in favor of effectiveness because the project team wrote them from the customer's/client's perspective and the customer/client is the right place to start. The team may therefore have to think more about metrics that address efficiency and adaptability. Customers or clients also care about the flexibility of the process, and the business cares about efficiency. If the measurements of success do not include any efficiency or adaptability items, consider adding additional measurements of success.

If we use Alistar's compensation budget process as an example, Figure 7-12 shows the measurements of success we defined. Using this information as a starting point, lead the project team through a discussion for each measurement to decide how to measure the item. Make sure to write specific metrics that are actionable and that have a time component. Everyone should understand what each metric means.

In the compensation budget process, we defined "on-demand knowledge of the budget balances" as the first measurement of success for Alistar. In other words, the half dozen senior-level executives want assurance that they can identify how much money remains in their salary budget to spend at any time throughout the year. The executives care about the timeliness of the information, which relates to our discussion of cycle time in Chapter 6. In this case, the executives did not want to

---

Measurements of success:

1. On-demand knowledge for the president's direct reports of their budget balances (the right information at the right time)
2. A process viewed as a reliable tool for use in employee-related activities like planning promotions and developing succession plans
3. Accurate tracking of spending
4. The ability to make better decisions on allocating funds

Figure 7-12 Alistar Corporation Compensation Budget Process: Measurements of Success

wait for the normal monthly report; they wanted the information at their fingertips. So how do you meet their need?

Start by defining what *on-demand* means in this case. You may find that a weekly update adequately meets the requirement, or they may want daily or hourly updates. When the executives said "on-demand," they may have simply meant something more frequent than the monthly report that they now receive. After defining what *on-demand* means, think about the work involved in delivering against the need and the value of achieving this measurement. In other words, how much labor does it take to provide on-demand information, and how much is it worth?

The project team discussed this measurement of success for some time and considered things like what *on-demand* meant, where the department stored the budget information, whether the executives already had access to the information, and whether the executives knew how to run the reports. We found that the company's human resource system of record held the budget information and that the executives had access to the information any time they wanted it, but they never ran the reports. The project team evaluated several options:

▶ Redesign the report if it did not provide the executives with the information they wanted.

▶ Create a variant (a predefined report format) and teach the executives how to run the report in the system of record using the variant.

▶ Have compensation run the report for the executives, and download the information into a spreadsheet.

It turned out that weekly updates would provide senior executives with the information they wanted in the appropriate timeframe. Although the budget information resided in the system of record and the executives could retrieve the information at any time, even hourly if they preferred, they did not want to take the time to learn how to run the report. Sound familiar? As a result, the compensation department decided to run the report and download the information into a spreadsheet for the executives. Because this had to be done for only a half dozen executives, meeting this requirement added an additional 15 minutes per week to the overall business process, a labor investment deemed worth the cost.

Pete Hodges, our sales executive from Chapter 3, defined success in multiple ways, but the number of new customers became a key metric that directly led to the lead-generation process. One of his measurements of success read, "Increased number of new customers." Initially, this may seem like an efficiency metric because the statement seems to focus on volume. However, once we discussed how to measure an increase in the volume of new customers, it became obvious that Pete cared about more than the volume; he was also concerned about the *quality* of new customers. So remember not to assume what a word means. Clarify the terminology for each measurement of success before defining a metric. As a result of our discussion, Pete defined the metric as a "30 percent increase in the number of qualified new customers over the next six months."

Look at the second Alistar measurement of success in Figure 7-12, and you find the term *reliable* used. Again, what does that term mean?

In the third measurement, it sounds like the Compensation department had trouble accurately tracking past spending. The first job is to uncover what occurred in the past so you understand what this measurement means, and the next step is to establish controls so the same problem does not happen again.

The fourth identified measurement is an internal metric for the Compensation department. When you have internal measurements, spend time discussing how the department knows when it achieves success. Because it gets easier to create a metric once the project team can share what success looks like, simply ask, "What does success look like?" "How will you know when you achieve success?" For Alistar, this measurement of success really meant how much money remained at the end of the year for each of their compensation funds. Because they forfeit any money remaining at the end of a year, similar to a health flexible spending account, they wanted to make sure that they spent every last dollar. We defined the metric for this last item as "Less than 1 percent of budget remains at year end."

Once you understand what to measure, establish a baseline measurement to help the organization recognize whether the new business process moves them in the right direction. In the previous internal metric example, compensation had about 10 percent of the budget left at the end of the prior year. With their new goal of less than 1 percent, they can tell whether they are moving in the right direction.

A department that has responsibility for system support provides another example. If reducing the number of reported problems in a specific area like security is important, then they have to start by identifying the number of problems reported today, which becomes the baseline. We could then state the metric as "20 percent reduction in security issues over the next year."

Chapter Summary: Step 7

Identifying points in the business process where a mistake can occur provides the opportunity to introduce internal controls. Using a warning symbol to mark those spots makes the problem areas visible and obvious. Developing an internal control document, which contains the details about how to avoid common errors, provides an effective training tool for new process workers.

Developing tools to support the business process helps train new process workers to avoid errors. Create job aids to simplify or standardize a step in the process, use the Microsoft Office Suite to create simple forms, or create checklists and other reminders about important steps in a process. If you have a system of record in place or other applications, you can recommend changes to those systems to support the business process.

Creating metrics to support the measurements of success defined in the scope definition document allows you to evaluate whether the process works as planned. Review the metrics from the three business process perspectives of effectiveness, efficiency, and adaptability, and include metrics from each of the three perspectives. Show caution in developing metrics because you can easily create too many of them. Always balance the usefulness of having a metric against the expense of capturing the data required to supply it.

Time Estimate

Figure 7-13 summarizes the time you should allow to create the internal controls, tools, and metrics (step 7).

Project Team Meeting

This meeting is a continuation of the project team meetings. It generally takes several hours to identify the points in the process where mistakes can happen because most process maps are more complex than our intentionally simple example. After identifying the potential problem areas, spend sufficient time identifying how to avoid the potential mistakes. I generally dedicate an entire meeting to this topic because it takes some time to identify solutions to potential errors. Identifying the possible

Event	Time	Purpose
Project team meeting: identify internal controls	3–5 hours	■ Add internal control symbols to the process map and document potential errors. ■ Determine how to make certain that mistakes do not happen.
Postmeeting work: create tools	Varies: ■ 40–80 hours (simple items); ■ 1–2 months (for databases); ■ longer (if system of record changes)	■ Create the job aids and tools identified.
Project team meeting: identify metrics	3–4 hours	■ Identify how to meet the measurements of success.

Figure 7-13 Time Estimate—Step 7: Create Internal Controls, Tools, and Metrics

errors is easy; determining how to avoid the problems is the hard part.

Postmeeting Work

During this time, the project team creates the tools identified during the process improvement phase. Depending on the number of internal controls and tools you have to create, this time takes from one to two weeks for simple job aids, a month or more to create databases, and significantly longer if you plan to make changes to your company's system of record.

Project Team Meeting

During this meeting, your entire focus is on reviewing what you identified as the measurements of success on the scope definition document and talking about how you can deliver against those goals.

What You Have Achieved

In this chapter, you have achieved the following:

▶ The ability to identify internal controls to avoid potential problem points in a business process

- ▶ The knowledge of how to create a variety of tools to simplify the process
- ▶ The wisdom of when to include a metric and how to use the measurements of success as a starting point
- ▶ Most important, the *power* to bring the business process to life by including internal controls, tools, and metrics that employees can use

KNOWLEDGE CHECK

Use this knowledge check to validate your understanding of the material covered in step 7. Answer True or False to the following questions.

1. Internal controls help prevent errors in a business process.   True   False
2. The Sarbanes-Oxley Act requires officers of a company signing financial reports to confirm they have evaluated internal controls within the previous year.   True   False
3. List *all* potential problem areas in a business process *first*, before discussing possible solutions.   True   False
4. Job aids are a simple tool to help drive consistency in a business process.   True   False
5. You should insert a metric at every step in a business process.   True   False
6. A business process should have at least one metric focused on effectiveness, efficiency, and adaptability.   True   False
7. The scope definition document can help you in developing metrics.   True   False
8. Add internal control symbols as you draw the process map in step 4.   True   False
9. Discuss possible solutions for an identified error only after the team has identified all possible errors.   True   False

Answers

1–true, 2–false, 3–true, 4–true, 5–false, 6–true, 7–true, 8–false, 9–true

Explanations for False Answers

Question 2: The requirement is to evaluate internal controls within 90 days, not one year.

Question 5: Balance the usefulness of a metric with the expense of capturing the data.

Question 8: Wait until after the entire process map is drawn before identifying potential problem areas to keep the team focused on identifying the correct steps.

CHAPTER 8

Step 8: Test and Rework

Making Sure It Works

Joanne Wu, training and development manager for a mid-size computer manufacturer, redesigned a half dozen of her department's business processes to increase her department's responsiveness to its clients. She often received complaints that it took too long to design and develop courses to address unexpected training needs that surfaced throughout the year.

Joanne and I worked together for several weeks to change steps in her business process, reduce the time required for the approval cycle, and realign resources. Now we had to make certain that the changes worked before introducing the new process on a wide scale. Joanne identified the area training managers as the test group because she considered them a crucial client group who routinely brought unplanned regional training requirements to her attention. The area training managers had geographically dispersed employees, so using them as the test group would also enable us to assess how the process worked in multiple locations. If the new process worked for the area training managers, it would work for Joanne's remaining clients. We decided to conduct the test during December, a traditionally slow time for the manufacturer.

At this point in the roadmap, you have completed the formidable work. You redesigned the business process so the customer/client sees the process as effective and so it runs efficiently for the organization. You have also documented the process and created new tools and metrics to support the process. Now you want to validate that the process, documentation, and tools work as you expect.

The custom Microsoft Outlook form I created to support the salary rate process in Chapter 7 provides an example of what to test and what you might discover in this step. The form worked fine when entering information and calculating formulas; however, we found a problem with the form in testing. Once the recruiter received an email from compensation providing the salary rate, the recruiters could not forward the email to the hiring manager because we had not enabled the forwarding capability when we designed the form.

Before introducing a new, improved process to the organization, test it and work out any bugs before communicating the change on a wide scale. Testing the business process helps to determine how well the business process will perform in the organization so you meet your goals, whether they are increased productivity, minimizing errors, or anything else. Testing helps in identifying bottlenecks and provides the chance to fix the problems or rework the process, thus ensuring that the implementation proceeds as smoothly as possible.

In this phase of the work, you think about the who, what, where, when, and how of testing:

> **Whom** do you involve in the testing? Consider who will use the process and tools created. If the business process involves only a single department, you may have a small list of people to include in the testing. On the other hand, multiple departments often share responsibility for a business process. In this case, the list of people to include may consist of employees who work with the process daily because they will act as subject-matter experts, managers who have a role in the process, and stakeholders who have an interest in the process.

If you suspect dissimilarity between local and global sites, include both sites in the testing phase. Ideally, you should include local and global site team members early in the overall process work itself, instead of just during the testing phase. This saves rework time in the end.

▶ **What** do you have to test? Test the business process itself, the associated documentation, the tools created to support the process, and the metrics. This includes any job aids created, new technologies introduced, and metrics designed.

Even though you may not have any actual data yet for the measurements, create a mock-up of what the measurement will look like, and validate that the information meets the requirements of the data recipients. If you plan to create a report, include a mock-up of the report during testing to validate that it works.

▶ **Where** should the testing occur? Define the different locations where testing must happen.

- If employees use the process in multiple locations, you may have to test the tools at various business sites because each location may use a different technology or have unusual technical challenges. You may encounter firewall or server challenges at different sites depending on the function of your tools.

- If you have local and global sites, include key locations in the testing to validate that the process and tools work at both types of sites. You may find a step in the process that does not work because of a country's legal requirements. If you work in the United States and have locations in Europe, for example, think about challenges that can arise because of the Safe Harbor framework developed between the United States and the European Union. The following excerpt, taken from the U.S. Department of Commerce Web site, provides an overview of Safe Harbor's concern with protecting a citizen's privacy. You can read additional information at http://www.export.gov/safeharbor/index.asp:

> While the United States and the European Union share the goal of enhancing privacy protection for their citizens, the United States takes a different approach to privacy from that taken by the European Union.
>
> In order to bridge these different privacy approaches and provide a streamlined means for U.S. organizations to comply with the Directive, the U.S. Department of Commerce in consultation with the European Commission developed a "Safe Harbor" framework.

- Another decision revolves around whether to test the tools from the work location and from home. Do managers frequently work from home? What mobile devices do managers use?

Think about who will use the business process, where the users work, and how they do their work to identify the parameters to include in the testing.

► **When** should the testing occur? Identify the timeframe for the testing period. Think about the best time to conduct the testing, and avoid any peak periods for the organization. For example, if you work with finance, avoid month- and year-end time periods. If you work with a company that has a seasonal business, avoid those busy times.

In Joanne Wu's case, she wanted to conduct the testing in December, a customarily slow period for the computer manufacturer because the company had already built and distributed product for the holiday season. However, other businesses may consider December a busy holiday season.

► **How** will the testing happen? Define your testing approach, which you can think of as the series of steps involved in testing. If you participated in a system implementation in the past, you will see similarity with the steps involved in the user acceptance testing phase of those implementations because this testing focuses on subject-matter experts who test, through trial and error, that the new or improved process and tools work.

In systems testing, three key types of testing occur: functional testing, user acceptance testing, and regression testing. Of course, an implementation includes other varieties of testing (like unit, interface, performance, or stress testing), but the three I mention generally involve business partners versus the technical staff. User acceptance testing has the most applicability to business process work because of the similarity of the steps.

The Five Steps in Testing the Business Process

Figure 8-1 shows the five steps to follow in testing the business process.

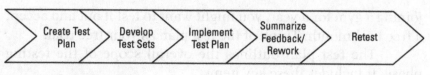

Figure 8-1 The Five Testing Steps

1. Create the test plan.
2. Develop the test sets (test scripts and data sheets).
3. Implement the test plan.
4. Summarize the feedback received and the challenges encountered, and then rework the process and tools.
5. Retest (if appropriate).

Step 1: Create the Test Plan

The test plan provides structure and a systematic approach to testing the business process. Test plans are created when implementing new systems, and you will find them just as beneficial when implementing new or improved business processes. The test plan brings the who, what, where, when, and how together in one location.

▶ Who will perform the tests?
▶ What items constitute the test plan?
▶ Where will the testing occur?
▶ When will the testing occur?
▶ How will you communicate with the testers?
▶ How will you report, track, and resolve problems?

Some of your colleagues may have a negative view of test plans because there is sometimes an inclination to overuse them, but I find that, if you keep them simple, test plans help you avoid mistakes. The discipline alone of developing a test plan forces you to think about things you might otherwise overlook. So think of the test plan as simply a tool used to verify that the business process works as expected. Before signing up and joining a gym for a year, you might want to test it out and accept a free trial month. Think of the test plan as your free trial.

The test plan outlines the overall scope of the testing phase. It includes these key items:

▶ **Testing Goal:** The goal is a statement of the overall purpose for the testing.

▶ **Testing Resources:** The resources include people, software, and equipment requirements.

▶ **Test Items and Objectives:** The objective for each test item assists the project team in writing appropriate test scenarios. For the team to do a thorough job, they have to understand what you want to accomplish for each test item.

▶ **Communication and Feedback Process:** This provides information on how the team will stay connected during the testing timeframe and how the team will report issues they encounter.

▶ **Time Frame:** Identifies what will be done by when.

Figure 8-2 shows a completed test plan for Alistar Corporation's salary rate process.

The table at the end of Figure 8-2 shows the expected completion date for each of the items in the test plan. The project manager can perform two activities while the project team writes the test scripts:

1. **Gain Support for Resources:** You can secure approval from the appropriate managers to include the testers during the scheduled testing period.

2. **Create a Feedback Collection Tool:** In formal system testing, companies use automated tools that house test sets and enable issue tracking. Hewlett-Packard's Application Lifecycle Management tool is a popular choice. This level of formality seems too complex for business process testing, but if you have software available, use it. A simple spreadsheet, though, usually works fine.

TESTING GOAL:

To validate that the salary rate process is simple to use on a global basis for the recruiters, compensation, and the hiring managers, and that the tools created to support the process work as expected with no defects.

TESTING RESOURCES:

The following employees have a role in testing the process:

- Recruiters located in Chicago, San Francisco, and London
- Compensation analysts at corporate headquarters in Chicago
- Managers located in Chicago and London

The following software is required:

- Microsoft Outlook, Version 2010 Professional
- Microsoft Excel, Version 2010 Professional
- Microsoft PowerPoint, Version 2010 or later
- Microsoft Word, Version 2010 or later
- Adobe Acrobat Reader, Version 11 or later

TEST ITEMS and OBJECTIVES

The test plan includes the following items:

Task	Objective	Tools
End-to-end business process	To make certain each step in the business process works for every site and that the documentation supports the work.	■ Microsoft PowerPoint process map ■ Microsoft Word detail document
Salary rate quotation form	To validate the fields work as expected (including data entry fields, mandatory fields, and formula-driven fields), that the form appropriately flows through the email system, and that the calculation button works.	■ Microsoft Outlook
Salary rate calculation tool	To make certain the formulas work, that the user cannot change the field values, and that the tool includes the appropriate scenarios.	■ Microsoft Excel
Job aid focused on the recruiter's ability to use the form and tool	To validate the help content answers recruiter questions that may surface and the file converted to the PDF format correctly.	■ Adobe PDF
Sample report that summarizes quarterly salary rate quotations	To validate the report includes information required to help senior management understand the cost of hire.	■ Microsoft Excel

Figure 8-2 Salary Rate Process Test Plan   *(continues)*

COMMUNICATION AND FEEDBACK PROCESS

A daily 30-minute phone meeting will occur to discuss testing progress and issue resolution at:

- 8:30 a.m. San Francisco time.
- 10:30 a.m. Chicago time.
- 4:30 p.m. London time.

At the first meeting, the project manager will review the test plan and the testing responsibilities.

An issue resolution log will reside on the shared network drive, and each tester will enter:

- Problems that surface during testing.
- Points of confusion that surface in the process.
- General feedback on the process.

All entries will have a category and severity level attached:

- Category: Usability or Technical Problem
- Severity Level: High, Medium, or Low

TIME FRAME

The testing will occur from June 2 through June 15.

ID Number	Task	Person Responsible	Due Date
1	Define testing goal.	Project manager	May 15
2	Define test items and objectives.	Project manager	May 15
3	Develop scenarios for test items.	Project team	June 1
4	Gain support for resources.	Project manager	June 1
5	Create feedback collection tool.	Project manager	June 1
6	Conduct testing.	Project team	June 2–15
7	Rework, as required.	Project team	June 30

Figure 8-2 (continued)

Design the spreadsheet that the testers will use to report issues and feedback throughout the testing period. Figure 8-3 shows a simple example of an issue resolution log I have used to capture problems that surface during testing. When entering an issue in the tool, the testers choose either *Usability* or *Technical* in the *Category* column by selecting from the drop-down list, and they choose *High*, *Medium*, or *Low* from the *Severity* column. Use the issue resolution log during the project team's daily phone meetings to discuss the problems encountered and the status of resolving the problems.

ID Number	Test Item	Date	Description	Category	Severity	Detected By	Assigned To
1	Calculation tool	6/4	No scenario for an external hire with greater than 10 years' experience	Usability	High	Sarah Jones	Jesus Carrabba
2	Job aid	6/5	Missing step: what to do after you enter the desired percentage	Usability	Low	May Chang	Sue Sams
3	Quote form	6/5	Cannot forward form to hiring manager	Technical	High	Liz Fleet	Jesus Carrabba
4							
5							

Figure 8-3 Salary Rate Quotation Process: Issue Resolution Tool

Step 2: Develop Test Sets

When the resources you identified for testing are ready to start, what do they do? Where do they begin? You do not want them sitting around making up their own scenarios because this wastes time and they might not test the items that you want them to test. The test sets, which include scripts and data sheets, provide the resources with step-by-step guidelines so they understand how to test the process and tools. Figure 8-4 shows the relationship between test sets, test scripts, and data sheets.

This figure shows that one test set has multiple test scripts depending on the functionality you want to test. Each test script has data sheets to cover the number of scenarios you want to test.

Let us revisit the Alistar Corporation's salary rate quotation form created in Microsoft Outlook to see an example of a script and data sheet. Figure 8-5 shows the overall workflow for the quotation form. The six steps involved in the process are repeated under each process worker with their responsibility for the form highlighted. This figure shows that:

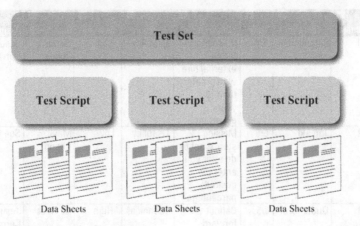

Figure 8-4 *Test Set Components*

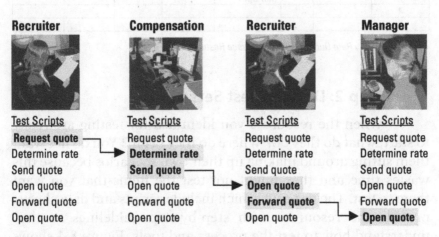

Figure 8-5 *Workflow for Salary Rate Quotation Form*

► The *Recruiter* requests the quotation from *Compensation*.

► *Compensation* determines the salary rate and sends the quotation back to the *Recruiter*.

► The *Recruiter* then opens the quotation and forwards the salary quote to the hiring *Manager*.

► The hiring *Manager* opens the quote on the desktop computer, home computer, or mobile device.

Test Scripts and Data Sheets

The information in Figure 8-5 assists in creating appropriate test scripts because each highlighted task, under *Test Scripts* in the figure, must be accompanied by a separate test script. For example, look at the first test script under the recruiter's list, *Request Quote*. Figure 8-6 shows the steps involved in testing that step. The text at the start of Figure 8-6 provides the following general information:

▶ **Test Set:** The overall grouping of related tests that represent a portion of the business process (the salary rate quotation form)

▶ **Test Script:** The activity or test item (request a quotation)

▶ **Responsible Tester:** The person conducting the test (recruiter)

As Figure 8-6 shows, the test script gives testers (in this case, the recruiter) the details required to test the form. The *Data* column provides the information they should enter as they move through the test script. By providing information in the *Data* column, you speed up the testing because the tester does not have to spend time making up information to enter. Providing data also enables you to control the test and to test specific scenarios. If you want to test various versions of a report, you can include the report parameters you want used.

The *Expected Result* column tells testers exactly what they should see after they complete the step, and the *Actual Result* column provides the testers space to document what they observe or encounter during testing.

If you want to test many different scenarios, you should separate the test script from the data by using a separate data sheet instead of using the *Data* column in the test script, because using data sheets in this case saves everyone time. Figures 8-7 and 8-8 show what Figure 8-6 looks like if you separate the test script from the data. Notice that the test script in Figure 8-7 provides only the steps involved in testing, not the data. The test

Test set: Salary rate quotation form
Test script: Request quote
Responsible tester: Recruiter

Step	Description	Data	Expected Result	Actual Result
1 of 8	Open Microsoft Outlook® salary rate quotation form.	None	Normal Microsoft Outlook® email opens.	
2 of 8	Click in *to* field and search the global address list for compensation consultant's name. Enter the name.	Abigail Adams	Email is addressed to Abigail Adams.	
3 of 8	Enter candidate's name in the subject line after "New hire quote for."	Dennis Schwartz	Subject line shows "New hire quote for: Dennis Schwartz."	
4 of 8	Type a general message on the main page.	Please note that Dennis has been in his present job for fewer than six months.	General message appears on Email message tab.	
5 of 8	Click on the *internal candidate* tab.	None	Outlook message switches to a new screen.	
6 of 8	Enter information for candidate using the *current* salary field, and hit *calculate* button when done.	■ Candidate name: Dennis Schwartz ■ Employee no.: 7489 ■ Current title: Assistant Manager, Retail ■ New title: Manager, Retail ■ Current salary grade: 29 ■ New salary grade: 31 ■ Current salary: $65,000 annually	The hourly and weekly sums under current salary are automatically filled in after $65,000 is entered in the current salary (annual) field and the *calculate* button is clicked.	
7 of 8	Change the form by using the *new* salary field and hit *calculate* button when done.	■ New salary: $77,000 annually	The hourly and weekly sums under new salary are automatically filled in after $77,000 is entered in the new salary (annual) field and the *calculate* button is clicked.	
8 of 8	Click *send*.	None	Email arrives in Abigail Adams's inbox. (Confirm receipt of email in Abigail Adams's inbox.)	

Figure 8-6 Example of Test Script

script refers the tester to the data sheet to find the exact field values to enter.

The data sheet in Figure 8-8 provides the data elements to enter for the various scenarios. In this example, you see three data sets, one in the *Data Set 1* column, a second one in the *Data Set 2* column, and a third in the *Data Set 3* column. To make certain that you include the different scenarios you want to test, you can add as many columns as desired.

When you separate the test script from the data, the testers run through the test script multiple times using a different column of data in the data sheet each time until they have tested all the scenarios. If you use data sheets because you want to test many scenarios, you can move the *Expected Results* and *Actual Results* columns to the data sheet instead of including these two columns as part of the test script.

In systems testing, you perform positive and negative testing.

▶ **Positive Testing** confirms the application works as expected based on appropriate inputs. If you encounter an unexpected result, the test fails.

▶ **Negative Testing** ensures the application appropriately handles invalid data input or unexpected usage behavior.

You may find the need to include negative tests in your business process scenarios, particularly with any new tools you introduce.

Step 3: Implement the Test Plan

During the specified time frame, the identified resources use the supplied test sets, which include scripts and data sheets, to follow the new process and use the new tools. You monitor the progress as the testers enter problems they encounter in the issue resolution tool. As you conduct the daily meetings, the project team discusses known problems and possible resolutions. If the project team resolves a problem, remove the item from the issue list by moving the problem to a new worksheet in

Test set: Salary rate quotation form
Test script: Request quote
Responsible tester: Recruiter

Step	Description	Data	Expected Result	Actual Result
1 of 8	Open Microsoft Outlook® salary rate quotation form.	See data sheet 5, request quote	Normal Microsoft Outlook® email opens.	
2 of 8	Click in *to* field and search the global address list for compensation consultant's name. Enter the name.	See data sheet 5, request quote.	Email is addressed to Abigail Adams.	
3 of 8	Enter candidate's name in the subject line after "New hire quote for."	See data sheet 5, request quote.	Subject line shows "New hire quote for: <name>."	
4 of 8	Type a general message on the main page.	See data sheet 5, request quote.	General message appears on Email message tab.	
5 of 8	Click on the *internal candidate* tab.	See data sheet 5, request quote.	Outlook message switches to a new screen.	
6 of 8	Enter information for candidate using the *current* salary field, and hit *calculate* button when done.	See data sheet 5, request quote.	The hourly and weekly sums under current salary are automatically filled in after <salary amount> is entered in the annual salary field and the *calculate* button is clicked.	
7 of 8	Change the form by using the *new* salary field and hit *calculate* button when done.	See data sheet 5, request quote.	The hourly and weekly sums under current salary are automatically filled in after <salary amount> is entered in the annual salary field and the *calculate* button is clicked.	
8 of 8	Click *send*.	See data sheet 5, request quote.	Email arrives in Abigail Adams's inbox. (Confirm receipt of email in Abigail Adams's inbox.)	

Figure 8-7 Example of Test Script—no data

Test scenario: Salary rate quotation form
Data sheet: 5, Request quote
Responsible tester: Recruiter

Step	Data Set 1	Data Set 2	Data Set 3
1 of 8	None	None	None
2 of 8	Abigail Adams	Yvonne Chan	Becky King
3 of 8	Dennis Schwartz	Henrie Bette	Susan Sharp
4 of 8	Please note that Dennis has been in his present job for fewer than six months.	Henrie is transferring from the Brussels branch.	Susan is a new external hire.
5 of 8	None	None	None
6 of 8	■ Candidate name: Dennis Schwartz ■ Employee no.: 7489 ■ Current title: Assistant Manager, Retail ■ New title: Manager, Retail ■ Current salary grade: 29 ■ New salary grade: 31 ■ Current salary: $65,000 annually	■ Candidate name: Dennis Schwartz ■ Employee no.: 2009 ■ Current title: Sales Promotions Coordinator ■ New title: Marketing Communications Specialist ■ Current salary grade: L3 ■ New salary grade: L8 ■ Current salary: $47,000 annually	■ Candidate name: Susan Sharp ■ Employee no.: 8015 ■ Current title: Not applicable ■ New title: Vice President, Marketing ■ Current salary grade: Not applicable ■ New salary grade: L35 ■ Current salary: Not applicable
7 of 8	New salary: $77,000 annually	New salary: $52,500 annually	New salary: $135,000 annually
8 of 8	None	None	None

Figure 8-8 Example of Data Sheet

your spreadsheet called *Closed*. Continue working through the issue resolution log until the team fixes the major problems.

Step 4: Summarize Feedback and Rework

Once the test period ends, summarize the findings and determine the next steps. If you do not obtain the results expected, identify the steps required to gain acceptance. You may have to adjust the business process itself, fix errors in spreadsheets, or rectify other problems that surfaced during the testing phase.

Step 5: Retest

Based on the number and severity of problems that surfaced, you may or may not have to retest a portion of the process. View testing as an iterative process when you test an item.

If the item does not work, you fix it, but then you have to test it again.

Chapter Summary: Step 8

Creating a plan to test the new business process helps to make certain that it works as expected and that you do not experience too many surprises during implementation. Consider it your test drive.

The discipline of creating a test plan forces you to answer questions such as whom to involve in testing, what items to test, where to conduct the testing, when is the best time to conduct the test, and the steps involved in the testing.

Test scripts provide structure for the resources by giving them step-by-step instructions for conducting the test. Gathering information in an issue resolution log or a similar tool gives you the information to understand what may have to change in the business process or tools. Include as many different scenarios in the testing phase that may occur in real life. If you have multiple scenarios, separate the data from the test script by using data sheets.

Once the testing is done, summarize the feedback and make adjustments. If you make a substantial number of changes, retest either the entire business process or the impacted tools.

If you suspect deviation between local and global locations, include participants from both locations in the overall process work itself because including them early in the process saves rework time in the end.

Time Estimate

To plan the time it takes to work through this step, Figure 8-9 summarizes the time you should allow to test the process (step 8).

Event	Time	Purpose
Create test plan.	16 hours	■ Identify the who, what, where, when, and how of testing.
Create test sets, secure resources, create collection tool.	40 hours	■ Prepare information for testers. ■ Write test sets and data sheets for test items. ■ Develop feedback method. ■ Gain resource approval.
Implement test plan/rework.	40 hours (over two weeks)	■ Validate that the process works as expected. ■ Resolve problems.

Figure 8-9 Time Estimate—Step 8: Test and Rework

Create the Test Plan

During this time, think about how you want to conduct the business process testing. This should not take long, but answer the who, what, where, when, and how questions. You should find yourself spending the majority of your time on the how, or testing approach.

Create Test Sets, Gain Resource Approval, Develop Feedback Tool

During this time, the project team writes the detailed test sets, which include test scripts for different functionality and data sheets for the scenarios you want to test.

While the team writes the test sets, you should use this time to gain support from the managers who own the resources you want involved in the testing phase. Create a feedback collection tool, like an issue resolution log.

Implement the Test Plan and Rework

During this time, the testing occurs. You can establish the exact hours you want testing to occur, or you can let the testers plan their own calendars. In Figure 8-9, I estimated 40 hours over two weeks. This period also provides additional time to make any minor revisions as the testing progresses.

What You Have Achieved

In this chapter, you have achieved the following:

▶ Insight into how to make certain that the business process works as you expect

▶ The awareness to include both local and global locations in the business process improvement work, or at least in testing the process

▶ The importance of identifying whom to include in testing, what to test, where to test, when to test, and the method for testing

▶ The steps involved in the testing cycle

▶ Knowledge of how to create test scripts and data sheets

▶ Most important, the *power* to make certain that you introduce a workable business process into your company

KNOWLEDGE CHECK

Use this knowledge check to validate your understanding of the material covered in step 8. Fill in the blanks with the correct answer.

1. The first step in testing the business process is to create a _____.
2. The testing _____ is a statement of the overall purpose for the testing.
3. The testing _____ for each test item assists the project team in writing appropriate test scenarios because the team understands what you want to accomplish for each test item.
4. The test _____ includes test scripts and data sheets.

5. Test scripts provide _____ for a tester to follow and the data sheets provide the specific _____ to enter.

6. _____ testing ensures an application or business process will appropriately handle invalid data.

7. _____ testing confirms an application or business process works as expected.

8. During testing, collect defects in a feedback collection tool and categorize defects by either _____ or _____.

9. To denote the _____ level of a defect, allow testers to choose high, medium, or low.

10. Based on the number and severity of problems encountered, you may have to retest so view testing as a(n) _____ process.

Answers

1. test plan
2. goal
3. objectives
4. set
5. step-by-step directions; information or data
6. Negative
7. Positive
8. usability; technical
9. severity
10. iterative

CHAPTER 9

Step 9: Implement the Change

Preparing the Organization

Now that you know your business process and tools will work, think about how to introduce the change to the organization. Who needs to know? What do they need to know? When should you inform them? How should you communicate the change?

The term *change management* simply means taking people in an organization from the current state to a future state. This chapter focuses on managing change because, as we know from our own experiences, change is a constant and "nothing endures but change," as the Greek philosopher Heraclitus wrote.

When the banking industry went through a cycle of rapid acquisitions and mergers, I was asked by an industry giant to help them merge two separate business processes. At the beginning of the work, I developed an implementation plan that included all the roadmap steps, which kept the work organized while ensuring that we did not miss anyone or anything along the way.

The implementation plan acts as your guide to ensure successful implementation of a new or improved business process. Think of it as a project plan that focuses on either an individual business process or a group of processes. It includes everything from start to finish:

▶ Developing the process inventory

▶ Establishing the foundation and creating the scope definition document

▶ Drawing the process map and developing the documentation
▶ Estimating the time and cost
▶ Verifying the process map
▶ Applying the improvement techniques
▶ Creating internal controls, tools, and metrics
▶ Testing and reworking the business process
▶ Implementing the change
▶ Developing a continuous improvement plan

In this chapter, I cover three topics to include in an implementation plan that will help you identify the work. The implementation plan acts as the organizing umbrella that pulls the following three components together in one location:

1. The *impact analysis*, developed in step 6, outlines the changes that must happen in the organization to ensure a successful implementation of the business process.
2. The *communication plan* provides clarity about who needs to know about the change, what they need to know, when they need to know the information, and the best method of communication for each of the defined audiences.
3. The *training plan* covers who requires training on what, who owns the responsibility to conduct the training, where the training will occur, and when and how to deliver the training.

The sponsor, as the champion for the change, has increased responsibility in the implementation phase, and that responsibility includes advocating the change, aligning the business process changes with the organizational strategy, and helping to resolve any resistance or remove roadblocks.

The Implementation Plan

The best implementation plans include phases that break the work down into reasonable chunks that function as a guide to keep the work on track. Figure 9-1 shows an example of an implementation plan with three phases identified.

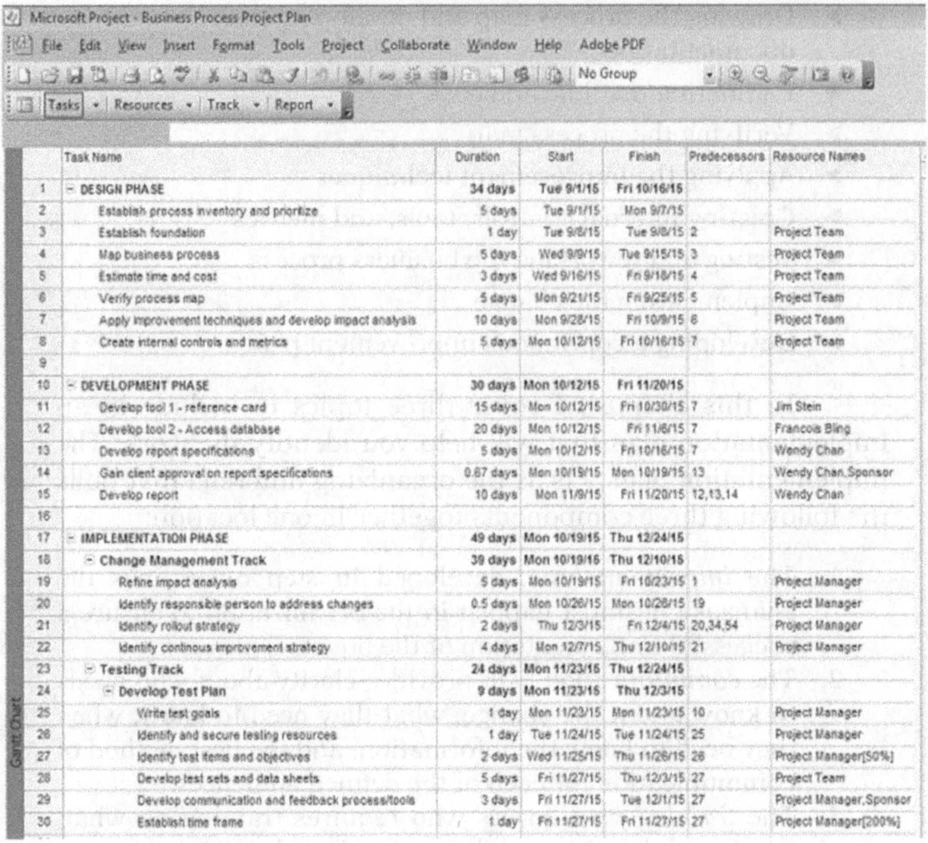

	Task Name	Duration	Start	Finish	Predecessors	Resource Names
1	**DESIGN PHASE**	**34 days**	**Tue 9/1/15**	**Fri 10/16/15**		
2	Establish process inventory and prioritize	5 days	Tue 9/1/15	Mon 9/7/15		
3	Establish foundation	1 day	Tue 9/8/15	Tue 9/8/15	2	Project Team
4	Map business process	5 days	Wed 9/9/15	Tue 9/15/15	3	Project Team
5	Estimate time and cost	3 days	Wed 9/16/15	Fri 9/18/15	4	Project Team
6	Verify process map	5 days	Mon 9/21/15	Fri 9/25/15	5	Project Team
7	Apply improvement techniques and develop impact analysis	10 days	Mon 9/28/15	Fri 10/9/15	6	Project Team
8	Create internal controls and metrics	5 days	Mon 10/12/15	Fri 10/16/15	7	Project Team
9						
10	**DEVELOPMENT PHASE**	**30 days**	**Mon 10/12/15**	**Fri 11/20/15**		
11	Develop tool 1 - reference card	15 days	Mon 10/12/15	Fri 10/30/15	7	Jim Stein
12	Develop tool 2 - Access database	20 days	Mon 10/12/15	Fri 11/6/15	7	Francois Bling
13	Develop report specifications	5 days	Mon 10/12/15	Fri 10/16/15	7	Wendy Chan
14	Gain client approval on report specifications	0.67 days	Mon 10/19/15	Mon 10/19/15	13	Wendy Chan,Sponsor
15	Develop report	10 days	Mon 11/9/15	Fri 11/20/15	12,13,14	Wendy Chan
16						
17	**IMPLEMENTATION PHASE**	**49 days**	**Mon 10/19/15**	**Thu 12/24/15**		
18	**Change Management Track**	**39 days**	**Mon 10/19/15**	**Thu 12/10/15**		
19	Refine impact analysis	5 days	Mon 10/19/15	Fri 10/23/15	1	Project Manager
20	Identify responsible person to address changes	0.5 days	Mon 10/26/15	Mon 10/26/15	19	Project Manager
21	Identify rollout strategy	2 days	Thu 12/3/15	Fri 12/4/15	20,34,54	Project Manager
22	Identify continous improvement strategy	4 days	Mon 12/7/15	Thu 12/10/15	21	Project Manager
23	**Testing Track**	**24 days**	**Mon 11/23/15**	**Thu 12/24/15**		
24	**Develop Test Plan**	**9 days**	**Mon 11/23/15**	**Thu 12/3/15**		
25	Write test goals	1 day	Mon 11/23/15	Mon 11/23/15	10	Project Manager
26	Identify and secure testing resources	1 day	Tue 11/24/15	Tue 11/24/15	25	Project Manager
27	Identify test items and objectives	2 days	Wed 11/25/15	Thu 11/26/15	26	Project Manager[50%]
28	Develop test sets and data sheets	5 days	Fri 11/27/15	Thu 12/3/15	27	Project Team
29	Develop communication and feedback process/tools	3 days	Fri 11/27/15	Tue 12/1/15	27	Project Manager,Sponsor
30	Establish time frame	1 day	Fri 11/27/15	Fri 11/27/15	27	Project Manager[200%]

Figure 9-1 Implementation Plan

- **The design phase** identifies the work involved in defining and improving the business process.
- **The development phase** includes creating the tools required to make the improved business process work before moving to step 8, where you test the process.
- **The implementation phase** includes testing the process, determining how to roll out the new business process, how to communicate and train the affected people, and how to continually improve the business process so it remains relevant over time.

For a complex business process, it helps to use project management software. For a simple business process, on the

31		Implement test plan	10 days	Fri 12/4/15	Thu 12/17/15	24	Project Team
32		Rework, as necessary	5 days	Fri 12/18/15	Thu 12/24/15	31	Project Team
33	⊟ Communication Track		16.5 days	Mon 11/23/15	Tue 12/15/15		
34	⊟ Develop Communication Plan		8 days	Mon 11/23/15	Wed 12/2/15		
35		Define audience	1 day	Mon 11/23/15	Mon 11/23/15	10	Sam Boyer
36		Develop communication goals	1 day	Tue 11/24/15	Tue 11/24/15	35	Sam Boyer
37		Develop key message points	3 days	Wed 11/25/15	Fri 11/27/15	36	Sam Boyer
38		Identify communication vehicles	2 days	Mon 11/30/15	Tue 12/1/15	37	Sam Boyer
39		Determine vehicle deadlines	1 day	Wed 12/2/15	Wed 12/2/15	38	Sam Boyer
40	⊟ Develop Communication Vehicles		8.5 days	Thu 12/3/15	Tue 12/15/15		
41	⊟ Vehicle 1: Client Meeting		5.5 days	Thu 12/3/15	Thu 12/10/15		
42		Develop presentation	5 days	Thu 12/3/15	Wed 12/9/15	34	Project Manager
43		Conduct meeting	0.5 days	Thu 12/10/15	Thu 12/10/15	42	Project Manager
44	⊟ Vehicle 2: Client Email Follow Up		3 days	Thu 12/10/15	Tue 12/15/15		
45		Write email	1 day	Thu 12/10/15	Fri 12/11/15	43	Project Manager
46		Gain sponsor approval	2 days	Fri 12/11/15	Tue 12/15/15	45	Project Manager
47	⊟ Vehicle 3: Stakeholder Email		3 days	Thu 12/3/15	Mon 12/7/15		
48		Write email	1 day	Thu 12/3/15	Thu 12/3/15	34	Project Manager
49		Gain sponsor approval	2 days	Fri 12/4/15	Mon 12/7/15	48	Project Manager
50	⊟ Vehicle 4: Employee Meeting		4.5 days	Thu 12/3/15	Wed 12/9/15		
51		Develop presentation	4 days	Thu 12/3/15	Tue 12/8/15	34	Project Manager
52		Conduct meeting	0.5 days	Wed 12/9/15	Wed 12/9/15	51	Project Manager
53	⊟ Training Track		20 days	Mon 11/23/15	Fri 12/18/15		
54	⊟ Develop Training Plan		5 days	Mon 11/23/15	Fri 11/27/15		
55		Define audience	1 day	Mon 11/23/15	Mon 11/23/15	10	Jim Stein
56		Write training objectives by audience	2 days	Tue 11/24/15	Wed 11/25/15	55	Jim Stein
57		Identify approach	1 day	Thu 11/26/15	Thu 11/26/15	56	Jim Stein
58		Identify tools and due dates	1 day	Fri 11/27/15	Fri 11/27/15	57	Jim Stein
59		Identify facilitator/gain approval, if necessary	0.5 days	Fri 11/27/15	Fri 11/27/15	57	Jim Stein
60		Develop/customize training materials	10 days	Mon 11/30/15	Fri 12/11/15	54	Jim Stein
61		Schedule training	0.5 days	Mon 11/30/15	Mon 11/30/15	54	Jim Stein
62		Conduct training	5 days	Mon 12/14/15	Fri 12/18/15	60,61	Project Team

Figure 9-1 (continued)

other hand, a table or a spreadsheet may work fine. If you use a table or spreadsheet, though, you must manually calculate how long a task takes (the duration), which can be a disadvantage because manual calculations increase the time required to create the original timeline and then to make adjustments to the dates as the work progresses. Figure 9-1 shows an implementation plan created with Microsoft Office Project. That figure shows the following standard Microsoft Office Project columns:

► **Task Name:** Create the phases in this column and include specific tasks associated with each major phase. Figure 9-1 shows three phases (*Design*, *Development*, and *Implementation*). The implementation phase then includes four separate tracks (change management, testing, communication, and training). Using tracks within a phase helps to further organize the work. Although this layout works well for general business process implementations, feel free to customize the list of tasks to fit your situation.

▶ **Duration:** This column states how long a task will take to complete. After entering the number of days for each task, Microsoft Office Project automatically rolls up the subtasks and shows the total duration for a phase in bold text. For example, Figure 9-1 shows a duration of:
- 34 days for the design phase (row 1).
- 30 days for the development phase (row 10).
- 49 days for the implementation phase (row 17).

▶ **Start/Finish:** Microsoft Office Project automatically calculates the start and finish dates once you enter the beginning date of the project and the duration for each task.

▶ **Predecessors:** This column shows the dependency of one task on another and allows you to identify whether one task has to occur before another can start. If you make one task a predecessor to another, Microsoft Office Project appropriately schedules the start and finish dates to ensure that the first task is completed before scheduling the second task. In Figure 9-1, row 4 has the number 3 listed in the *Predecessors* column, indicating that you cannot begin mapping the business process (task 4) until you have established the foundation (task 3). In this example, Microsoft Office Project automatically set the task 4 start date *after* the completion of task 3, once I entered the number 3 in the predecessor's column in row 4.

▶ **Resource Names:** Identify the people responsible for a task.

As an alternative to using project software for the implementation plan, Figure 9-2 shows a portion of Figure 9-1 created using Microsoft Word. In this case, think through the task dependencies and schedule the tasks using the predecessor concept. Microsoft Excel works well too.

Overview of the Three Phases of the Implementation Plan

The next few sections help you to develop an implementation plan by explaining the three phases in greater detail.

Task ID	Task Name	Duration	Time Frame
	Design phase	**34 days**	**April 1–May 6**
1	Establish process inventory and prioritize.	5	April 1–7
2	Establish foundation.	1	April 8
3	Map business process.	5	April 9–15
4	Estimate time and cost.	3	April 16–20
5	Verify process map.	5	April 21–27
6	Apply improvement techniques.	10	April 28–May 11
7	Create internal controls and metrics.	5	May 12–18
	Development phase	**30 days**	**May through June**
8	Develop tool 1: reference card	15	May 12–June 1
9	Develop tool 2: access database	20	May 12–June 1

Figure 9-2 Implementation Plan (Alternative)

The Design Phase

The design phase tasks in Figure 9-1 or 9-2 should seem familiar because these include the roadmap steps covered in previous chapters:

▶ **Step 1:** Develop the process inventory: identifying and prioritizing the process list.

▶ **Step 2:** Establish the foundation: identifying the scope and process boundaries.

▶ **Step 3:** Draw the map process: flowcharting and documenting the business process.

▶ **Step 4:** Estimate time and cost: estimating the process/cycle times and calculating the process costs.

▶ **Step 5:** Verify the process map: validating and gaining buy-in.

▶ **Step 6:** Apply improvement techniques: improving the business process.

▶ **Step 7:** Create internal controls and metrics: error-proofing the process and creating measurements.

The Development Phase

In this phase, identify the tools that the project team has to create to enable the business process to work (refer to step 7 in the roadmap). Figure 9-1 shows that the team has to develop a reference card (row 11) and a Microsoft Access database (row 12) to support the process. The team also determines the data elements required for the report (row 13), gains agreement from clients to verify that the report meets their needs (row 14), and then develops the report (row 15).

The *Predecessors* column on row 15 tells us that the report development cannot begin until after the project team creates the database (task 12), develops the report specifications (task 13), and gains client approval (task 14).

The Implementation Phase

This phase, which covers roadmap steps 8–10, includes several different tracks that require further explanation. Tracks break down a phase and help organize a large phase into manageable chunks of work. Often a different project team member can handle each of the tracks.

▶ **The Change Management Track** includes refining the impact analysis, validating who has responsibility for each proposed change, determining the overall rollout strategy, and developing the continuous improvement plan. I discuss continuous improvement as a separate topic in Chapter 10.

▶ **The Testing Track** focuses on step 8 of the roadmap and includes the tasks that must happen to make sure the process works.

▶ **The Communication Track** includes developing the communication plan and associated communication vehicles.

▶ **The Training Track** includes developing the training plan, course materials, scheduling the training, securing facilitators for the training, and conducting the training.

The Four Tracks in the Implementation Phase

Now that you have an overview of the four tracks in the implementation phase, let me explain each of them in more detail.

Change Management Track

When you improved the business process in step 6, you created an impact analysis. At this time, you review the analysis with the project sponsor and gain agreement on how the discussions with the organization will occur. You want to understand what you have responsibility to do and what the sponsor will handle.

This track also includes deciding the best time to introduce the change to the organization and developing the continuous improvement strategy.

Testing Track

I do not cover the testing track here because it is discussed in depth in Chapter 8, and you can refer to that chapter for the list of items included in Figure 9-1.

Communications Track (Communication Plan)

The third track in the implementation phase involves the communication plan. In developing this plan, think about what communication has to occur to make sure that all parties receive the appropriate information to prepare them for the change. Introducing a new business process is like introducing any other change to an organization. After defining the audience (the *who*), determine the following for each audience:

▶ The key message points (the *what*): What each audience group has to know about the change

▶ The best communication vehicles to use (the *how*): The best way to communicate with each audience

▶ The right timing for the communication (the *when*): The best time to communicate with each audience

If you have an internal communication group in your company, and you have limited experience with communications, ask whether they have a communication template they use when introducing a new system, initiative, or benefit. Then adapt it for the business process implementation.

Figure 9-3 shows an example of a general communication plan to use when implementing new business processes. Each of the columns in the communication plan has its role to fill.

Audience	Communication Goal	Key Message Points	Communication Vehicles (Method)	Due Date
Customer/ Client	Feedback and support	■ What's changing linked to the client needs defined in the scope definition document ■ Benefits to the customer/client ■ Timeline	Meeting; email follow-up	July 5 July 7 (email)
Stakeholders	Awareness	■ What's changing and why ■ Benefits ■ Timeline	Email	July 8
Process Workers	Education	■ What's changing and why ■ Their role and responsibility ■ Training schedule ■ Contact resources to help	Meeting (live and via video conference); intranet site; SharePoint site	July 9

Figure 9-3 Communication Plan

Audience

List the different categories of people who need to know about the process change. Figure 9-3 lists three different audiences: *Customer/Client*, *Stakeholders*, and *Process Workers*.

Communication Goal

State what you hope to accomplish with each audience. Typical examples include providing awareness, gaining approval, obtaining feedback, gaining support, or educating.

In the example, the goal for the customers/clients is to gain their feedback and support for the changes, whereas the stakeholders simply need awareness of the changes, and the process workers require education on the changes so that they can support the new process.

Key Message Points

List the key points to cover for each audience. Think about different cultures that you may have to communicate with because you may have to design different messages to work for those audiences.

Notice in the example that for the customers/clients, a key message point is to connect the process changes back to what the project team defined as important to the customers/clients in the scope definition document created in step 2. Getting the key message points correct is critical to a successful implementation, so do not rush through this step. The *Key Message Points* make writing the presentation or emails easier because they guide you through the creation of the communication vehicles.

Communication Vehicles

Identify the methods to use to communicate with each audience. Consider the different vehicles available, including face-to-face meetings, email, brochures, flyers, newsletters, and video conferencing. The method(s) chosen may differ because of local cultures; for example, some cultures prefer face-to-face communications.

For customers/clients, our example shows that we plan to conduct face-to-face meetings with them, along with a follow-up email to reinforce the key message points. A simple email message suffices for the stakeholders, and a video conference meeting will occur for the process workers to engage the geographically dispersed employees. The project team also plans to replace content that resides on the company's intranet and on the SharePoint collaboration site.

Due Date

Identify the timeline for each communication piece. Think about who needs to know the information first, second, and third.

In our example, we wanted to communicate with the customers/clients first to gain their support before letting the stakeholders and process workers know about the new process. In this way, any changes that have to occur to the business process can happen before introducing the new process on a wide scale.

As part of the communication plan, develop responses to any anticipated concerns, in the form of a frequently asked questions list. This may seem similar to the *Change Management* column in the impact analysis, but in this case the list is much broader and has to include questions or concerns that could surface from anywhere, both within and outside the department making the changes. If the new process significantly changes the current work of any of the process workers, you should include this fact in the impact analysis so the sponsor can assume responsibility for presenting the change to the affected employees.

The keys for successful communication include using simple language and terminology that the audience understands, as well as putting the message in the appropriate context so the recipients of the message can relate to the key points.

Training Track (Training Plan)

The fourth track in the implementation phase involves the training plan. In developing this plan, think about what training has to occur to make sure that all parties understand and can perform their process responsibilities. Consider:

▶ Who needs training
▶ Who owns the responsibility to conduct the training
▶ What they need training on
▶ Where to conduct the training

► When to train

► What methods to use to conduct the training

Although some people use the terms *training* and *communication* interchangeably, they are two different streams of work, and anyone in the training field probably has experience with a client trying to make a communication problem a training problem. I differentiate the two terms this way:

► **Communication** transmits or exchanges information and messages.

► **Training** provides a person with knowledge and skills to perform a task.

If you have an internal training group in your company, and you have limited experience with training, ask for the group's help on this part of the implementation. Tools may exist that you can use when analyzing audience needs, deciding how to deliver the training, and developing the training.

Figure 9-4 shows a general example of a training plan that you can use as a starting point for implementing any new business process. Let us look more closely at each of the columns in the training plan.

Audience	Learning Objectives	Approach	Tools	Facilitator	Due Date
Customer/ Client	■ *Run* the newly designed report.	Meeting	Reference card	Sponsor, project manager	July 16
Process Workers	■ *Identify* the five steps in the business process. ■ *Explain* how to handle an exception to the business process. ■ *Complete* the <name> template.	Instructor-led training session	■ Process documentation ■ Job aids ■ Personal computers with access to email	Project team member	July 12–15

Figure 9-4 Training Plan

Audience

Here you list the different categories of people who require training on the process change.

You may notice that we omitted the stakeholders from the training plan in Figure 9-4, although we included them in the communication plan because our only priority with this group is awareness. We do not have to train the stakeholders on anything.

Learning Objectives

State the learning (or training) objectives in this column, or what the audience will learn as a result of the training. In our example, the project team plans to train the client on how to run a new report and train the process workers on multiple items. If we had different groups of employees with different training needs, we could have added additional rows in the training plan to identify the learning objectives and approach for each group of learners.

Although developing learning objectives falls into an entire field of study called instructional system design, I share the relevant highlights to support what has to occur in this step.

Notice in Figure 9-4 that each learning objective starts with an action verb: *run, identify, explain, complete*. An action verb denotes the ability to do something. What should a person be able to do after completing training? In business process work, you generally want a person to either:

▶ Know something.

▶ Absorb or grasp something.

▶ Apply something.

Each of these three action verbs denotes a different level of cognition with *know* at the lowest level, *absorb* at a higher level, and *apply* at an even higher level. Figure 9-5 summarizes how these action verbs relate to one other.

The *know–absorb–apply* example demonstrates a hierarchy that exists where the person attending training achieves a

Action Verb	General Description	Learning Objectives	Example
Know	If people can identify or define something, they have proved that they *know* something.	*Identify* the five steps in the business process.	If people can state the five steps, then they obviously *know* them.
Absorb	If people can explain or summarize something, they have proved that they *absorbed*, or grasped, something because they can translate the concept into their own words.	*Explain* how to handle an exception to the business process.	If an employee can explain how to handle exceptions, then they *absorbed*, grasped, or comprehended the concepts presented in the training.

The ability to explain constitutes a higher level of knowledge than simply identifying the five steps because you need to know the five steps before you can identify an exception. |
| *Apply* | If people can complete or demonstrate something, they have proved that they can *apply* what they learned. | *Complete* the <name> template. | If people can successfully complete the template, then they *applied* what they learned.

The ability to apply constitutes an even higher level than either identifying or explaining, because people can perform a task as a result of the training. |

Figure 9-5 *Levels of Learning Objectives*

higher level of competence as they move up in the hierarchy. Figure 9-6 shows another way to depict the hierarchy of learning. In this figure, first you *Know*, then you *Absorb*, and finally you *Apply*. When you write learning objectives, try to reach the *apply* level so that employees demonstrate their knowledge. Confucius said, "What I hear I forget, what I see, I remember, but what I do, I understand."

Avoid using verbs that do not support the ability to observe a result, for example, *understand*. How can you tell if people understand something because the process of comprehension is an internal mental process? Unless they can define,

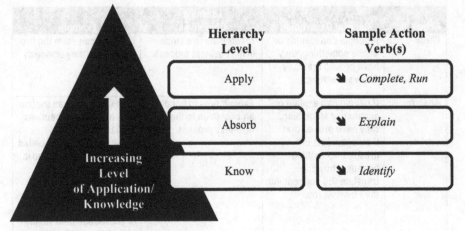

Hierarchy Level	Sample Action Verb(s)
Apply	↘ *Complete, Run*
Absorb	↘ *Explain*
Know	↘ *Identify*

Increasing Level of Application/ Knowledge

Figure 9-6 Training Objectives Hierarchy

identify, explain, or demonstrate their understanding, you do not know if they truly understand.

To continue explaining the columns in Figure 9-4, the remaining columns include:

Approach

Identify how you plan to deliver the training. Will you conduct face-to-face training, Web-based training, blended learning, or something else?

Tools

List the training tools required to deliver the training. These should include the process documentation but define what other tools you require. For example, do you need personal computers so that the people attending the training can access your company's intranet and email system, or do you require a wireless connection?

Facilitator

Identify who will deliver the training to each audience. You, a project team member, or your sponsor may own a portion of this responsibility.

Due Date

Identify the timeline for the training, and think about who needs the training first, second, and third, similar to the way we thought about the order in the communication plan. In our example, we trained the employees first so they could support the clients when they had questions running the report.

The keys for successful training include developing good learning objectives that articulate what the participants should know at the end of training, matching delivery styles with learner preferences, and delivering the training at the right time.

Chapter Summary: Step 9

Planning the entire business process improvement endeavor up front, by creating the implementation plan, will give you confidence that you have the right steps and the right people in place to improve the business process and implement the changes required to bring it to fruition. The implementation plan is the framework that brings the separate components together.

The topics discussed in this chapter include the:

► *Impact analysis*, originally introduced in Chapter 6, which identifies the changes that have to occur, the rationale for the changes, the area and population impacted, and potential pushback.

► *Communication plan* that identifies who needs to know what about the new process.

► *Training plan* that tells who needs training on what.

If you leave one of these components out of the implementation plan, you risk decreased productivity caused by confusion or anxiety, as well as the inability to deliver customer/client satisfaction. Spend the time at the beginning of the work developing the implementation plan and continually adapt it as the work progresses.

The hierarchy of learning helps you to build accurate

learning objectives that address the level of application or knowledge you desire.

Time Estimate

To plan the time that it takes to work through this step, Figure 9-7 summarizes the time you should allow to complete the implementation plan and its components (step 9).

Event	Time	Purpose
Develop the implementation plan.	5 days	■ To make sure that you understand the individual tasks that have to occur to address the business process
Refine the impact analysis.	3 days	■ To determine who has responsibility to handle each of the changes that must occur to implement the new business process
Develop the communication plan.	1 day	■ To identify who has to know about the process changes, what they need to know, and when and how you will communicate with them
Develop the training plan.	3 days	■ To identify who requires training on the new process, who will deliver the training, where you will deliver the training, when you will deliver the training, and how you will deliver the training
Gain sponsor buy-in.	1 day	■ Ensure that the sponsor agrees with the components of the implementation

Figure 9-7 Time-Estimate—Step 9: Implement the Change

Develop the Implementation Plan

Develop the details for each of the implementation phases, determine how long each task will take, identify the responsible person, and sequence the tasks. Developing the plan goes faster if you have the project team help develop the separate components of the overall plan. For example, have one person work on communications, another on training, and another on testing.

Refine the Impact Analysis

This can take quite some time to complete. While you started creating the impact analysis in step 6, take the time now to review the analysis and refine it. Do not rush developing the impact analysis because it can have a significant effect on the success of the implementation of the new business process.

Develop the Communication Plan

During this time, develop the audience profile, using the matrix introduced to identify the audience for the communication, what they need to know, and when they need to know the information.

Develop the Training Plan

Develop the detailed training plan, and spend sufficient time writing the learning objectives. If you have no experience writing learning objectives, try to find someone, if possible, with a training background to validate them.

Gain Sponsor Buy-In

Once you complete the implementation plan, review it with the sponsor and make adjustments to either the content or the timeline. In my experience, the timeline generally needs adjustments because the sponsor wants to have the work done sooner than you estimate.

What You Have Achieved

In this chapter you have achieved the following:

► An understanding of the tasks required to implement the new business process

► Insight into how to use phases and tracks to organize implementation tasks

► An updated analysis of the changes that have to occur

► A grasp of how to develop a communication plan that provides details surrounding who needs to know about the changes and what they need to know

▶ A plan to train those affected by the change

▶ A tool to help you stay on track

▶ Most important, the *power* to have a successful implementation

KNOWLEDGE CHECK

Use this knowledge check to validate your understanding of the material covered in step 9. Select the best answer in the following multiple-choice questions by circling the best choice.

1. What do implementation plans include?
   a. A series of tasks that you must complete
   b. Phases and tracks to help organize the work
   c. A design, development, and implementation phase
   d. All of the above

2. The *Predecessors* column in Microsoft Project tells you what?
   a. What task must occur before another task can begin
   b. The start and finish of a task
   c. What task follows the task with the predecessor
   d. The duration of a task

3. Tracks can help in an implementation plan by:
   a. Differentiating the design and development phases
   b. Identifying what to include in the impact analysis
   c. Organizing a large phase into manageable chunks of work
   d. None of the above

4. A continuous improvement plan is part of what track in the implementation phase?
   a. Testing track
   b. Communication track
   c. Change management track
   d. Training track

5. What comprises an effective communication plan?
   a. Audience and key message points
   b. Communication goal
   c. What vehicles to use and due dates
   d. All of the above

6. A learning objective helps to do what?
   a. Identify what the presenter of training must do
   b. Identify what the participants of training will learn as a result of the training
   c. Define what to test
   d. Transmit or exchange information and messages

7. The following is true regarding learning objectives:
   a. They should start with an action verb
   b. There is a hierarchy associated with learning objectives
   c. As one moves up the hierarchy of learning, the level of application and/or knowledge increases
   d. All of the above

8. The sponsor should be involved in which of the following?
   a. Building the implementation plan
   b. Taking action on the impact analysis
   c. Developing the communication and training plans
   d. All of the above

CHAPTER 10

Step 10: Drive Continuous Improvement

Embracing the New Mindset

Joanne Wu, the training and development manager from Chapter 8, led the effort each year to create the annual budget for the training department, which required her to gather the training requirements for the next year from client groups, determine priorities, and allocate the department's resources to address the forecasted training needs. Joanne found the time required to conduct this annual process excessive, just as in every prior year. Only about 40 percent of the projects specified in the plan ever happened. Joanne felt her clients requested unnecessary projects, which did not allow her to plan her department's resources or budget as tightly as she would like.

My first observation was that Joanne viewed the annual plan as an end in itself, not as an ongoing process. Although Joanne's team had streamlined the process of collecting input, she still did not like the result; so she asked me to evaluate the process and help make additional changes to improve the process. An analysis of the situation showed me that Joanne's staff spent most of their time focusing on the efficiency of the process, streamlining it so that their clients would find it simple. Although they did make the process easier for the clients, they overlooked the effectiveness of the process and that it could not adapt to changing business needs. Because the clients could not always foresee issues that might surface during the year, like new competitive products or a changing economy, the business process had to include flexibility so it could address new needs as they surfaced throughout the year.

Continuous improvement, a term derived from the total quality movement, means monitoring a business process and making adjustments to it so it continually improves over time. Developing a continuous improvement mindset ensures that the process continues to deliver the gains achieved. This means continually measuring the business process, regularly reevaluating customer/client needs and expectations, engaging the process workers on a regular basis, and not allowing the documentation to sit on the shelf.

Although you may consider skipping over this chapter because it sounds more like theory than practicality, I urge you to reconsider because this step enables you to sustain the effectiveness, efficiency, and adaptability introduced into the business process. If you decide to skip this step, you will find that the business process works fine for a while. Then it starts slipping backward a little, then a little more, until eventually it becomes outdated, and you have to start the improvement effort all over again. Think about losing weight. If you successfully lose 20 pounds but never weigh yourself, you will probably start regaining the pounds—perhaps not overnight, but gradually until you find yourself back at your original weight or higher.

The same scenario applies to business processes for a variety of reasons. You have to stay on top of your business processes in order to stay competitive, to continue meeting the changing customer/client needs, or to keep pace with the changing technology. Change and external factors demand that you continuously improve business processes.

Even business processes that went through reengineering in the 1990s required a focus on continuous improvement to retain the strategic gains made. During the reengineering rage, though, continuous improvement did not enter many people's minds, probably because it stems from the total quality management field. Proponents of reengineering dismissed total quality management as too slow because total quality techniques delivered incremental, not dramatic change. Some people incorrectly theorized that when you reengineered a business process, it would remain competitive. The same applies to business process management.

Continuous improvement requires the mindset that improvement never ends and that you may never achieve perfection. Practitioners of yoga or followers of Buddhism strive to reach nirvana with the full knowledge that, at best, they may only become more serene and self-disciplined. Just as you set goals to fulfill your personal vision, also set goals to sustain the improvements made to a business process.

As you follow the ten steps to business process improvement, you acquire a unique level of understanding about the business process, which positions you to act in the role of innovator, influencer, and communicator. You can then:

► Demonstrate innovation by continually identifying new ways to improve the business process.

► Influence others to continuously think about their work from a process perspective.

► Talk and communicate with the customers/clients, stakeholders, and process workers to make sure the process continues to deliver what they require.

So let me share a model that will help you think about continuous improvement and some tools that can help. Because continuous improvement can seem like an obscure concept, the model and tools assist in keeping this step at the forefront and in perspective.

The Continuous Improvement Cycle

The continuous improvement cycle wheel in Figure 10-1 shows four phases that can help you achieve the new mindset. Each phase in the wheel provides a degree of structure to keep you thinking about how to continually improve a business process. You can move through the four phases quickly, but do so often. The four phases are:

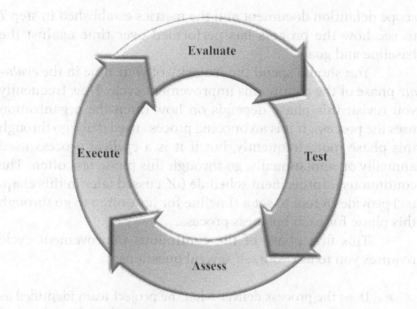

Figure 10-1 *Continuous Improvement Cycle*

1. **Evaluate:** Determine the opportunities.
2. **Test:** Make the change and try it out on a limited basis.
3. **Assess:** Determine whether the change worked.
4. **Execute:** Deploy the change on a wide scale.

Evaluate

In this phase of continuous improvement, examine all aspects of the business process to identify opportunities for improvement. To accomplish this, you have to understand the expectations for the business process. Start by asking a few questions. Does the process continue to deliver the effectiveness, efficiency, and adaptability intended? What bottlenecks exist? Have customer/client needs changed?

To answer these questions, go back and review the customer/client needs defined when the project team created the scope definition document in step 2. Review the needs and expectations to see if the business process still delivers against them. Also look at the measurements of success defined in the scope definition document and the metrics established in step 7 to see how the process has performed over time against the baseline and goals.

You should spend the majority of your time in the *evaluate* phase of the continuous improvement cycle. How frequently you revisit this phase depends on how often the organization uses the process. If it is an ongoing process used daily, go through this phase more frequently, but if it is a cyclical process used annually or semiannually, go through this phase less often. The continuous improvement schedule (discussed later in this chapter) provides a tool to set a timeline for how often to go through this phase for each business process.

This first phase of the continuous improvement cycle requires you to ask yourself several questions:

▶ Does the process deliver what the project team identified as customer/client needs? Customers and clients have a way of raising the bar over time because, as the process meets their expectations, they tend to expect a new level of service. They may not be explicit about their expectations, so stay focused on how the customers/clients feel about the business process. To stay on top of their expectations, revisit the customer/client needs and measurements of success over and over again. Make sure you do the right things well, and stay fresh and connected to any new expectations. As Joanne Wu learned, client needs do not stay static but change as the business changes. Joanne required increased flexibility in her budget to accommodate changing business needs.

▶ Do the process workers follow the documented process? Keep the documentation up-to-date, make sure employees use the documentation and tools created, and see that new employees receive training on the business process. Problems can easily occur simply because no one thoroughly trains new employees.

▶ Do the stakeholders receive what they require from the business process? Although the customer/client is our primary focus, do not ignore the stakeholders. Review the scope definition document, and validate that the process continues to meet their requirements.

▶ Do identified third parties deliver what they said they would deliver? Make sure that vendors or suppliers follow through on their commitments.

Thinking about the customer/client, process workers, stakeholders, and vendors/suppliers makes it easier to regularly evaluate the effectiveness, efficiency, and adaptability of a business process.

In step 7 the project team developed metrics and established the baseline. Evaluating these metrics becomes one of the most important components of the evaluate phase because it immediately highlights a problem. As you collect the quantitative and qualitative data, evaluate the performance of the business process against the metrics and identify any trends. Plot the data and compare it to your baseline data.

As an example of the need for evaluation, recall Pete Hodges, the regional sales manager from Chapter 7, who cared about the number of new customers. The metric we established said that Pete wanted a "30 percent increase in the number of qualified new customers over the next six months." To track the number of new customers, Pete used the table in Figure 10-2, where he captured the:

Evaluation Criteria	1st Quarter	2nd Quarter	3rd Quarter	4th Quarter
Number of leads generated	250	400	450	
Number of customer calls	100	150	250	
Number of qualified leads	50	75	100	
Number of new customers	25	45	50	
Ratio of qualified leads to new customers	2:1	5:3	2:1	
Percentage of qualified leads converted to new customers	50%	60%	50%	
Percentage increase of qualified new customers		80%	11%	

Figure 10-2 Sales Metrics: Percentage Increase in New Qualified Customers

▶ Number of leads generated (supplied by the marketing department)

- ► Number of customer calls (the number of leads that sales representatives followed up)
- ► Number of qualified leads (the number of leads that fell within the sales department's definition of "qualified," ones that the sales representatives would call on)
- ► Number of new customers (the number of new accounts closed)
- ► Ratio of qualified leads to new customers
- ► Percentage of qualified leads converted to new customers
- ► Percentage increase of qualified new customers

According to Figure 10-2, something seems to have happened between the second and third quarters because the *Percentage of qualified leads converted to new customers* dropped by 10 percent (from 60 percent to 50 percent), although the total increase of qualified new customers increased by 11 percent. Pete was happy with the second quarter results, which exceeded his expectations, but not with the third quarter results.

At this point, Pete came to me wanting to dig deeper into the decrease in the ratio between the second and third quarters. I tried to determine the cause for the drop, and we set new goals for the next measurement period. Pete had to reach a number equal to or greater than the second quarter to at least get back to the 60 percent conversion rate. This would put him back on track to achieve his overall target of a 30 percent increase in the number of qualified new customers over a six-month period. With two months behind him, he was averaging a 45.5 percent increase, which looked good, but he knew that he had to focus on the monthly statistics to ensure meeting his 30 percent target.

After assessing how the sales representatives performed their day-to-day responsibilities, it appeared the problem rested with a dozen new sales representatives who did not follow the guidelines established for qualifying leads. As a result, Pete did not have to introduce any new steps in the process; he simply had to make certain the new sales representatives received the appropriate training on how to qualify sales leads. Pete added this training to the onboarding process to help new sales representatives in the future.

In Joanne Wu's case, we designed flexibility into her annual budgeting process to accommodate new client expectations, technology improvements, or changing business priorities. We changed the process so Joanne's staff captured only a handful of initiatives for the next year, ones that clearly supported the company's stated priorities and that would not change. We introduced changes to allow Joanne and her staff to regularly evaluate incoming requests. Having a half dozen identified projects gave Joanne a sense of control and gave her clients the flexibility they wanted.

During the evaluation phase, look at the process itself and confirm that everyone follows the process, uses the tools as planned, and gathers the metrics as defined. This includes items like:

▶ Determining the effectiveness of the internal controls put in place: Do they help in eliminating errors?

▶ Talking to the customers/clients and stakeholders to assess how they feel about the effectiveness of the process: This provides qualitative feedback instead of numbers, and both qualitative and quantitative data aid in determining the effectiveness of the process.

▶ Evaluating the roles and responsibilities and making changes if appropriate.

▶ Making sure that the organization trains new employees.

▶ Evaluating the effectiveness of any communication processes.

▶ Making sure employees share information and knowledge.

▶ Making sure that vendors or suppliers deliver what the process expects.

After conducting some analysis and talking to the appropriate people, propose any needed changes, either to the business process itself, to customer/client needs, to the measurements of success, or to the process metrics.

By the end of this phase, you have identified the points in the process that present improvement opportunities and have created a plan of action to focus on them.

Test

Once you have identified a problem or opportunity, made the process changes, and established an improvement goal, implement the change on a small scale to validate that the change(s) work. In this phase of continuous improvement, you want to make certain that any changes work before introducing them on a wide scale.

This task should seem familiar since Chapter 8 covered testing in detail. You can use many of the same techniques from that chapter here, just on a smaller scale. Remember to think about the who, what, where, when, and how of testing the change:

▶ **Whom** to involve in the test
▶ **What** items to test
▶ **Where** the test should occur
▶ **When** the test should occur
▶ **How** to measure the success of the change

During the second phase of the continuous improvement cycle, plan how to test the change. Identify who will participate, what part of the business process to test, what location or area to include in the test, how long the test will run, how to collect and analyze the data, and how to define success. Include the process owner or sponsor to make sure you have the appropriate support.

Testing in the continuous improvement phase should be on a smaller scale than what we covered in Chapter 8, so involve a smaller number of participants and test items in the testing. A good example of the extent of testing is the follow-up on the bank merger from Chapter 9, where we merged the business processes from two banks into one after an acquisition. In this example, the merger of two highly visible areas, private banking and investment banking, worked fine because the merger team placed significant effort on making their transition seamless. However, after evaluating the new process three months later as part of our continuous improvement plan, problems surfaced at the retail banking sector with their decreased level of customer service and increased operating expenses. This sector had not received as much attention during the merger, and so the retail team made adjustments to their business processes. In deciding where to test the changes, the project team decided to test them with one branch before implementing the changes at all branches.

Depending on what you uncover in the evaluate phase of continuous improvement, you may not always have to test because in some cases employees simply require training, as in the Pete Hodges case, or the project team may simply make adjustments to the measurement data. At other times, though, as in the retail banking example, the project team may make significant changes and you have to test those changes before implementing them on a wide scale. If you find yourself making major changes, revisit Chapter 8 and create a test plan.

It often helps to look first at the process workers if a problem in the measurement data surfaces, because you will find it easier to retrain employees on the process or tools than to change the process. Understand why employees perform the way they do, and make sure to differentiate between an employee and a process issue.

At the end of this phase, you have data available to help assess whether the proposed changes to the business process work.

Assess

In this phase of continuous improvement, keep track of how the changes work as you implement the change on a small scale to understand what has to occur to introduce the change on a wider scale. Did the change deliver the value expected? What other criteria should you consider?

In this phase, review the data collected during the testing phase, make any adjustments deemed appropriate, and decide whether to proceed with the changes. You may also want to bring in benchmark data to help you form an opinion on what changes to introduce.

Benchmarking consists of measuring a business process against a standard of excellence, either an internal group in your company or an external company well-known as being of world-class or best-in-class caliber. For example, Disney is known for delivering outstanding guest service, Apple for its innovative designs, and Bosch for its quiet, stylish appliances. Benchmark data can help introduce greater effectiveness, efficiency, and flexibility into your business processes so they can be adapted to changing needs. Chapter 13 includes a real-life example of a benchmarking study.

Gathering external benchmark data can present a problem because some companies do not like to share information about their business processes. Not all external companies present a problem, though, particularly if they belong to a different industry and do not compete in the same market as your company. Internal benchmarking can be just as effective as external benchmarking, and it may seem easier because you do not have to worry about confidentiality.

If you choose to proceed with benchmarking, work with a colleague who has designed a benchmark study in the past because conducting an effective benchmark study requires experience. Spend enough time planning the benchmark study, and have a solid understanding of your own business process before talking to other people about their processes.

To conduct a benchmark, start with the customer/client needs identified in the scope definition document and prioritize them so that your benchmarking study focuses on the most important customer/client needs. Joanne Wu, a training and development manager, identified "quality training experience" as one of her client's top needs.

Start a benchmark study by conducting internal interviews because these assist in defining terminology and in developing a list of external companies and internal groups to benchmark. As you conduct the internal interviews, ask the interviewee to define terms. In Joanne's case, for example, I had to find out what a *quality training experience* meant. By talking to Joanne's clients, I found that they wanted their employees who attended training to apply what they learned on the job upon their return, and they wanted their employees to have reference materials that they could use on the job. The clients also wanted only experienced instructors teaching classes. Once you understand what a term means, ask the interviewee to identify best-in-class companies or internal groups who demonstrate excellence in the type of customer/client need being discussed. For example, I asked Joanne's clients if they knew of any companies or internal groups that delivered a quality training experience.

As this example shows, the internal clients interviewed can help you develop a clear list of customer/client needs and build the list of companies to benchmark because they know their field and they know the best-in-class companies. Once you identify the benchmark list, comprised of both internal and external contacts, develop a set of questions that focus on the business processes' critical success factors. The questions should delve into how the benchmark companies or internal groups achieve the critical success factors.

The project team can also use benchmarking during the evaluate phase of the continuous improvement cycle and during step 6 (when looking at improving the business process) to help determine how the business process compares to best-in-class companies, which in turn can help establish improvement goals.

At the end of this phase, you have all the information necessary to make a decision on how to proceed.

Execute

After assessing the success of the changes to the business process and perhaps comparing the process to other internal groups or external companies, in this phase of continuous improvement you deploy the updated business process across the organization.

This phase should seem similar to the implementation step discussed in Chapter 9, but on a smaller scale. In this phase, communicate the change and train the process workers on the change. Although you may not have to create a communication plan or a training plan, you should create a new impact analysis.

The same audience defined in the original communication plan has to know about the process changes if the changes affect them. You can probably use the same goal, key message points, and preferred communication vehicles defined in the plan.

The training plan will have a reduced number of learning objectives and perhaps a different, simpler approach, and the audience probably remains the same.

Create a new impact analysis any time a change occurs because it ensures that nothing falls through the cracks. Always engage the sponsor in introducing the proposed changes.

At the end of this phase, you have introduced the business process change(s) to the organization.

Continuous Improvement Plan

Although continuous improvement introduces many new points to remember, the continuous improvement plan assists you in developing a continuous improvement mindset. The plan summarizes the activities necessary to maintain a focus on the business process and outlines how frequently to perform each activity, any sources of data used, the technique or method used, and who performs the activity.

Before leaving the business process you just worked on and moving on to the next one, create a continuous improvement plan for the existing process so that everyone can see the tasks required to keep the process alive and adaptable to the changing business climate. Figure 10-3 shows a sample plan for Joanne Wu's training department. Use this template as a starting point to create a plan for your own business process. The activities listed in Figure 10-3 remain fairly consistent for any business process because they represent the components of the foundation established in Chapter 3 or the process map created in Chapter 4. Make sure to include these activities in your continuous improvement plan:

Activity	Frequency	Data Source	Method	Person Responsible
Review measurement data	Monthly	Weekly activity reports	Observation; conversation	Training manager
Revisit customer/ client needs	Quarterly	Scope definition document	Conversation (phone call)	Director, training and development
Test internal controls	Monthly	Process map and internal control checklist	Observation; conversation	Training manager
Validate that process workers follow process	Quarterly	Process map	Observation; conversation	Training manager
Revisit stakeholder needs	Semiannual	Scope definition document	Conversation (phone call)	Director, training and development
Evaluate third-party vendors/suppliers	Annual	Process map	Phone call	Training manager

Figure 10-3 Continuous Improvement Plan

▶ **Review Measurement Data**: Review what the project team identified as measurements of success in Chapter 3 and how you decided to measure those items in Chapter 7.

▶ **Revisit Customer/Client Needs:** Look at the expectations identified by the customers/clients in Chapter 3.

▶ **Test Internal Controls:** Review the process map created in Chapter 6, looking for the internal control icon and reviewing how the project team stated the organization would overcome the potential problems in the internal control checklist.

▶ **Validate That Process Workers Follow Process:** Go through the process map and validate that the employees involved in the process follow the steps outlined.

▶ **Revisit Stakeholder Needs:** Look at the expectations identified in Chapter 3.

▶ **Evaluate Third-Party Vendors/Suppliers:** Go through the process map and validate that the vendors or suppliers are delivering what the process specifies.

If you customized the scope definition document and added additional sections, include them in the activity column in the continuous improvement plan.

Over time, as you improve multiple business processes, keeping track of all your business processes becomes more difficult. As the inventory of improved business processes increases, create one continuous improvement *schedule* that covers all the business processes to keep track of the various activities. Translate the frequencies, from Figure 10-3, to actual dates so that the organization has an annual schedule to follow.

Figure 10-4 shows an example of a schedule with the activities from Figure 10-3 now listed horizontally as columns. This allows you to list the business processes vertically down the left-hand column, which provides a summary of all business processes in one continuous improvement schedule. Figure 10-4 shows a continuous improvement schedule for part of a recruitment department's hiring processes. Notice how the table lists the requisition, sourcing, and orientation business processes down the left-hand column.

You can see how much easier it gets to manage multiple

Business Process	Review Measurement Data	Test Internal Controls	Revisit Customer/ Client Needs	Validate Process Workers	Revisit Stakeholder Needs	Evaluate Third Parties
Requisition	1st of month	1st of month	Q1–3/1 Q2–6/1 Q3–9/1 Q4–12/1	Q1–3/1 Q2–6/1 Q3–9/1 Q4–12/1	5/1 11/1	January
Sourcing	15th of month	15th of month	Q1–3/15 Q2–6/15 Q3–9/15 Q4–12/15	Q1–3/15 Q2–6/15 Q3–9/15 Q4–12/15	5/15 11/15	April
Orientation	30th of month	30th of month	Q1–3/30 Q2–6/30 Q3–9/30 Q4–12/30	Q1–3/30 Q2–6/30 Q3–9/30 Q4–12/30	5/30 11/30	August

Figure 10-4 Continuous Improvement Schedule

business processes by having this snapshot because you can quickly see what the organization has to focus on at any point in time. In this example, the business decided to look at the metrics for the requisition process on the first of each month, sourcing on the fifteenth, and orientation on the thirtieth. Figure 10-4 also demonstrates that the organization wants to review the measurement data and test internal controls the most frequently (monthly) and the third-party performance the least frequently (annually).

In developing the continuous improvement plan, the project team identified how often to evaluate each activity, but, after creating the combined schedule, you may decide to reduce some of the frequencies because it may seem overwhelming. Continue to develop the continuous improvement plan for each business process as you update the continuous improvement schedule because the plan provides additional data that the organization requires to conduct the appropriate evaluations.

Chapter Summary: Step 10

The continuous improvement cycle confirms that the business process continually delivers effectiveness, efficiency, and flexibility to the organization. The four phases (evaluate, test, assess, and execute) provide the necessary structure. You can move through the four phases quickly, but do so often. Let the frequency of how often the organization uses a business process drive the continuous improvement schedule. During continuous improvement, spend the majority of your time in the evaluate phase because improvement opportunities surface in this phase.

Throughout continuous improvement, you will find yourself using some of the tools created during previous steps, like the scope definition document from step 2, the impact analysis from step 6, or the communication and training plans from step 9. Continually evaluate the information defined in the scope definition document because it helps to keep the business process aligned with the changing business needs.

Benchmarking can influence how to approach a business process and assist you in thinking about different goals. Focus any benchmarking effort on the most important customer/client needs, use internal and external parties in the benchmarking, and use data available in research studies as part of the analysis. Identify how best-in-class companies deliver against your customer/client needs.

The continuous improvement *plan* lays the foundation for verifying that the business process remains relevant and adapts to changing business needs. Combining all your business processes into one continuous improvement *schedule* provides a tool to better manage the work throughout the year.

Time Estimate

To plan the time that it takes to work through this step, Figure 10-5 summarizes the time to allocate to this step.

Event	Time	Purpose
Develop continuous improvement plan (evaluate phase); create or add to schedule.	3 days	■ To put a focus on ongoing improvement and to confirm that everyone involved understands their responsibility ■ To either start a continuous improvement schedule or add the newly completed process to the existing schedule
Gain sponsor buy-in.	1 hour	■ Make certain that the sponsor agrees with the components of the plan
Test/assess/execute.	Varies	■ To validate that the proposed changes work before introducing them on a wide scale

Figure 10-5 Time Estimate—Step 10: Drive Continuous Improvement

Develop the Continuous Improvement Plan and Schedule

Outline the details for the steps to follow in the evaluate phase of the continuous improvement cycle. Identify how frequently to conduct each item in the plan, where the data comes from, the persons responsible for the items, and how they will handle them. Implementing the plan goes faster if you include the people identified as the responsible parties in the overall planning. Creating the plan only takes an hour or two, but gaining other people's support adds to the time it takes to complete this step. Also develop the continuous improvement schedule during this time, or add the newly improved business process to the existing schedule and make any adjustments.

Gain Sponsor Buy-In

Once you complete the continuous improvement plan, review it with the sponsor and adjust the tasks as necessary. If you created a continuous improvement schedule, show the sponsor how the newest business process fits into the overall schedule. You may need the sponsor to gain agreement from executives if you list them as responsible for any action items in the plan.

Test, Assess, Execute

During these phases, you or a project team member makes the decision on how to test the changes on a small scale, evaluate the effectiveness of the proposed changes, and then implement them on a full scale.

What You Have Achieved

In this chapter you have achieved the following:

► An understanding of what continuous improvement means and why you should care

► Details about how to keep adapting the business process to changing business needs

► A plan that includes the appropriate steps to regularly review the business process

► A schedule that provides a snapshot of when to evaluate

multiple business processes so you can manage a group of business processes

► Most important, the *power* to sustain the improvements

KNOWLEDGE CHECK

Use this knowledge check to validate your understanding of the material covered in step 10. Match the correct answer to the statement by placing the appropriate letter on the blank line.

_____ 1. Phase where you determine whether the changes worked on a small scale

_____ 2. Monitoring a process and making adjustments so that it continually improves

_____ 3. Why continuous improvement is important

_____ 4. Phase where you implement the change on a small scale

_____ 5. Phase in which you examine all aspects of the process to identify opportunities for improvement

_____ 6. A tool to assist in managing continuous improvement across processes

_____ 7. Phase in which you deploy the improved process

_____ 8. Measuring a process against a standard of excellence

_____ 9. Summarizes tasks required to keep a process relevant and the associated time frames

A. Evaluate; B. Continuous improvement plan; C. Benchmarking; D. Execute; E. Continuous improvement schedule; F. Continuous improvement; G. Sustain process improvements; H. Assess; I. Test

CHAPTER 11

Create the Executive Summary

Getting the Recognition

After all the work you have gone through with each step of the roadmap, now is your time to get some well-deserved recognition. Do not relax yet, but rather help management recognize what you have accomplished. Recognition for improving a business process does not come as easy as getting a compliment on a new haircut or a new suit because the new process may not immediately stand out. You have to let management know, in an acceptable way, the work you have done, and that becomes the challenge. This chapter shows how you gain recognition in a professional way by summarizing your business process work in an executive summary, a package that management will find useful.

Executive summaries always seem to differ, and I do not recall any two that looked exactly alike. Every executive summary I completed for the scenarios presented throughout this book has a different look because each has its own unique circumstances. My executive summaries have ranged from two to ten pages, but there is no standard, so feel free to create what seems right for your particular situation.

The most important point when writing an executive summary is to make certain that it addresses what the sponsor cares about, so tailor the summary to address those known concerns. For example, let me summarize the chief concerns of some of the people discussed so far:

► Stuart Wang, the compensation director, wanted to understand the labor requirements to support the business processes that his team delivered and how to sustain the improvements that the project team achieved.

▶ Joanne Wu, the training and development manager, cared about adequately planning her resources.

▶ Kendall Smith, the senior vice president of human resources, cared about processes that impacted bringing new employees on board, which meant that his initial interest lay with the training process.

▶ Wendy Chan, the manager of workforce analysis, wanted accurate head count reporting for the entire company to use.

The executive summary is usually one part of a larger document, like a business plan, and most busy executives read only that section. In business process work, the executive summary provides a high-level overview of the entire project. Write the summary in a clear and concise manner, but provide sufficient detail of the completed work; then provide additional information in an appendix, as needed. When writing the executive summary, remember that not every reader has the same degree of familiarity with the topic as you and the project team, so write with the novice reader in mind.

The Six Sections of the Executive Summary

Always start the executive summary with an intriguing or compelling statement that grabs the reader's attention, and remember to include the following sections:

▶ Project focus
▶ Goals
▶ Summary
▶ Key findings
▶ Deliverables
▶ Appendix (if applicable)

Let me walk through an explanation of each section of the executive summary and provide some examples.

Section 1: Project Focus

Start the executive summary with a story about the current predicament, which illustrates the problems that caused you to take on the work. I use *project focus* instead of problem statement, because the word *focus* is more positive than *problem*, putting the reader in a more positive mindset. Include information in the project focus that shows the business need that drove the analysis; for example, did the work result from a reorganization, the formation of a new business, an increase in errors, or another reason? The following four examples illustrate several different project focus statements, one for each of the three themes just mentioned, plus one for the recognition bonus award process:

EXAMPLE 1: A REORGANIZATION

The fall 2015 reorganization of the home improvement segment caused the human resources organization to realign its support network. Departments no longer have responsibility for employees at a single geographic location, but now have employees who reside in multiple worldwide locations.

The sales and marketing department executives, for example, now have employees that reside in multiple countries and . . .

EXAMPLE 2: A NEW BUSINESS

The project focused on developing the orientation process that the new Los Angeles division will use to onboard their front-line employees. We expect a high turnover rate because of the local market. Due to the expected turnover, the project team paid close attention to the timing of each activity in the process.

The team also kept in mind the local . . .

EXAMPLE 3: ERROR REDUCTION

Transactions that cause a change to employee data usually involve multiple departments, and, as a result, handoffs between departments become critical. Over the last 18 months, we have noticed a lack of integration between the departments, causing ineffective handoffs, increased errors, and ultimately inefficient business processes.

Although each department does a thorough job at their individual responsibilities . . .

EXAMPLE 4: RECOGNITION BONUS AWARD PROCESS

Managers have increasingly complained about the turnaround time associated with providing their employees recognition bonus awards. As the company faces increasing competition in the labor market, the Compensation department wanted to streamline the business process and make it easier for managers to give employees a bonus award as part of the company's retention strategy.

The project team focused its work on reducing the overall time required to process a bonus award, which now averages 11 days. The . . .

The intent of these opening paragraphs is to enable the reader to instantly understand why the project team focused on the specific business process(es). Provide enough detail so you paint the picture of the current situation from the reader's perspective rather than from your own. Often when we write emails, it is natural to include everything we know about a subject, believing that everything is important and losing sight that most readers care only about a quarter of the information provided. Make an effort to keep the project focus simple, and give readers only what they want to know. They should grasp the issue and want to read further.

In the previous four examples, the reader cares that:

▶ The human resources organization is proactively supporting the company's reorganization.

▶ The recruitment department is concerned with high turnover and the speed of onboarding new employees.

▶ Management is focusing on integration across departments to make sure that the process runs smoothly.

▶ Compensation is concerned with retaining employees in competitive times.

From reading the project focus alone, the reader either continues reading the remainder of the executive summary or loses interest and decides to stop. The more engaging this section, the more likely it is that the reader will continue reading.

Section 2: Goals

The project goals become the second part of the executive summary. Think of a goal as an objective or the purpose of your work. When listing the goals of the project, revisit the scope definition document you created and review what the customer/client and stakeholders told you they wanted from the process. Then look at the measurements of success you defined. This information assists you in articulating the goals to include in this section. Simply state the goals in bulleted fashion and keep them short. For example:

▶ Provide executives with up-to-date budget balances.

▶ Develop a common understanding of the end-to-end business process.

▶ Balance customer/client needs of the learning environment with prevailing technologies.

If you feel that you have to provide additional detail, write the information as a subset of the main point. For the first example, it might read:

PROVIDE EXECUTIVES WITH UP-TO-DATE BUDGET BALANCES:
Make certain that executives can see the dollar amounts that they have already spent on a compensation program, the amount of money they have planned for the next quarter, and the remaining balance that they have to spend for the current year.

If you worked on multiple business processes, you might identify general goals, not specific ones targeted at a business process. In this case, the goal section of the executive summary may start with a statement like:

THE GOALS OF THE PROCESS IMPROVEMENT WORK WERE TO ENSURE THAT THE BUSINESS PROCESSES:
■ Provide our customers/clients with an effective process.
■ Deliver efficiency to the operation.
■ Integrate with our key stakeholders.

- Drive consistency across the business groups.
- Have the appropriate internal controls.
- Reflect the future direction.

Section 3: Summary

The summary should tell the story of your journey. You can think of this third section of the executive summary as an executive summary within the executive summary. I find that executives generally spend their time reading the project focus and the summary sections, skimming over goals and deliverables. As a result, devote sufficient time to this section.

If your work included a cross-functional group of employees, identify the project team members to show the integration between departments, a point that management will appreciate. Link what you write in this section to the goals identified in the prior section, and include various analytical results to give the reader a few concrete statistics to identify with, like a labor summary or information from the impact analysis or implementation. A few examples of different ways to include statistical information in an executive summary might help you better understand what I mean.

Example 1

An executive I worked with at a consumer products company accepted responsibility for a new department, and he did not have familiarity with the new group's work. While the new department was located in California, Jim resided in New Jersey, so he rarely had occasion to interact with them face-to-face. He wanted to understand the details of their work, if the department had the right number of employees, and if he should change any reporting relationships.

With Jim's goals defined, I worked with the employees in the personnel administrative services group over six weeks to better understand what they did. I started by identifying the business processes that the department owned, and then identified the process activities and timing involved. I used the simple process map template, presented in Chapter 4 (Figure 4-32), as a tool to capture my discussions with employees.

When talking to employees one-on-one, I do not enlarge the template, as I would when I work with project teams, or draw the process map on a dry-erase board because that seems too formal and perhaps threatening. I simply use the template to jot down the activities as an employee explains them to me. Sometimes, I do not even bring this template with me, but just make notes on a pad of paper. I always have a mental picture of this template, though, and complete it, including the inputs and outputs.

After documenting the process, I revisit each activity and ask employees for an estimate of the time they believe each step takes. As discussed in Chapter 5, strive to get the activities correct before asking for time estimates. After I draw the process map using process mapping software, I find it helpful to ask the employees to review it and validate the data. Rarely do I need to make significant changes after doing this, only some minor tweaks. Having employees validate the information removes any later concerns about estimating process times.

Over six weeks, I gathered process data and conducted some follow-up analysis for Jim's personnel administrative services group. My analysis revealed several areas for improvement that led me to create the work analysis shown in Figure 11-1. The labor calculation box at the top of the figure should look familiar; we discussed it in Chapter 5. This figure shows:

▶ The personnel administrative services department responsibilities listed in the *Process* column.

▶ Current total time employees spend on each process, broken into annual hours and full-time equivalent (FTE, or head count) in the *Current* columns. (Recall from Chapter 5 that we use the full-time equivalent to account for percentages of an employee's time spent on a business process.)

▶ Future projections of the total time employees will spend on each process, if Jim follows the recommendations, appear in the *Future* columns.

Labor calculation used: 1,840

Annual hours	2,080
Less 3 weeks vacation	(120) (due to long-term employees)
Less 1 week sick	(40)
Less 10 paid holidays	(80)
	1,840

Current head count: 18

PAS (Personnel Administrative Services) Work Analysis Table

Process	Current		Future	
	Annual Hours	FTE	Annual Hours	FTE
Maintain personnel records	2,157	1.2	1,500	0.8
New employee orientation	500	0.3	450	0.2
Payroll processing and issue resolution	4,129	2.2	2,800	1.5
Benefits administration	1,950	1.1	1,300	0.7
Terminations and exit interviews	481	0.2	240	0.1
Administrative activities (for example, leaves of absence, bereavement pay, minor work permits)	4,095	2.2	2,020	1.1
Employee complaint resolution	7,868	4.3	3,500	1.9
Time card maintenance	894	0.5	650	0.4
Policy and procedures manual maintenance	1,114	0.6	950	0.5
Annual survey participation	160	0.1	150	.08
Workers compensation management	1,780	1.0	1,780	1.0
Audit support	1,445	0.8	1,445	0.8
Reporting (standard and ad-hoc)	2,976	1.6	1,500	0.8
Grand total	29,549	16.1	18,285	9.9

Figure 11-1 Executive Summary Work Analysis

You can skip this paragraph unless you want a reminder of how I arrived at the calculations. I calculated the FTE number in Figure 11-1, just as we did in Chapter 5: Divide the annual hours for each business process by the labor calculation number (1,840) shown at the top of the figure. For example, for the *Maintain personnel records* process, divide 2,157 hours (the annual hours spent on this process) by 1,840 (the labor calculation used for employees in this work group) to arrive at 1.2 FTE.

Figure 11-1 shows that if Jim applies the improvement recommendations, he can reduce his full-time equivalents from

16 to 10. These figures do not account for the amount of time employees become involved in other administrative activities, like attending staff meetings or writing weekly reports. Taking these factors into consideration, the future full-time equivalent number probably looks more like 11 or 12.

I also included an impact analysis in the executive summary to show the changes that had to occur to achieve the projected savings. In Chapter 6 you learned that an impact analysis shows the changes required to implement an improved business process.

Figure 11-2 shows one portion of the impact analysis for the *Administrative Activities* process from Figure 11-1. The analysis includes:

Activity	Current		Recommended Change	Rationale	Change Management	Future	
	Annual Hours	FTE				Annual Hours	FTE
Administrative activities ■ Leave of absence (LOA) ■ Bereavements ■ Minor work permits	4,095	2.2	LOA tracking: Assess East and West Coast group processes (very different) and drive toward process consistency. Bereavements: Move responsibility for checking an employee's right to take a bereavement leave to his or her manager.	West Coast group's LOA process takes half the time as the East Coast's process. Managers own responsibility for implementing company policies.	East Coast has to feel comfortable with automatic letter generation. Managers have to learn employee eligibility rules.	2,020	1.1

Figure 11-2 Executive Summary: Impact Analysis

> ➤ A description of the change, in the *Recommended Change* column.

> ➤ The rationale for the change, in the *Rationale* column.

► The department or population affected and the potential controversy or pushback with each proposed change, in the *Change Management* column.

Example 2

Sometimes my clients only want a summary of the total time their organization spends on their business processes to understand how their staff spends most of their time. Usually, this analysis leads to new business process improvement work.

Figure 11-3 shows an example of what this might look like for a training department. In this figure, I used 1,880 as the labor calculation number (or the standard annual employee hours) to perform the FTE calculations. The figure shows the training processes in the order of how the work is performed, starting with needs analysis and ending with logistics management.

Process	Annual Hours	FTE
Needs analysis	12,480	6.6
Program design/storyboard	10,400	5.5
Content development	16,620	8.8
Evaluation plan	3,120	1.7
Course material development	4,160	2.2
Delivery	29,120	15.5
Logistics management	10,816	5.8
Total	86,716	46.1

Figure 11-3 Executive Summary: Training Example 1

Figure 11-4 shows the same processes organized by the most labor-intensive process first. In this figure, we can tell that delivery is the most labor-intensive process. Using the format in Figure 11-4, you can immediately spot the time-consuming processes and quickly know where to focus your attention.

So far, I have shared two different ways to present a statistical component to the summary section of the executive summary. Let me share one more example.

Process	Annual Hours	FTE
Delivery	29,120	15.5
Content development	16,620	8.8
Needs analysis	12,480	6.6
Logistics management	10,816	5.8
Program design/storyboard	10,400	5.5
Course material development	4,160	2.2
Evaluation plan	3,120	1.7
Total	**86,716**	**46.1**

Figure 11-4 Executive Summary: Training Example 2

Example 3

A program management group asked me to help them move responsibility for some business processes from human resources to the operations department. In this case, the goal did not include reducing head count, but instead required me to examine the business processes and make certain that activities resided closest to where the work originated, thus reducing handoffs, cycle time, and errors.

Figure 11-5 shows the final summary analysis in this case. You can see that I listed the business processes, current labor requirements, and future labor requirements on the left three-quarters of the figure and summary information on the right quarter of the figure. It took eight weeks to obtain the information necessary to put together this analysis, but having all this information in one table provided the sponsor with a snapshot of the business.

Figure 11-5 shows:

▶ What work the program management group will keep (*PMG Retain . . .* columns).

▶ What work my process evaluation recommends eliminating (processes in the *New Responsible Party* column marked *Eliminate* to denote they are not required).

▶ Work that should move to other departments (also reflected in the *New Responsible Party* column).

Labor calculation used: 1,840		
Annual hours	2,080	
Less 3 weeks vacation	(120)	(due to long-term employees)
Less 1 week sick	(40)	
Less 10 paid holidays	(80)	
	1,840	

Current head count: 16
Program Management Group Analysis

	Current		Future				Labor Shifts	
Process Number	Annual Hours	FTE	PMG Retain Annual Hours	PMG Retain FTE	New Responsible Party	Labor Shifts	Department	FTE
1	2,157	1.2	1,563	0.8	Department A	0.4	Department A	6.3
2	166	.09	0	0	Eliminate		Department B	0.5
3	4,129	2.2	1,763	1.0	Department A	1.2	Department C	0.6
4	7,868	4.3	459	0.2	Department A	4.1	Total	
5	4,095	2.2	3,050	1.7	Department A	0.5	Labor	7.4
6	1,152	0.6	0	0	Eliminate		Shift	
7	894	0.5	0	0	Department B	0.5		
8	1,114	0.6	0	0	Department C	0.6		
9	572	0.3	572	0.3	Retain			
10	481	0.3	481	0.3	Retain		Grand Summary	
11	35	0.02	35	0.02	Retain		PMG retains	5.4
12	607	0.3	607	0.3	Retain		Labor shifts	7.4
13	50	0.03	0	0	Eliminate		Head count	
14	92	0.05	0	0	Department A	0.05	Reduction	0.7
15	1,445	0.8	1,445	0.8	Retain			
Grand total	24,857	13.5	9,975	5.4		7.4	Total	

Figure 11-5 Executive Summary: Labor Analysis

In addition, this figure shows two summaries on the right-hand side: the total labor moving to each of the new departments in the *Labor Shifts* section and a total summary of all movements in the *Grand Summary* section. As this figure shows, the program management group retained 5.4 head count, shifted 7.4 head count to the operations, and reduced head count by 0.7 (the *Eliminated* items).

Figures 11-1 through 11-5 show examples of including important analytical information in the executive summary. They also show different ways to provide this type of analytical data. Base this section on whatever drove you to do the work in the first place, and strive to summarize a multitude of data into a single table to show the big picture.

Section 4: Key Findings

The purpose of this section of the executive summary is to make management aware of the key points uncovered during the work. The topics may relate to what the project team learned or to caution management about crucial points in the process. Here are some examples:

▶ The project team developed a shared knowledge of the end-to-end process and the effect one action can have on another part of the process. Prior to the business process improvement work, each department completed their actions independently without an understanding of their effect on the overall process.

▶ We created internal controls to address crucial points in the business process where the highest likelihood of error existed.

▶ Human errors will persist if the department does not follow the processes put in place and bypass the internal controls. Although internal controls add time to the overall process, they offset the increased time by mitigating human error.

▶ The department should review the business process at least annually.

The information included in this section should focus on the few points important for the reader to remember.

Section 5: Deliverables

In this section, identify the materials created as a result of the business process work. List the title and description of each deliverable. The recap helps readers understand what information to ask for if they want additional details. Deliverables can include documents like:

- ► **Process Overview:** A narrative description explaining the purpose of the process, boundaries or scope, customers/clients and their needs, key stakeholders and their needs, measurements of success, and other relevant information.

- ► **Process Maps:** A visual representation of the business process outlining key activities.

- ► **Detail Document:** A narrative description of the process map to assist in understanding the process and to provide a framework for additional training.

- ► **Internal Controls Document:** The crucial points in the process where an error can occur, the potential reasons for the errors, and the proposed solution.

- ► **Checklists:** Tools that document the internal controls or other important information.

- ► **Impact Analysis:** A summary of the changes that have to occur to ensure the success of the new business process.

- ► **Implementation Plan:** A project plan that identifies the key phases of the work and the associated timelines.

- ► **Training Plan:** An outline of who requires training on the new business process, what they require training on, who owns the responsibility for the training, and how to conduct the training.

- ► **Communication Plan:** An audience profile of who has to receive communication on the new business process, the key message points, the best vehicles to use, and when the communications should happen.

Section 6: Appendix

Include any additional content in the appendix. If you want to include numerous pieces of information, break the appendix down into separate ones and number them. The appendix may include feedback you received from the project team, how the team completed the work, a customized version of the roadmap, the scope definition document, process definitions if you addressed multiple business processes, and perhaps the process map(s). Include whatever material you feel supports your conclusions.

Chapter Summary

Creating an executive summary gives you the opportunity to summarize your work for management and gain recognition, while appearing like a normal part of any project closure.

Keep the readers in mind when writing the executive summary, and include the information you know they care about reading. The project focus sets the tone for the entire executive summary and either draws readers in or bores them. Include the goals of the work, a summary of the work itself, the key findings, and a list of the deliverables. Include process data in the summary section of the executive summary to show the analytical nature of your work because managers always care about the efficient use of head count and the delivery of effective processes to the customers/clients. Keep effectiveness, efficiency, and adaptability in your thoughts as you write the executive summary.

Time Estimate

To plan the time it takes to work through this step, Figure 11-6 summarizes the time you should expect to spend creating the executive summary.

Event	Time	Purpose
Create analytical tables.	40 hours (for 1 process)	■ Summarize data into tables that are appropriate to include in the executive summary.
Write executive summary.	40 hours	■ Write the project focus, goals, key findings, and deliverables sections of the executive summary.

Figure 11-6 Time Estimate—Create Executive Summary

Create Analytical Tables

During this time, study the information you gathered and decide what you can summarize in a table format. Build your labor or work analysis using the process times from the process map. Completing this analysis for one business process can easily take a week. If you worked on multiple business processes and have to summarize a group of them, you might need more than 40 hours.

Write the Executive Summary

At this time, take a step back and reflect on what you accomplished. Write each of the sections, and have a colleague—who is not familiar with the work—review what you wrote. Keep streamlining the executive summary until you feel it tells the story of your journey in a tight, compressed way.

What You Have Achieved

In this chapter, you have achieved the following:

▶ The opportunity to summarize your work

▶ The knowledge of how to write an executive summary

▶ An understanding of how to create analytical summaries of the work

▶ What senior managers care about reading

▶ Most important, the *power* to gain the recognition for your work

CHAPTER 12

Business Process Management

BPM and Other Improvement Techniques

Process improvement techniques—such as continuous improvement, reengineering, Hoshin Kanri, total quality management (TQM), Kaizen, Lean, Six Sigma, and Lean Six Sigma—can confuse anyone new to the world of business process improvement (BPI). Now add in business process management (BPM) and business process modeling and notation (BPMN), and how does anyone decide which technique to use to improve a business process?

Every one of these methods has the same goal—to attain process improvement. This improvement may drive increased effectiveness for the customer/client and increased efficiency for the business. Each technique has its advocates and detractors. As techniques come into and out of grace, an innovator may put a new spin on an existing technique, or techniques may merge. For example, reengineering was the rage in the 1990s, and BPM has come into the forefront in this and the prior decade. This ongoing change in the process improvement landscape causes confusion and can lead companies to do nothing. Which technique should they use, and how long will the company use one technique before a new and better one surfaces?

Every method draws its basis from the total quality management movement, introduced in the 1950s, which continually grew in the 1980s as American companies competed against the quality of Japanese products. In 1987, the U.S. Congress announced the Malcolm Baldrige National Quality Award, named for President Ronald Reagan's Secretary of Commerce, which recognizes companies for performance excellence.

This chapter provides an overview of the different process improvement techniques, starting with the newest entry into the mix—BPM.

Business Process Management

If you search for the definition of business process management (BPM), you will find a plethora. My simple definition? The application of multiple BPI steps directed at the alignment of an *enterprise-wide* view of business processes (instead of a functional view) and strategic goals.

BPM practitioners focus on the end-to-end process, including every party who interacts with a business process such as employees, vendors, and customers. BPM focuses on the *whole* (or enterprise), instead of individual functional processes, and you can find a linkage between the concept of "whole" to other philosophies and management techniques introduced over the years, including:

▶ Aristotle spoke of the "whole being greater than the sum of the parts" thousands of years ago.

▶ Peter Senge, in his work on learning organizations, discussed systems thinking as a discipline for seeing wholes. He stressed the importance of seeing interrelationships instead of individual things. Think of how this applies to an enterprise view of business processes. Senge also said that small, well-focused actions can produce substantial improvements, referring to this principle as leverage.

▶ Reengineering, which impacts the entire business system including employees and their jobs, information systems, administrative processes, rewards and recognition, and measurements, attempted to move companies to a process view instead of a functional view, similar to BPM. Leading companies first involved in reengineering included those with a substantial number of transactions such as banks, airlines, and retailers.

You can never go wrong taking an enterprise view of business processes because you will see interrelationships that are otherwise invisible. Focusing on enterprise-wide processes is valuable because it helps you to understand the complexity of your business, provides you with the skill to perform a systemic analysis of your company's processes and relationships among processes, lets you identify key processes to improve for competitive performance, and facilitates an understanding of your resource allocation and its relationship to corporate strategy. The challenge surfaces around authority: Do you have the authority to perform business process improvement at the enterprise level? If not, what degree of continuous improvement opportunity will you lose as you wait?

BPM started out as another information technology approach to business process improvement, and it has evolved. Initial vendors in the marketplace had software products to sell, and the cost of implementation was high because automation is implicit in the technique. Today, BPM has incorporated select Six Sigma concepts into the method. Again, this technique is the repackaging of existing methods and tools. You should remember the nucleus of BPM because the bias toward automation exists, and, as mentioned in Chapter 6, you should think about automation last in order to make certain you automate an efficient process, not an inefficient process.

You also hear the term *optimization* commonly used with BPM, and that term, when first used in the mid-1800s, related to mathematics, later to programming code, and most recently to search engines. As companies struggle to increase profits, additional revenues help, but reducing cost certainly does not hurt in achieving this goal. In companies today, you hear more and more about optimization efforts. The majority of optimization efforts now focus on maximizing process productivity or minimizing waste. In BPI terminology, this signifies improving *efficiency*. The same efficiency-related improvement techniques used to improve a business process work for optimization: eliminating bureaucracy, removing duplication, simplifying, and introducing automation as appropriate.

The key to success in an optimization endeavor is to balance efficiency with *effectiveness* so the customer/client remains in full view of any decisions made. Does the new process produce the anticipated results that meet the customer's/client's needs? (Not just does the process minimize the use of resources?)

To focus on business processes at the enterprise level, you require senior leadership support. You cannot just start changing enterprise processes because you want to approach the work that way. If you have senior leadership support, use the ten steps to business process improvement at the enterprise level. If you do not have this level of support, examine how the processes in your department or function interact with the rest of the company (or enterprise), and start building a systemic analysis of the enterprise's business system. You can influence others in the company and perhaps gain support to perform a degree of cross-functional analysis.

Although some BPM proponents might liken the method to nirvana, my apprehensions with BPM include:

▶ Do you have authority to examine the enterprise's business processes?

▶ How long do you have to wait for your company to adopt this approach, and what degree of improvement do you lose in the meantime?

▶ What will it cost to automate the enterprise's business processes, and do you have the financial approval?

Business Process Modeling (BPM)

BPM can also stand for business process *modeling*, the approach to producing a visual representation of a business process, showing the sequence of activities from end to end with the goal of improving business performance.

The model may include an as-is version, depicting the way the process works today, or a to-be version, showing how the future process works. Business process modeling is a basic step in any improvement effort and serves as foundational information to share across your company. As companies shift from focusing on production workers in the twentieth century to knowledge workers in the twenty-first century, capturing knowledge that resides in employees' heads will lead to an increase in institutional knowledge.

My guess is that the next big idea in the process improvement arena will combine business process management and knowledge management, with a focus on the *quality* of the information.

Business Process Modeling and Notation (BPMN)

This technique adds the *notation* feature to the definition of business process modeling, and it introduces an increased number of symbols to use in drawing a business process map. The symbols add complexity to a process map beyond the simple ones covered in Chapter 4. Any symbols used in process mapping should enable technical and nontechnical employees to understand the business process, and remember that your colleagues may not have the background required to understand the BPMN symbols.

Gaining industry consensus on a standard is still a work in progress. The closest group to developing a global standard is the Object Management Group (OMG), a computer industry standards consortium whose specifications focus on interoperable, portable, and reusable enterprise architectures. This implies that the use of OMG standards is of utmost importance in supporting the technical implementation of processes, that is, working with enterprise architectures.

Unless you work with information technology employees, you might find the BPMN symbols causing extra confusion among your colleagues. Although a standard is a respectable notion, many employees already find process maps difficult to read without the added complexity of unfamiliar symbols.

Let me share a few of the main BPMN symbols and terminology, so you can decide if you want to incorporate any in your process improvement work.

Gateways

The use of gateways instead of a simple decision symbol will work if everyone in your company understands the variations of the gateway symbol. You have the:

▶ **Parallel gateway symbol**, showing tasks that can occur in parallel

▶ **Exclusive gateway symbol**, showing alternate paths where you can *only* follow one path

▶ **Inclusive gateway symbol**, showing alternate paths where you always do one task even though you may also perform the other task

Figure 12-1 shows these three gateway symbols and a decision symbol. I prefer to use the decision symbol, with the decision expressed inside the symbol, because it highlights the required decision and every employee understands the question.

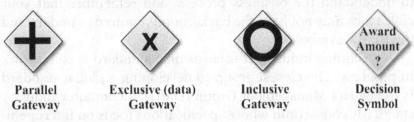

| Parallel Gateway | Exclusive (data) Gateway | Inclusive Gateway | Decision Symbol |

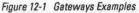

Figure 12-1 Gateways Examples

Figure 12-2a and 12-2b shows two versions of how the beginning of a process map might look when two parallel activities occur at the start of the process. In this figure, presume that budget guidelines and timelines exist for the process to begin. In Figure 12-2a, you see the two parallel activities that occur: The learning consultant gathers client requests while the business analyst gathers historical data. In Figure 12-2b, you see the parallel gateway symbol indicating that activities one and two occur at the same time. You also see, in Figure 12-2b, the use of a cross-functional process map, explained in Chapter 4, with

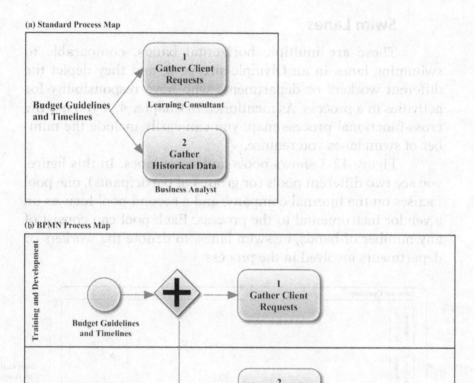

Figure 12-2 Process Map Alternatives—Standard vs. BPMN Examples

two bands, or swim lanes: one for training and development and a second for finance.

Pools

The use of pools may assist in clarifying a cross-functional process map if you want to show different groups of participants, especially useful for depicting internal versus external groups. A pool is simply multiple cross-functional process maps stacked one on top of another, each depicting a different group.

Swim Lanes

These are multiple horizontal bands, comparable to swimming lanes in an Olympic-size pool, and they depict the different workers or departments who have responsibility for activities in a process. As mentioned in Chapter 4, if you use the cross-functional process map, you can easily include the number of swim lanes you require.

Figure 12-3 shows pools and swim lanes. In this figure, you see two different pools (or groups of participants), one pool focuses on the internal company, and a second pool focuses on a vendor instrumental to the process. Each pool can consist of any number of bands, or swim lanes, to denote the workers or departments involved in the process.

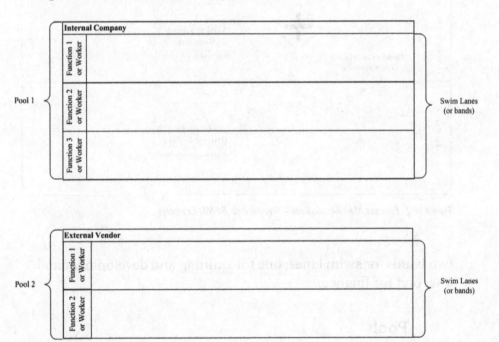

Figure 12-3 Pools and Swim Lane Examples

Events

In BPMN, many types of events exist (e.g., start, end, error), and you may find the *timer event* symbol a useful one to denote waiting for something to happen. This clock symbol is similar to the cycle time icon used in Chapter 4. The difference is that you insert this event icon directly on the process map as a step in the process instead of positioning it as a notation above an activity box.

Activity

In BPMN, you draw different styles of boxes to denote a normal task (a unit of work), a subprocess, or a transaction.

Loops

A way to depict a task that repeats until a defined condition occurs, similar to the cyclical/recurring symbol introduced in Chapter 4.

Flow Lines

In addition to the normal input/output flow lines, BPMN introduces other styles of lines, including the *message flow* line that identifies communication flowing across pools. Figure 12-4 shows an example of the message flow line where you see a communication message flowing from the *internal company* to the *external vendor*.

If you think that any of these symbols will improve your process map and that your colleagues understand their meaning, you should use them. Using extra symbols does not eliminate the need to write a *detail document* because the documentation helps explain the business process to new employees, and it should define any unfamiliar symbol(s) used.

Software Products

You will find numerous tools available to support BPM and BPMN. As mentioned in Chapter 4, the least expensive and most likely available software products in your company include Microsoft Visio and SmartDraw. However, if you have the

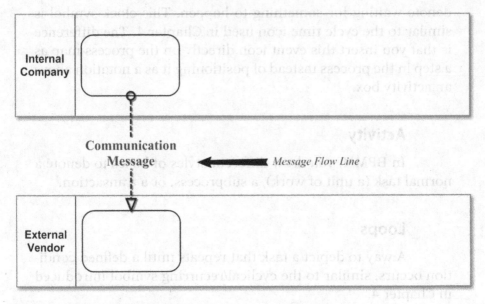

Figure 12-4   Message Flow Line Example

money and your information technology department supports a collaborative environment, you may want to consider a few of these tools, all of which offer a 30-day free trial.

IBM Blueworks Live

Originally Lombardi Blueprint, this product lets you build a process map using an outline feature, easily convert it to a process diagram, and include process documentation. You enter data regarding a process activity through a pop-up window, where you can enter the person responsible, cycle time, and systems used by the activity, among other facts. You can copy an activity and reuse the asset. All data you entered regarding the activity stays connected. You can also create subprocesses, quickly show and hide the subprocesses, and analyze points in the process where you should focus attention (e.g., high cycle time). You have to become familiar with the way the product uses *milestones* to organize activities associated with a business process, which is not necessarily intuitive, but you can master this feature. I found the product easy to use.

You can import Microsoft Visio files and export a process map you created in Blueworks to the Microsoft Office Suite (Word, PowerPoint, Excel), Adobe PDF, XPDL (XML Process Definition Language), and BPMN 2.0.

The downside of the product is the pricing approach. IBM licenses the software on an annual basis as a SaaS (software as a service) offering. SaaS is a method of delivering applications over the Internet, as a service, instead of installing the software on your computer. You may also hear this referred to as Web-based software, on-demand software, or hosted software.

IBM offers an *editor* license and a less expensive *contributor* license. While IBM offers a free version, the company limits the number of process maps you can create for free. I like this product and would use it as a single-user license if IBM offered a one-time charge to purchase the software, but paying an annual license fee is difficult for one person. In a corporate environment, it may not seem too expensive.

iGrafx Flowcharter

This process diagramming and modeling software is similar to Microsoft Visio. It has a few features I like (e.g., creating a cross-functional process map and subprocesses seems easy, and design warnings are helpful), but I found it not as intuitive to use as other products.

iGrafx has different versions of their product, each with different pricing: basic process mapping software, advanced process mapping software with analysis capability, and specialized versions for Six Sigma and SAP. Like Blueworks, iGrafx offers the products on an annual license fee at an increasing annual cost as you move up the product line.

Promapp

Another Web-based product, this software has a very user-friendly interface—a more social media style. You feel as if you are using Facebook or LinkedIn. I like the simplicity and overall organization of the product. You can hover over activity boxes and view the details without having to open another window, the dashboard provides information around process status, and you can save a business process as a favorite. This look and feel comes at a price, though, because the product locks you into a specific format or style, which I found inflexible. I found the online videos easy to use, and they helped me quickly learn the tool.

The cost can rapidly increase because you pay for each module (e.g., the improvement module, risk and compliance module, process approval workflow module). The product is licensed based on the number of network-connected users and, as of this date, requires a minimum of 30 users.

Other Process Improvement Techniques

In addition to BPM, the other techniques used to improve a process include well-known ones such as Six Sigma. Certain techniques offer more of a philosophical approach instead of a precise set of tools.

TQM (Total Quality Management), Continuous Improvement, and Kaizen

As mentioned at the start of this chapter, most improvement techniques have TQM at the core, although you see ample shifting and repositioning of the key components. The core of TQM includes adding value to customers, improving processes as learning increases, involving all parties (employees, customers, suppliers), and working together toward the common goal of customer satisfaction. TQM replaced TQC (total quality control) by incorporating the management activities related to process improvement. TQM requires a certain culture, well accepted in Japan. It stresses teamwork as part of the culture, and the Japanese do an exceptional job caring for the "roots" that allow the "culture" plant to grow. TQM requires employees who work with the process every day to control the quality of the processes, not management controlling the employees. Countless companies in the United States attempted self-directed teams years ago with mixed success because Americans appreciate individualism and competitiveness.

As I promote throughout this book, every employee can contribute to continuous improvement, and every employee benefits from those contributions. In the early days of continuous improvement, though, employees did not view themselves as contributors to the improvement process and thought it was something done to them. Employees did not believe they had the knowledge and skills required to participate. In reality, every employee has what is required to improve his or her business processes, which in turn helps their company thrive. One approach does not have to fit every scenario. Employees can contribute to process improvement with small, incremental changes. Numerous tools exist to assist with continuous improvement, such as brainstorming, fishbone diagrams, scatter diagrams, histograms, and process flowcharts. You can easily learn to use these tools in your day-to-day work to address challenges and ultimately improve a business process.

Kaizen is the Japanese word for continuous improvement. *Kai* means *continuous*, and *zen* means *improvement*.

Companies who have won the Baldrige Award see quality as an ongoing endeavor to improve continuously, not just a goal reached "once and done."

Hoshin Kanri

This strategic planning approach, developed in Japan in the 1960s, uses the collective thinking power of *every* employee to assist a company in rising to the top of its field. The concept of including "all" is key to Hoshin Kanri, so companies focus on a shared goal. Do you see the similarity with BPM's alignment of processes with strategic goals?

▶ Hoshin has two components based on two Chinese characters: *ho*, meaning *method* or *form*, and *shin*, meaning *needle* or *compass*. Thus, hoshins are breakthrough ideas.

► Kanri means *management*.

How does strategic planning correlate to process improvement? First, strategic planning (different from operational planning) focuses on defining a strategy that addresses the comprehensive concerns of a company over a long timeframe and on aligning resources to achieve its strategies, objectives, and goals. Second, the Hoshin Kanri approach encompasses the theories of systems thinking and continuous improvement because it requires practitioners to measure the system as a whole, uses inclusion as a guiding principle, has the W. Edwards Deming TQM model as its foundation, and uses customer expectations as key inputs.

Once a company has a strategic plan, the realization that improving the processes to support the business strategies becomes clear. A company can also use Hoshin Kanri, of course, for operational planning. You can find a source to read additional information about this technique at http://www.hos hinkanripro.com.

At this point, you should start to see how all the improvement techniques relate to one another and how every technique strives for process improvement.

Reengineering

An improvement technique popular in the 1990s, reengineering, is a methodical process that radically improves business processes to respond to customer needs and that challenges organizational boundaries. Practitioners saw processes as the hidden dimension of the business because, at the time, the majority of companies managed their business by product lines and functions. Because no one owned the processes, except perhaps for the CEO, processes went undermanaged, and, as a result, practitioners saw process improvement as a big opportunity.

Michael Hammer, the originator of reengineering (along with James Champy), used the phrase "don't automate, obliterate" in a *Harvard Business Review* article. This view caused TQM practitioners anxiety because it challenged the notion of incremental improvements. With Hammer's background coming from his engineering training and his experience as a professor of computer science at MIT (Massachusetts Institute of Technology), it should come as no surprise that his approach included the use of technology to improve business processes, although it may not seem so from the *Harvard Business Review* quotation regarding automation. The difference is that he wanted to use technology to enable the *redesign* of existing business processes, not just "pave the cowpaths," as the saying goes.

TQM and reengineering share certain notions such as customer focus, with the biggest contrast related to the degree of improvement. Reengineering proponents believe in reinventing processes, which requires a new way of thinking and radical change, while quality proponents focus on incremental improvements. Reengineering ignores the existing business process and starts by designing a new process from scratch based on customer needs. You can find both these approaches useful in different situations.

Figure 12-5 shows a visual for a reengineering project I led. This figure depicts a macro-level construct illustrating the major end-to-end processes by which the company both meets the needs of its customers and continuously renews itself. It provided a way to visualize the major processes and illustrate the interdependence of the processes. By removing the functional view of product lines and functions, the model enabled the discussion of ownership for processes instead of organizational accountability, similar to the BPM concept today.

The long-term success of reengineering seems to have suffered from poor change management strategies in the majority of companies. Even though managers recognize that many employees do not like change and understand that employees can resist change, I wonder how much blame lies with the way in which managers handled the human side of the radical redesign.

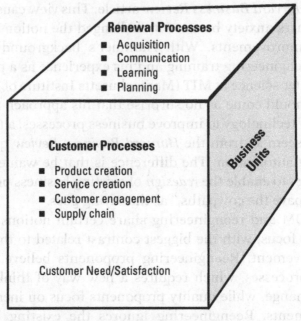

Figure 12-5 Business Process Reengineering Context

Six Sigma

You can view Six Sigma as a broad term referring to a method for achieving quality and as a statistical concept.

As a general term, Six Sigma started with measuring the statistical modeling of manufacturing processes, but it covers every type of work including engineering and manufacturing for a manufactured product; software product design, development, and maintenance; production; and other disciplines such as finance, education, marketing, purchasing, and personnel.

As a statistical method, Six Sigma (coined by Motorola) looks to reduce variation in process performance and strives for near perfection in products and services. The *Six* refers to six standard deviations, or how far a process deviates from perfection (or zero defects).

As you may recall from school, *standard deviation* is a statistic used as a measure of the dispersion or variation in a distribution from its mean: the more spread apart the data, the higher the deviation. For example, the number of human beings who exercise x hours a week, the number of women who earn x dollars, the number of countries with x terrorist attacks, or the number of days when the weather was x degrees.

Although various approaches exist to reach Six Sigma, the DMAIC method, inspired by Deming's Plan-Do-Check-Act cycle, is a widely adopted approach to achieving Six Sigma for existing business processes.

➤ **D** = *Define:* Identify project, processes, and goals.

➤ **M** = *Measure:* Evaluate existing process and collect existing measurements.

➤ **A** = *Analyze:* Identify the root cause of a defect.

➤ **I** = *Improve:* Make process improvements.

➤ **C** = *Control:* Establish control systems to fix any deviations and to maintain zero defects.

Can you see the ten steps to BPI reflected in the DMAIC approach?

Walter Shewhart, a predecessor to Deming, showed in the 1920s while at Bell Laboratories that processes required correction when they reached three sigma from the mean.

Six Sigma's focus on preventing defects and helping you understand process complexity makes it a viable tool, but no tool alone is adequate. If you use this technique, do not forget the cultural effect of process changes.

Lean

This technique focuses on the flow of value to the customer; anything else is considered wasteful. Companies who follow Lean have the goal of reducing the time between a customer order and shipment by eliminating waste.

Lean extends beyond manufacturing processes; it applies to every process and requires a shift in how employees think about the business. Lean companies think about what they do (purpose), how they do it (process), and the contribution of every employee (people). A key question asked by companies using this technique is, "Would the customer pay for this step in the process?" Do you recall that question from Chapter 6 when I discussed value added?

Lean Six Sigma

So then, what is *Lean* Six Sigma? Sometimes viewed as the best approach because it combines Lean and Six Sigma, this technique merges the *process variation* feature of Six Sigma with the *process flow* feature of Lean, both key concepts. Like other improvement methods, they have the same goal: delivering an effective and efficient process. These two techniques differ only in how each identifies the root cause of waste—removing variation in the process (Six Sigma) or removing steps that do not add value to the customer (Lean).

Chapter Summary

Every technique focuses on improvement, each has the customer/client at the core, and every approach wants to improve the effectiveness, efficiency, and adaptability of the business. While you will find variations, you will see more similarities than differences. For example:

▶ BPM's philosophy of enterprise process alignment with strategic goals seems similar to Hoshin Kanri's concept of focusing on the whole and shared goals.

▶ Six Sigma's tie to Deming's Plan-Do-Check-Act shows its relationship to TQM.

▶ Reengineering's enterprise-process focus and the use of technology seem similar to BPM.

▶ Lean has the customer as number one and shows ties to Hoshin Kanri with the inclusiveness concept of involving every employee.

▶ Six Sigma's constant evaluation to correct processes at certain points is similar to continuous improvement.

> ► TQM's concepts of customer focus and involving all parties relate to *all* the techniques.

Throughout this book, you find concepts used from the numerous process improvement methods sprinkled across the ten steps to business process improvement. Instead of calling myself a practitioner of any one discipline, I take the best of all methods and adapt them to accomplish my goals. You should do the same. Find a method you feel comfortable using and a software product that works in your environment, then add concepts from other techniques over time.

Because every method has quality as a basis, my advice is to pick a name for a BPI effort that resonates in your culture and that keeps the customer/client at the forefront of employee thoughts. Strive to incorporate continuous improvement as part of your company's DNA. You cannot change your DNA; it is inherent in who you are as a human being. Just think of the power your company can gain if every employee thinks of continuous process improvement every day. Eventually, it will become part of your company's culture, and then nothing can stop it. Until continuous improvement becomes part of your company's DNA, you will always see new trends coming and going.

Focus on the end-to-end enterprise processes if you have support to do so, but do not do nothing while you wait for consensus. Every technique wants to attain the perfect value stream to the customer/client, so simply think *process improvement* and spend time defining what *quality* means to you and your company.

What You Have Achieved

In this chapter, you have achieved the following:

- ► An understanding of business process management
- ► Knowing whether BPMN will work for process modeling in your company

▶ Recognizing the value and challenges of examining enterprise processes

▶ An understanding of the similarities among the process improvement methods

▶ The difference between Six Sigma, Lean, and Lean Six Sigma

▶ Knowledge of what tools exist in the market

▶ An understanding of Hoshin Kanri as a strategic planning approach

▶ Most important, the *power* to realize you can use any method or combination of methods to achieve business process improvement

CHAPTER 13

Case Study 1

Training and Development

Now let us put all the pieces together by stepping through a complete BPI project that I completed for a major bank I call BB&Z. We have all read stories about how someone lost weight, climbed a difficult mountain, or ran a marathon. If you are like me, you find them inspiring because reading what others went through helps me realize that I can do things I might previously have thought were impossible. I chose this case because it introduces several new bends in the road and demonstrates how you can adapt the ten steps to any situation. As we move through the study, you can reference the previous chapters in this book for clarification or for additional details. Hopefully, this case study motivates you and jump-starts you on your own road to improving business processes.

Background

Pam Borzak, senior vice president of human resources for BB&Z, called me for help with improving the business processes in her organization. As a result of that call, I spent the next year tackling each business process within her departments. Because Pam had responsibility for all the human resource functions, we decided to start her process inventory at the department level to decide which of the human resource departments we should start with first.

Step 1: Develop the Process Inventory

In Chapter 2, we built the business process inventory, created prioritization criteria, applied the criteria to each process, and created a process prioritization table that summarized the business processes. We did all that in one table to enable a process-by-process comparison, which then helped us decide where to start our improvement efforts.

I proceeded the same way in Pam's case, only this time I built the process inventory at her department level and applied the prioritization criteria used in Chapter 2 to the list of human resource departments. As you recall, the four main categories of prioritization criteria we used in Chapter 2 are impact, implementation, current state, and value.

I used the same 1–3 scale from Chapter 2 to keep the scoring simple and did not apply any weighting to the criteria.

Figure 13-1 shows the completed process prioritization table for Pam's human resource organization. This table shows that we should initially focus on the business processes within training and development (T&D) because that department has the highest total score (20). The high score for T&D resulted from the bank's ongoing acquisition of other financial institutions through mergers, forcing Pam's organization to have to continually integrate new employees into the company. You can see that the merger and acquisition focus is the driving force behind all four categories. Looking at the categories across the T&D row in Figure 13-1 leads to the following observations:

► Many employees are affected by the T&D processes (*Impact*).

► It will not take too long or require too much money to make the necessary changes, and the next cycle appears imminent because of an upcoming merger (*Implementation*).

► The T&D processes have an average client satisfaction and pain level (*Current State*).

► If new employees can quickly get immersed in the existing culture, the process will deliver a benefit to the bank (*Benefit/Return*).

Figure 13-1 BB&Z Process Prioritization Table: Human Resource Functions

	Impact		Implementation			Current State			Value	
	Number Affected	**Client Level**	**Time to Market**	**Funding**	**Timing of Next Cycle**	**Customer/ Client Satisfaction**	**Pain Level**	**Process Exists?**	**Benefit/ Return**	**Total Score**
	3 = large number 2 = average number 1 = small number	3 = senior 2 = management 1 = other	3 = short 2 = average 1 = long	3 = small 2 = medium 1 = large	3 = close/ongoing 2 = intermediate 1 = far	3 = low 2 = medium 1 = high	3 = high 2 = medium 1 = low	1 = no 0 = yes	3 = high 2 = average 1 = low	
Compensation and Benefits	3	2	1	2	2	2	1	0	2	15
Recruitment	2	2	2	3	2	2	2	0	2	14
Training and Development	3	1	3	3	3	2	2	0	3	20
Personnel Administration	3	3	1	1	2	2	2	0	1	11
Workforce Analysis	3	3	1	2	2	3	2	1	2	15

Once we decided to start by focusing on training and development, I built the department's process inventory by listing all the T&D business processes. Figure 13-2 shows the process prioritization table I created for BB&Z's T&D department. The figure shows the common business processes one might find in a training and development department, including:

▶ **Curriculum Development**, which includes designing and developing curricula and courses

▶ **Forecasting/Scheduling**, which involves estimating student demand and developing a class schedule to meet the demand

▶ **Enrollment**, which allows students to enroll in a learning event

▶ **Delivery**, which includes the facilitation of a class, either by an instructor or by alternative methods

▶ **Resource Management**, which involves securing all materials, equipment, and facilitators required to deliver training

▶ **Evaluation**, which assesses the impact of training

▶ **Budgeting**, which tracks all spending

Based on the results of the process prioritization table in Figure 13-2, I normally would start with the delivery process because it has the highest score (24), but before moving to the next step, I reviewed the results of this exercise with Pam. I expressed concern that the score given to delivery may be because it is one of the only business processes, besides enrollment, that her clients experience. All other processes reflect the internal workings in the department, not visible to clients.

At this point, a bend in the road occurred in my work with Pam. I encouraged her to think about the lack of client interaction throughout the process, and she agreed not to rush in and start with the delivery process just yet but rather to take a fresh look at how her organization functioned and interfaced with the client. Pam agreed that her key goal was making sure that her organization delivered training that supported the com-

	Impact		Implementation			Current State			Value	
	Number Affected 3 = large number 2 = average number 1 = small number	Client Level 3 = senior 2 = management 1 = other	Time to Market 3 = short 2 = average 1 = long	Funding 3 = small 2 = medium 1 = large	Timing of Next Cycle 3 = close/ongoing 2 = intermediate 1 = far	Customer/Client Satisfaction 3 = low 2 = medium 1 = high	Pain Level 3 = high 2 = medium 1 = low	Process Exists? 1 = no 0 = yes	Benefit/Return 3 = high 2 = average 1 = low	Total Score
Curriculum Development	1	2	2	3	2	3	1	0	2	16
Forecasting/Scheduling	1	2	3	3	3	3	3	0	2	19
Enrollment	3	2	3	2	3	2	3	0	3	18
Delivery	3	3	3	2	3	3	3	0	3	24
Resource Management	1	2	3	2	3	1	3	0	2	14
Evaluation	3	2	3	2	3	3	1	0	2	15
Budgeting	1	3	3	2	2	3	3	1	2	20

Figure 13-2 BB&Z Process Prioritization Table: Training and Development Group

pany's business objectives. As a result of our discussion, we decided to take a high-level look at the training and development process before getting into the details of any single business process.

The change in direction meant that I had to adjust how we approached step 2, building the foundation. Any change you make along the way subsequently causes other changes down the line as you move through the roadmap, and these changes are perfectly acceptable. In Pam's case, instead of developing a scope definition document on the delivery process, we created one for the entire training and development process.

The roadmap is a flexible and dynamic tool that provides overall direction on how to perform business process improvement work, and you can adapt it to changing circumstances.

Step 2: Establish the Foundation

In Chapter 3 we learned that in this step we create the scope definition document to establish the boundaries for the business process, so we can stay on track and avoid scope creep. At this point, you also form the project team, if necessary. Because we chose to look at the end-to-end training and development process, Pam elected to include on the team her training and development director, a delivery manager, an instructor, two instructional designers, one of her training specialists who helped with resource scheduling, and her business manager.

During the initial project team meeting, I walked the group through the roadmap in Chapter 1 (Figure 1-1) so they could see the steps we would go through and provide them with an opportunity to ask questions. Pam joined us for the first 15 minutes of the initial team meeting.

After reviewing the objectives of business process improvement, covered in Chapter 1, and answering the project team's questions, we moved on to setting the foundation for our work. All team members had a copy of the blank scope definition document so they could see the information we would discuss. I kept track of the team's conversation on an electronic dry-erase board so everyone could see the results of our conversation. Figure 13-3 shows the completed scope definition document the team created for the training and development process.

A look at the scope definition document tells us a great deal. We can see where the project team decided to start and end the process by reading the *Scope (boundaries)* section. It starts when Pam's organization works with the Finance department to establish T&D's annual budget and ends when Pam's management team reviews the annual summary of course evaluation results.

While reviewing the scope definition document with Pam after the first meeting, we made a few changes. Pam wanted to make it explicit that, going forward, business goals will drive where she invests her budget and she wanted to add another measurement of success related to return on investment. As a result, I added another sentence to the description stating that business goals drive training investments and a fifth measurement to show a linkage between the business goals and training. Figure 13-4 shows the updated scope definition document with these two additions (updated *Description* and a new *Measurement of success*).

At the second project team meeting, I reviewed the formatted scope definition document with the team and highlighted the changes that Pam and I made to the *Description* and *Measurements of success*. Because this is the first time the team sees the document typed, it seems more formal, and you should feel comfortable making edits. At our meeting, the team expressed concern over how to measure the linkage of training to business goals. I urged them to wait and discuss the *how* when we moved to step 7 on the roadmap, which addresses establishing metrics. This kept the team from veering off course. As side questions emerge in the meetings, refer to the roadmap to show how you will address a question at a later time. This assures participants that you heard them and you will not overlook their concerns.

Once the project team felt comfortable with the scope definition document, we moved to step 3 and began drawing the process map.

(text continues on page 298)

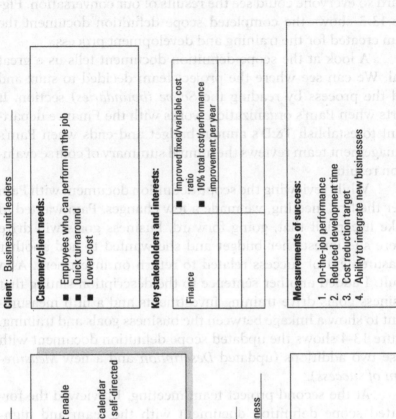

Process name: Training and Development

Process owner: Pam Borzak

Description (purpose):

This process covers delivering products and services that enable employee learning to support the business objectives.

All types of products and services are covered, including calendar classes, seminars, conferences, Web-based training, and self-directed learning, whether internally or externally delivered.

Scope (boundaries):

Start Establishing annual budget

End Annual management review to evaluate effectiveness

Process responsibilities:

- Forecasting/scheduling
- Curriculum/course development
- Enrollment
- Resource management
- Delivery
- Evaluation
- Communications
- Business planning/budgeting

Client: Business unit leaders

Customer/client needs:

- Employees who can perform on the job
- Quick turnaround
- Lower cost

Key stakeholders and interests:

| Finance | ■ Improved fixed/variable cost ratio |
| | ■ 10% total cost/performance improvement per year |

Measurements of success:

1. On-the-job performance
2. Reduced development time
3. Cost reduction target
4. Ability to integrate new businesses

Figure 13-3 BB&Z Preliminary Scope Definition Document

Process name: Training and Development

Process owner: Pam Borzak

Client: Business unit leaders

Description (purpose):

This process covers delivering products and services that enable employee learning to support the business objectives. In all cases, the business goals drive the learning investment.

Customer/client needs:

- Employees who can perform on the job
- Quick turnaround
- Lower cost

Scope (boundaries):

| Start | Establishing annual budget |
| End | Annual management review to evaluate effectiveness |

All types of products and services are covered, including calendar classes, seminars, conferences, Web-based training, and self-directed learning, whether internally or externally delivered.

Key stakeholders and interests:

| Finance | ■ Improved fixed/variable cost ratio
■ 10% total cost/performance improvement per year |

Process responsibilities:

- Forecasting/scheduling
- Curriculum/course development
- Enrollment
- Resource management
- Delivery
- Evaluation
- Communications
- Business planning/budgeting

Measurements of success:

1. On-the-job performance
2. Reduced development time
3. Cost reduction target
4. Ability to integrate new businesses
5. Clear linkage of training to business goal

Figure 13-4 BB&Z Final Scope Definition Document

Step 3: Draw the Process Map

As pointed out in Chapter 4, drawing the process map in step 3 gives the project team a tool to help them understand the end-to-end business process, shows them where handoffs occur between departments, and provides a background to apply the improvement techniques in step 6.

You may recall that, in this step, you decide whether to draw a standard or cross-functional process map, depending on how you plan to use the information, and select the level of detail for the map. You can draw a high-level map or a detailed process map.

In Pam's case, I decided to draw a high-level process map for three reasons:

1. Her organization had limited shared understanding of the end-to-end business process.
2. The process had numerous subprocesses, making it complex.
3. This level of detail would provide Pam with an overall view of the entire process.

Deciding to start at a high level of detail leads to both positive and negative repercussions for the facilitator. On the one hand, this decision makes it easier to draw the process map because you do not need a detailed level of understanding and you can do so quickly. On the other hand, managing the project team becomes more difficult because part of the team almost always likes to delve into detail. Although you will hear various, reasonable-sounding explanations for the need to go deeper, recognize that the root of team members' anxiety usually revolves around not seeing their own job reflected in the process map. Your challenge, as the facilitator, becomes keeping everyone grounded and feeling secure.

To draw Pam's high-level process map, the team met for three hours every week for four weeks to create the two-page, high-level process map shown in Figures 13-5 and 13-6. Between meetings, I created and updated the process map using Microsoft Visio.

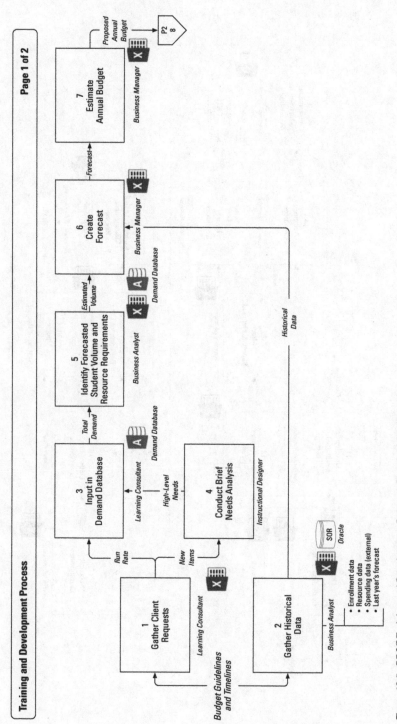

Figure 13-5 BB&Z Training and Development Process: Process Map (Part 1)

Training and Development Process

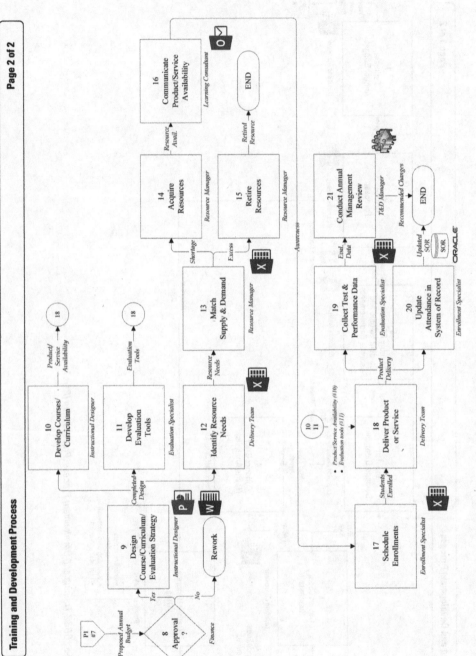

Figure 13-6 BB&Z Training and Development Process: Process Map (Part 2)

Notice in these two figures that the process map spans two pages because it did not fit onto a single page; notice how I used the two types of connectors discussed in Chapter 4 (Figures 4-26 and 4-27). The connector symbols help readers understand how to follow the process map by telling them where to move next. I used the off-page connector in Figure 13-5 to tell the reader to move to page 2, activity 8, after estimating the annual budget in activity 7. Also notice the off-page connector in Figure 13-6 entering activity 8, which lets the reader know that this activity comes from a prior page in the process map. After moving to activity 8 on the second page of the process map, the on-page connector in Figure 13-6 tells readers that, after activities 10 and 11, they move to delivery of the products and services in activity 18 on the *same* page of the map.

In reviewing Figures 13-5 and 13-6, we see that Pam's process starts after she receives the budget guidelines and timeline from the finance department. Figure 13-5 shows one way to draw a business process that starts with two activities occurring at the same time after an event enters the process. In Pam's case, as soon as her team receives the budget guidelines and timeline from finance, the learning consultants collect input from their clients to cover their needs for the next year. Simultaneously, the business analyst gathers historical data from the prior year. In looking at the process map, it becomes apparent, by the addition of the Microsoft Excel icon, that Pam's team uses a spreadsheet for many of the activities identified, as well as two databases: the demand database (a Microsoft Access database) and their system of record (an Oracle database).

Once finance approves the annual budget in activity 8, the instructional designers begin design work on courses, curriculum, and evaluation strategies. As the instructional designers design and develop the training products throughout the year, the evaluation specialists get involved and create the evaluation tools, and the delivery team identifies the resources required to facilitate the planned training.

Once the delivery team identifies the resources, the resource management team starts evaluating the available resources and secures any additional resources required. Once the resource management team secures the resources, communications can begin to tell employees of the upcoming training schedule. As students enroll and attend training, the evaluation specialists gather the performance data in preparation for the annual review meeting that occurs at the end of every year. Meanwhile, the enrollment specialist updates the system of record to reflect the employees' completion of training.

Figures 13-5 and 13-6 include many symbols to denote the various tools used to accomplish each activity, and you can include a legend page to explain the meaning of the symbols used, as discussed in Chapter 4. The legend page can go at the beginning or end of the map.

In addition to updating the process map between meetings, I spent time documenting the conversation in the detail document, a portion of which is shown in Figure 13-7. Remember to document the conversation as you proceed so you do not lose track of the rich dialogue, and include examples when possible.

After drawing the high-level process map and capturing the narrative to accompany the map, the team moved to step 4. We added the process timing to the process map and identified the cost of the business process.

Step 4: Estimate Time and Cost

In Chapter 5, we discussed process and cycle times and how to use this information to estimate what a process costs. Recall that:

> ► **Process time** is the time required to complete a single activity in a process.

> ► **Cycle time** is the time required to complete an entire process, from the first to the last step in a process. Sometimes you hear this called elapsed time.

In Chapter 5, I discussed how well estimating works for this step instead of using a formal data-gathering technique.

Number	Activity Description	Responsible Party	Tools	Output
1	**Gather client requests:** At this step in the process, the learning consultant, who works with a client group throughout the year, discusses the client's training needs for the upcoming year. They discuss existing and new courses that the client requires to meet their business objectives.	Learning consultant	Excel spreadsheet (phone, meetings)	**Run rate:** The products and services already delivered by the training and development organization that the client wants to continue using **New items:** New needs that the client identifies
2	**Gather historical data:** At the same time that the learning consultants gather client input, the business analyst gathers data for the prior year using existing sources to collect attendance numbers, identify resource usage, spending on external resources, and to compare last year's forecast to this year's actual.	Business analyst	Excel spreadsheet System of record	**Historical data:** All historical data is available to assist in creating the forecast for next year.
3	**Input in demand database:** Once the learning consultant determines the client's estimate on what existing training it plans to take advantage of during the next year, the learning consultant enters this information in the demand database to assist in forecasting the next year's demand. After the instructional designer conducts a high-level needs analysis with the client (4), the learning consultant enters the new items in the demand database.	Learning consultant	Demand database	**Total demand:** The run rate and new demand are available to help with forecasting student volume for next year.

Figure 13-7 BB&Z Training and Development Process: Detail Document   (continues)

Number	Activity Description	Responsible Party	Tools	Output
4	**Conduct brief need analysis:** If a client identifies a new need for which it does not seem that a training solution exists, the learning consultant works with an instructional designer to create a high-level needs analysis to understand the client's goals. This helps to gain insight into the potential demand and resource requirements that this new request may drive.	Instructional designer		**High-level needs:** This business has a brief summary of new demand items at this point.
5	**Identify forecasted student volume and resource requirements:** The run rate demand from existing courses and the high-level needs from newly identified products or services enter the process in this step. These two pieces of information assist the business analyst in forecasting the next year's student volume.	Business analyst	Excel spreadsheet Demand database	**Estimated volume:** The business has identified the estimated volume for run rate items and new items.
6	**Create forecast:** The business manager combines the forecast from step 5 and the historical data gathered from step 2, to create a forecast for the upcoming year. The forecast includes student volumes, resources requirements, and the number of new products.	Business manager	Excel spreadsheet	**Forecast:** A total forecast is available.

Figure 13-7 (continued)

However, when you work with such a high-level process map, as we did in Pam's case, you will not find the estimate as accurate because you do not have enough detail on all the subprocesses. You should still perform this task, though, because it provides directional information. When you draw a high-level process map, go back and revisit the timing estimates when you move to individual business processes.

During this step, I added process and cycle times to the process map for Pam's high-level T&D process. Figures 13-8 and 13-9 show the process and cycle times added to the training and development process map. As in Chapter 4, the white clock denotes process time, and the dark clock denotes cycle time.

After adding the process time to Pam's training and development process map and asking the project team to identify annual volumes, I had the data necessary to complete a high-level estimate of the labor cost for the T&D process. In Chapter 5, you learned that calculating the labor cost of a business process entails four components.

Part 1: List Process Activities and Process Time

After the project team completed the estimates for process and cycle time, I transferred the times shown on the process map to the next two tables. I completed this task after the project meeting, during which we identified process time, cycle time, and annual volume. Figure 13-10 shows the process time estimates for the training and development process, and Figure 13-11 shows the cycle time estimates.

Both tables include a range in some cases, depicted as the *Low End* and *High End* columns, because the team could not settle on a single number.

In these tables, I added a fourth column, *Frequency*, something I did not include in Chapter 5. I did this in Pam's case because we cannot count every step in the high-level process map the same way. The training and development organization performs the steps in the annual budgeting portion of the process map only once a year, so we cannot count the time con-

(text continues on page 308)

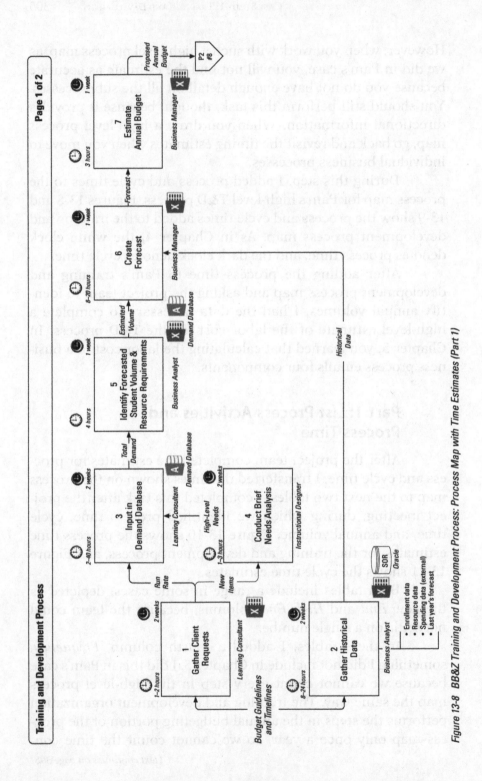

Figure 13-8 BB&Z Training and Development Process: Process Map with Time Estimates (Part 1)

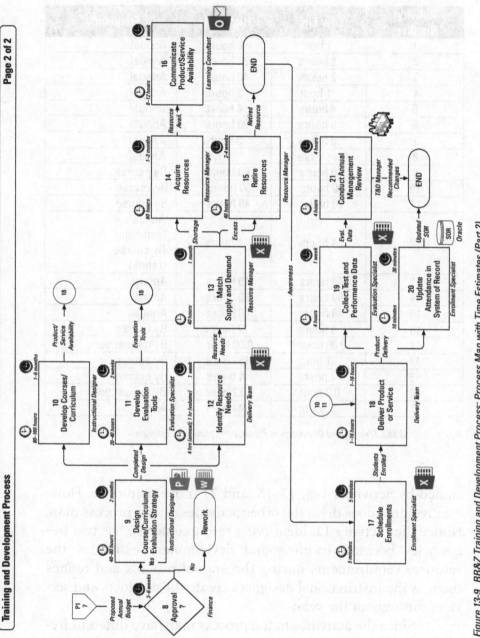

Figure 13-9 BB&Z Training and Development Process: Process Map with Time Estimates (Part 2)

Activity Number	Low End	High End	Frequency
1	1 hour	2 hours	Annual
2	8 hours	24 hours	Annual
3	2 hours	40 hours	Annual
4	1 hour	3 hours	Annual
5	4 hours	4 hours	Annual
6	8 hours	20 hours	Annual
7	3 hours	3 hours	Annual
8	n/a	n/a	Annual
9	40 hours	80 hours	By course
10	80 hours	160 hours	By course
11	20 hours	40 hours	By course
12	4 hours	4 hours	Annual (estimate) By course (refine)
13	40 hours	40 hours	Annual
14	80 hours	80 hours	Annual
15	40 hours	40 hours	Annual
16	8 hours	12 hours	By course
17	0.08 hour	0.08 hour	By transaction
18	1 hour	16 hours	By course
19	4 hours	4 hours	By course
20	0.2 hour	0.2 hour	By transaction
21	4 hours	4 hours	Annual

Figure 13-10   BB&Z Training and Development Process: Process Time Estimates

sumed by activities 1–8, 13–15, and 21 more than once. However, volume does drive the other activities on the process map. Notice that activity 12, identifying resource needs, has two frequencies because training and development estimates the resource requirements during the annual process and refines them as the instructional designers create the products and services throughout the year.

Since the activities in the process map have different frequencies, we have to reorganize the information from the process and cycle tables by frequency so we can calculate the labor costs. Figure 13-12 shows a combined view of process and cycle time information organized by the frequency of each activity.

Pam wanted to know how long the annual components

Activity Number	Low End	High End	Frequency
1	80 hours	80 hours	Annual
2	80 hours	80 hours	Annual
3	80 hours	80 hours	Annual
4	80 hours	80 hours	Annual
5	40 hours	40 hours	Annual
6	40 hours	40 hours	Annual
7	40 hours	40 hours	Annual
8	120 hours	240 hours	Annual
9	320 hours	320 hours	By course
10	160 hours	960 hours	By course
11	80 hours	80 hours	Annual
12	40 hours	40 hours	Annual (estimate) By course (refine)
13	160 hours	160 hours	Annual
14	160 hours	480 hours	Annual
15	80 hours	160 hours	Annual
16	40 hours	40 hours	By course
17	.08 hour	.08 hour	By transaction
18	1 hour	16 hours	By course
19	40 hours	40 hours	By course
20	0.5 hour	0.5 hour	By transaction
21	4 hours	4 hours	Annual

Figure 13-11 BB&Z Training and Development Process: Cycle Time Estimates

of the business process took in days or months, so I translated the hours consumed by the total annual activities in Figure 13-12 (229.5 and 1,264.0 hours) into days and months using the formula shown in Figure 13-13.

After performing these calculations, we knew that the annual portion of Pam's business process consumed 28½ days of process time, but it could take as long as five months of cycle time to complete.

Our next step included bringing in volume-related data.

Part 2: Identify Annual Volume

Before we can calculate the volume and associated labor cost for the activities affected by volume, we must first

Activity Number	Description	Process Time	Cycle Time
Annual Activities (performed once a year)			
1	Client requests	1.5 hours	80.0 hours
2	Historical data	16.0 hours	80.0 hours
3	Demand database	21.0 hours	80.0 hours
4	Needs analysis	2.0 hours	80.0 hours
5	Student volume	4.0 hours	40.0 hours
6	Forecast	14.0 hours	40.0 hours
7	Annual budget	3.0 hours	40.0 hours
8	Approval	n/a	180.0 hours
12	Resource needs	4.0 hours	40.0 hours
13	Supply/demand	40.0 hours	160.0 hours
14	Acquire resources	80.0 hours	320.0 hours
15	Retire resources	40.0 hours	120.0 hours
21	Mgmt. review	4.0 hours	4.0 hours
Total annual activities		**229.5** hours	**1,264.0** hours
Per-Course Activities (performed each time a course is developed)			
9	Design/develop	60.0 hours	320.0 hours
10	Develop	120.0 hours	560.0 hours
11	Evaluation tools	30.0 hours	80.0 hours
12	Resource needs	1.0 hours	n/a
16	Communications	10.0 hours	40.0 hours
18	Delivery	8.5 hours	8.5 hours
19	Collect performance data	4.0 hours	40.0 hours
Total per-course activities		**385.5** hours	**808.5** hours
Per-Transaction Activities (performed each time a student consumes a product or service)			
17	Enrollments	0.08 hour	0.08 hour
20	Update SOR	0.2 hour	0.5 hour
Total per-transaction activities		**0.28** hour	**0.58** hour

Figure 13-12 BB&Z Training and Development Process: Process and Cycle Time Estimates

separate the two volume categories (*by course* and *by transaction*) by the type of employees who do the work because these employees have different rates of pay. In Chapter 5, I used an intentionally simple process, the recognition bonus award process, and included only one compensation employee type, but in Pam's case, five types of employees affect the volume calculation:

Formula:

$$\frac{\text{Total process or cycle time hours}}{8 \text{ hours/workday}} = \text{Process or cycle time total in days}$$

Example 1—Process time:

$$\frac{229\frac{1}{2} \text{ hours}}{8 \text{ hours/workday}} = 28\frac{1}{2} \text{ days of process time}$$

Example 2—Cycle time:

$$\frac{1{,}264.0 \text{ hours}}{8 \text{ hours/workday}} = \frac{158 \text{ days}}{30 \text{ days/month}} = 5.3 \text{ months of cycle time}$$

Figure 13-13 *Calculating Total Process and Cycle Times in Days or Months*

1. Instructional designers
2. Evaluation specialists
3. Learning consultants
4. Instructors
5. Enrollment specialists

To incorporate these employee types into the calculation, Figure 13-14 shows the employee type that delivers the training and development activities added to the table. Notice that this new table shows only the process time for volume-related activities since, moving forward, we only care about this information. The new concept you should notice in this table is that one employee type can perform different activities. For example, the evaluation specialist develops evaluation tools (11) and collects performance data (19).

Next, I had to merge activities performed by one employee type into a single row to get us ready to incorporate the volume component. In Figure 13-15, I added the 60 hours that the instructional designers spend designing each course (9) to the 120 hours they spend developing the course (10), giving the instructional designer a 180-hour total in Figure 13-15. From a labor perspective, Figure 13-15 tells us that:

► Instructional designers require 180 hours, on average, for every course they develop.

Activity Number	Description	Employee Type	Process Time
Per-Course Activities			
9	Design	Instructional designer	60.0 hours
10	Develop	Instructional designer	120.0 hours
11	Evaluation tools	Evaluation specialist	30.0 hours
12	Resource needs	Instructor	1.0 hours
16	Communications	Learning consultant	10.0 hours
18	Delivery	Instructor	8.5 hours
19	Collect performance data	Evaluation specialist	4.0 hours
Per-Transaction Activities			
17	Enrollments	Enrollment specialist	0.08 hour
20	Update SOR	Enrollment specialist	0.2 hour

Figure 13-14   BB&Z Training and Development Process: Employee Type and Process Time Estimates for Volume-Related Activities

Activity #	Employee Type	Process Time
Per-Course Activities		
9, 10	Instructional designer	180.0 hours
11, 19	Evaluation specialist	34.0 hours
12, 18	Instructor	9.5 hours
16	Learning consultant	10.0 hours
Per-Transaction Activities		
17, 20	Enrollment specialist	0.28 hour

Figure 13-15   BB&Z Training and Development Process: Process Time Estimates by Employee Type

▶ Evaluation specialists require 34 hours per course.

▶ Instructors require 9.5 hours.

▶ Learning consultants require 10 hours for this part of the process.

▶ Enrollment specialists require 0.28 of an hour for every transaction.

Now that I knew how much time each instance of an activity took and who performed the work, I had to determine the annual labor required for each employee type. To perform this calculation, I had to identify the yearly volume. Figure 13-16 shows the volume listed in the *Annual Volume* column, which shows that, every year, the training and development organization:

▶ Designed and developed about 30 new courses.

▶ Delivered 1,000 classes.

▶ Had a total of 25,000 students attend classes.

Employee Type	Process Time/Activity	Annual Volume	Annual Labor
Instructional designer	180.0 hours	30	5,400 hours
Evaluation specialist	34.0 hours	30	1,020 hours
Instructor	9.5 hours	1,000	9,500 hours
Learning consultant	10.0 hours	130	1,300 hours
Enrollment specialist	0.28 hour	25,000	7,000 hours

Figure 13-16   BB&Z Training and Development Process: Labor and Labor Estimates

Notice that the annual volume for the learning consultant shows 130, instead of just 30, because this employee not only communicates the 30 new products and services developed, but also markets the ongoing calendar of almost 100 products and services.

The last column in Figure 13-16 shows the *Annual Labor* calculation, which I derived by multiplying the process time by the annual volume that Pam's team gave me, to arrive at the annual labor hours. So now we know that the instructional designers, for example, require 5,400 hours a year to perform their job.

Next, we had to determine how many employees the 5,400 hours equate to, using the full-time equivalent formula (FTE) discussed in Chapter 5.

Part 3: Determine the FTE Formula

The FTE number denotes the total number of hours that an employee can be paid for in a work year. So, if an employee works 40 hours in a week and we multiply that number by 52 weeks, we get 2,080 hours, a starting point for the FTE formula. However, I could not simply use 2,080 hours in the labor calculation because I had to deduct vacation, sick, and holiday hours available to an employee, as explained in Chapter 5 (Figure 5-8).

I used 1,880 as the labor calculation number to apply to the annual labor hours from Figure 13-16. You can see the formula I used to perform this calculation in Figure 13-17, using the instructional designer's 5,400 hours as the example.

Formula:

$$\frac{\text{Annual labor hours}}{\text{FTE hours}} = \text{Total FTE required to support the business process}$$

Example:

$$\frac{5,400 \text{ hours}}{1,880 \text{ FTE hours}} = 2.9 \text{ FTE required}$$

Figure 13-17 FTE Calculation

So now we know that Pam requires three instructional designers to handle the level of work in the training and development organization. I then went on and performed the same calculation on Pam's other employee types, and the table in Figure 13-18 shows the result of this calculation on the five employee types.

Employee Type	Process Time	Annual Volume	Annual Labor	FTE
Instructional designer	180.0 hours	30	5,400 hours	2.9
Evaluation specialist	34.0 hours	30	1,020 hours	0.5
Instructor	9.5 hours	1,000	9,500 hours	5.1
Learning consultant	10.0 hours	130	1,300 hours	0.7
Enrollment specialist	0.28 hour	25,000	7,000 hours	3.7
Total FTE required				**12.9**

Figure 13-18 BB&Z Training and Development Process: Labor Process Time Estimates

At this point, we know that the training and development process requires about 13 employees to support the development and delivery of training. However, remember that we created this process map at a high level and I did not include the annual component of the process in the labor estimate. I also did not include other day-to-day tasks that Pam's organization must perform to keep the business running. Because Pam wanted only a high-level estimate, we agreed to revisit the labor estimates after we completed the improvement phase.

The next step is normally to introduce the employee salaries into the mix.

Part 4: Determine Employee Costs

In Pam's case, we did not calculate the employee costs, even though we had the necessary information. I recommended we wait to perform the employee cost calculations until after we finished our work because creating the process map at such a high level would guarantee changes in the estimates.

To calculate the employee costs, follow the process outlined in Chapter 5. Start by identifying the pay rate for each employee type, and add an employee benefit rate (EB rate) to each salary. For example, we could say the instructional designers earn $80,000 a year, that Pam's company uses a 30 percent EB rate, and that the designers dedicate 100 percent of their time to design and development activities.

These numbers show that each instructional designer costs Pam about $104,000 a year. Even though Pam wanted to move to the improvement phase, we had one additional step to complete.

Step 5: Verify the Process Map

Before moving to the improvement phase, we did a quick check-in with Pam's managers to test whether we had captured the big pieces of work and used the right volume numbers. We completed this task at her weekly staff meeting and made minor changes to the volume numbers.

Step 6: Apply Improvement Techniques

Chapter 6 covered how to use six techniques to improve a business process, including eliminating bureaucracy, evaluating value-added activities, eliminating duplication and redundancy, simplifying the process/reports/forms used, reducing cycle time, and applying automation tools.

I began this step by discussing what happens in activity 1 with the project team, to find places where we could reduce bureaucracy. As the conversation progressed to the value-added technique, we found few value-added activities. I asked why gathering client requests occurred only once a year. The more the team talked, the more they came to realize that activity 1 appeared to be the only activity in the *entire* business process where the client interacted with the process. The team became more and more concerned about the limited interaction their clients had with the business process.

As we talked about their clients and what their clients wanted from the process, the project team began doubting whether they truly understood their client needs. Going back to the scope definition document the team completed earlier, they thought their clients cared about their employees' ability to perform on the job, quick turnaround on training requests, and lower cost. But now the team questioned the validity of those needs and did not even agree on what a particular need meant. Failing to reach any satisfactory conclusions, we chose to stop and conduct a benchmark study to determine how best-in-class companies meet certain customer/client needs.

Benchmarking

In Chapter 10 we touched on benchmarking, which consists of measuring a business process against a standard of excellence (either of an internal group in your company or of an external company well-known as best in class). Before you can benchmark a process against best-in-class companies, you first have to understand the crucial points in your own business process. Figure 13-19 shows a visual depiction of how to approach a benchmarking exercise, with three distinct phases.

Now let us look at how I led Pam's training and development organization in conducting a benchmark study and how to apply each of the three phases.

Phase 1: Customer/Client Interviews

In the first phase, the project team had to understand:

► What Pam's clients deemed important, to see whether they matched what the project team identified as client needs

► How the clients recognize when their need is met

► Whom the clients would identify as best in class for each of their needs

So I directed the project team to begin the benchmarking exercise by conducting 55 client interviews over a four-week period. We then validated the interview results by using a survey that we sent to 700 end users of training and their managers. We received 519 surveys back. As a result of gathering and analyzing the data, we determined that Pam's clients wanted the following from their training investment:

► Quality instructors

► Training alternatives

► The ability to customize courses

► Employees applying the training on the job

During the interviews, we asked interviewees how they would know when a need was met. For example, how would they know if they had a quality instructor? What does *quality* mean? In asking how clients would measure a quality instructor, I found out that quality, in their eyes, meant they wanted instructors who had industry experience to teach classes. I now had a new gauge by which Pam could evaluate her instructor pool: How many of Pam's instructors taught courses in which

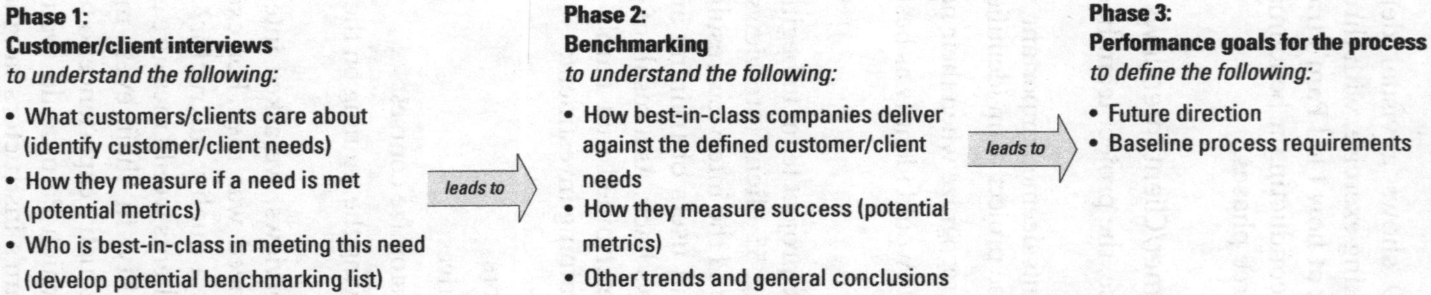

Phase 1:
Customer/client interviews
to understand the following:

- What customers/clients care about (identify customer/client needs)
- How they measure if a need is met (potential metrics)
- Who is best-in-class in meeting this need (develop potential benchmarking list)

leads to

Phase 2:
Benchmarking
to understand the following:

- How best-in-class companies deliver against the defined customer/client needs
- How they measure success (potential metrics)
- Other trends and general conclusions

leads to

Phase 3:
Performance goals for the process
to define the following:

- Future direction
- Baseline process requirements

Figure 13-19 Benchmarking Phases

they possessed real-world experience? As it turned out, not many.

The final question in the interview asked clients to identify any companies they felt did an outstanding job at meeting a particular need. Could they identify a company that did a good job at having quality instructors, instructors who bring their real-life experience to their teaching? Their answers to this question helped me build a list of companies that we could benchmark against.

At the end of the first phase, we had a validated list of client needs for the training and development business process, we knew how Pam's clients measured success, and we had a list of companies and internal groups that we could benchmark against to find out how they delivered against client needs.

Phase 2: Benchmarking

Now that we understood what Pam's clients cared about, how they would measure success, and who they thought were best-in-class companies, it was time to move the project team to phase 2. Next, I asked the team members to focus on:

▶ Writing the interview questions and creating a tool to collect the data.

▶ Working with Pam's internal productivity group to identify contacts at the companies that we wanted to benchmark and then scheduling appointments.

▶ Reviewing benchmarking studies available in the market on education and training.

We created two sets of questions. One set focused on general information to ask every benchmark company, and the second addressed the list of client needs. We did not ask every benchmark company about all four client needs, but rather focused each interview on the single client need for which the company was identified as best in class. We asked certain companies about quality instructors, another group about training alternatives, others about course customization, and finally a

fourth group about how they evaluated an employee's performance on the job.

The first list of general questions, which we asked all
companies, included items like:

▶ How many employees do you have in your company?

▶ How many employees do you have in your training and
development organization?

▶ How do you organize your training and development group
(centralized, decentralized, or other)?

▶ How do you organize your resources to support your client
base (by business, geography, or other)?

▶ How do you fund the training and development group
(tuition, fully budgeted, other)?

▶ What do you consider the top-priority goals for the training
and development organization?

▶ What do you consider the training and development group's
critical success factors (the key goals your organization
must attain to compete in your market)?

▶ What do you feel differentiates you from other companies
in the training and development business (your primary
strengths)?

For the second set of questions, we started the interview
by providing each best-in-class company with a definition of the
client need we wanted to discuss with them. For example, we
started an interview on *quality instructors* by defining what we
thought quality instructors should possess: industry expertise,
technical competence, exceptional platform skills, and credi-
bility.

We then asked five main questions to understand how
the particular benchmark company met the client need, for
example:

1. How are you organized to support _____?
2. What approach or process do you use to gain _____? How
   do you determine the best approach?

3. What process do you use to measure the effectiveness of _____?
4. What problems do you encounter?
5. What, if anything, would you change? Why?

Phase 3: Performance Goals

After the project team completed the benchmark interviews, I summarized the findings and translated them into performance goals, that is, what Pam's organization cared about:

▶ **Instructor Expertise:** Pam wants her organization to become known for having instructors with real-world experience, which suggests that she will:
  ■ Focus on acquiring instructors with industry and/or product expertise.
  ■ Build a core of instructors/developers and outsource delivery, if appropriate, to acquire the content expertise required.
  ■ Use the same resource, if possible, for the development and delivery of training.
  ■ Use team teaching/consulting to provide required content expertise.

▶ **Training Delivery Alternatives:** A significant percentage of Pam's training is instructor-led training, and she wants to move toward offering a wider range of formats and increase the use of technology.

▶ **Ability to Customize Courses:** Pam wants to increase the modularity in her course design to enable quicker customization, to offer training for intact groups that uses examples and scenarios from her client's business, and to deliver training at her client's site.

▶ **On-the-Job Performance:** Pam wants her organization to focus on measuring an employee's ability to perform on the job, to offer refresher training in self-paced formats, and to give managers reinforcement tools to support their employees' learning.

Conducting a benchmark study can take some time, so remember these keys to a successful benchmarking study:

▶ Identify the right contacts in the right companies.

▶ Discuss one critical success factor, or client need, per interview.

▶ Recognize that internal benchmarking can be as effective as external benchmarking.

▶ Include research study findings in your summary.

A New Approach

After reviewing the results of the benchmark study, we took another bend in the road. Pam and the project team did not see how their present process, even after it was improved, would get them to their desired end state. As we discussed the activities involved in the current process map, the team identified instances of bureaucracy, and they created a value-added analysis, but the importance of increasing the client interaction throughout the overall process became obvious. The process map showed that Pam's team interacted with the client most often once a year during the two weeks when they collected annual needs. I helped the project team to recognize that the organization asks the wrong questions during the annual data collection process by focusing on volume instead of on business objectives and that they had not provided a means of addressing changing needs throughout the year. In reviewing the scope definition document created in step 2, I reminded the team of the process definition they wrote:

This process covers delivering products and services that enable employee learning to support the business objectives. In all cases, the business goals drive the learning investment.

I helped the project team think about how they would redesign the front end of the process to see whether they could simplify the process, how they might reduce the five-month cycle time, and how they could make the planning process more of an ongoing one instead of just an annual process. With the client identified as the central point of the process, we designed a totally new approach to planning for client needs that influenced a redesign of the activities that followed.

Pam's case demonstrates the flexibility required when working on business process improvement. You saw one bend in the road in step 1 when we built the process inventory at the department level, which influenced a change in step 2 and the writing of the scope definition document. Now we had taken another twist because we are about to redesign BB&Z's training and development business process from scratch to place the emphasis on the client.

As you perform process work, try not to put labels on the work other than business process improvement. Avoid the use of terms like *quality improvement* or *reengineering* because it does not matter what you call it or whether you switch between the two, as long as you focus on improving the process.

Over the next week, we developed a new process map, depicted in Figure 13-20, that placed the client at the center of the process. The project team devoted significant time to identifying the data flow throughout the process (i.e., having the right data at the right time) because of its importance in supporting a more integrated process in the future. Figure 13-20 shows three new databases that support the process:

1. **Client Profile:** Holds information about training and development clients, their needs and preferences, and how training and development handled their needs, rejections, and acceptance.
2. **Offering Profile:** Holds solutions, performance goals, designs, learning objectives, and delivery requirements.
3. **Process Performance Profile:** Holds evaluation data and other general data on how the learning process performs.

Four major business processes began to surface, which moved Pam's group away from the traditional view of training and development work:

1. **Need/Solution Identification:** This business process becomes the focal point for the client partnership and

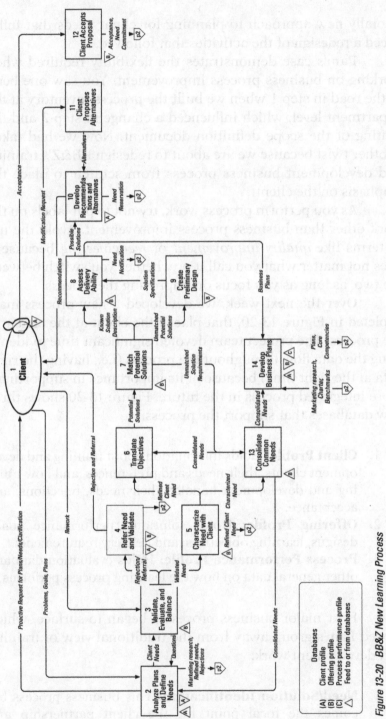

Figure 13-20 BB&Z New Learning Process

includes the identification of needs and solutions, proposal creation, return on investment, and client acceptance.

2. **Business Direction and Measurement:** This business process sets the foundation for the business of the training and development organization and includes the rules for running the business, measuring the overall performance of the learning process, and the development/coaching/reward of employees who work throughout the learning process.

3. **Resource Development and Delivery:** This process secures and develops resources (internal and external) to enable development and delivery of solutions. The process includes managing vendor relationships, assembling the multiple components, and overall applied research and technology.

4. **Promotion and Communication:** This process creates the promotional and/or communication strategy, and it reviews the results of the strategy. It includes managing the creation of the materials and the distribution of those materials.

In summary, the new learning process delivers the following improvements to the business process:

► The new business process has ongoing client interaction, increasing the value-added activities of the process.

► Performing data collection throughout the year minimizes the time required during the annual planning process, thus reducing cycle time.

► The learning process expresses client needs as performance goals, which the training and development employees translate into measurable, observable learning objectives, increasing the value-added activities of the process.

► The creation of three databases helps to streamline the information and organize the data around clients, offerings, and performance results.

► The offering profile database provides a searchable tool that assists in eliminating duplication. Once the training and development employee translates a client's performance needs into learning objectives, the objectives become the basis for reconciling common needs.

► Streamlining the business process delivers a more adaptable process that can react more quickly to changing business needs.

Pam and the project team liked the new process and reviewed it with a few clients to gain their support. Once the team felt comfortable with the design, we moved to the next step on the roadmap, identifying internal controls, creating tools, and developing metrics.

Step 7: Create Internal Controls, Tools, and Metrics

In Chapter 7, we discussed how internal controls help to identify points in the business process where a mistake can occur and to explain how to prevent those errors; how tools can support and streamline the process, avoid errors, and assist with training new employees to perform their jobs easier; and how metrics show whether the process works as planned.

Internal Controls

I started this step by asking the project team to identify where something could go wrong in the new process. We then created internal controls to address each of those areas. Having a discussion about what can go wrong in a business process helps the organization to circumvent the potential problems.

Tools

The next part of step 7 involves developing the tools to support the process. Pam's team had to develop several new items to support the learning process, including:

► Creating three new Microsoft Access databases to store the client, offering, and performance data.

► Creating standards for the documents used throughout the learning process, such as a design document and a business plan.

➤ Establishing a process for obtaining and storing external research, competitive analysis information, and the company's corporate charter.

➤ Evaluating solutions to enable class registration and manage resources.

➤ Creating job aids to help employees perform their jobs.

I asked the project team members to think about the various tools they had to create and how they would explain the new process to their clients and stakeholders. One job aid we created helped validate that only correct data entered the offering profile database. Because the learning process views the new offering database as a crucial tool to enable the matching of common needs, thus reducing duplication, this job aid provides examples of how to translate client needs into performance goals and performance goals into learning objectives.

I also suggested that a model would help people outside the department understand the new process because it included so many changes. The model I developed in Figure 13-21, working with the project team, illustrates the interaction throughout the learning process:

➤ The business direction/measurement process acts as the foundation for the entire learning process, supporting Pam's concept that business goals drive learning investments.

➤ Client needs flow through the needs/solution identification business process, while the business direction/measurement process and the resource development and delivery processes support those client needs.

➤ Ultimately, the promotion/communication process interacts with the clients to share details about the available products and services.

➤ The horizontal arrows depict the employees in the learning process and show the interaction between client needs and the delivery of products and services.

➤ The learning/information utility reflects the databases that hold information to make the entire process functional, and the model shows that all employees use the utility.

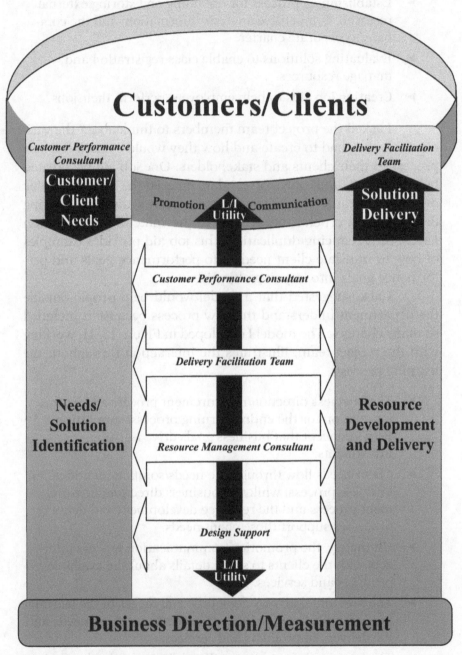

Customers/Clients

Customer Performance Consultant

Customer/
Client
Needs

Promotion · L/I Utility · Communication

Delivery Facilitation Team

Solution
Delivery

Customer Performance Consultant

Delivery Facilitation Team

Needs/
Solution
Identification

Resource Management Consultant

Resource
Development
and Delivery

Design Support

L/I
Utility

Business Direction/Measurement

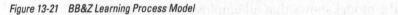

L/I Utility = Learning/Information Utility

Figure 13-21   BB&Z Learning Process Model

Notice that the learning consultant's job title changed in the new model to *customer performance consultant* to stress the importance of focusing on the clients' businesses and helping them to achieve their goals.

I highly recommend that you spend time creating a visual representation of how your business process works because using a model helps explain a complex business process to people outside the day-to-day business better than a process map, which can seem overwhelming.

Metrics

In the scope definition document we created in step 2, Pam's clients seemed to care about performance on the job and two efficiency-oriented metrics (quick turnaround and lower cost). With this information, we listed five measurements of success in the document:

- ▶ On-the-job performance
- ▶ Reduced development time
- ▶ Cost reduction target
- ▶ The ability to integrate new businesses
- ▶ The linkage between training and business goals

After completing the benchmarking study, we learned that training and development's clients also cared about quality instructors, alternative delivery methods, and course customization. Although Pam and the project team cared about every measurement of success, I encouraged them to recognize that the learning process had too many potential measurements to start. I suggested they limit their metrics for the first year to one metric for each of the following: effectiveness, efficiency, and adaptability. The project team agreed, and after discussing the measurements of success, we developed metrics for the following items:

- ▶ **Effectiveness:** On-the-job performance (We felt that having quality instructors could help us to meet this measurement of success.)

▶ **Efficiency:** Reduced development time (We thought that course customization and a new approach to modularity could help reduce the time required to develop courses.)

▶ **Adaptability:** The ability to integrate new businesses

We then took each of Pam's measurements of success and translated them into the metrics shown in Figure 13-22.

Measurement of Success		Metric
On-the-job performance	➡	20% improvement of on-the-job performance after attending training.
Reduced development time	➡	100% of new products and services developed will incorporate a modular design.
Ability to integrate new businesses	➡	New employees are trained within two weeks of an acquisition.

Figure 13-22 BB&Z Learning Process: Year 1 Metrics

Using the effectiveness measurement of on-the-job performance as an example, let me share how we approached this item. I suggested they start with instructor-led training, the most expensive type, to measure employees' ability to perform on their jobs after they attended training.

In the training and development field, you typically hear about four levels of training evaluation, depending on what you want to measure: satisfaction, learning, application, or return on investment.

We decided to create an evaluation to measure employees' application of what they learned on the job. Pam committed to focus on five high-volume courses throughout the first year. She chose to start with an evaluation of Beating the Competition, a course delivered to the company's financial sales representatives that targets BB&Z's biggest competitor. She felt that she could use the results of this evaluation to demonstrate a linkage between training and business goals.

The evaluation specialist developed a pre- and post-assessment for the course; then we established a process where the instructors would capture a student's baseline at the beginning of the course by administering a brief survey. Three months later, the evaluation specialist would follow up with the students using a telephone survey to measure increases in their on-the-job performance. In addition to the assessment and survey, I suggested that the evaluation specialist track the sales figures of employees who attended the training.

Pam now had a newly designed business process that included increased client interaction, necessary internal controls, tools to support the process, and metrics to evaluate the effectiveness, efficiency, and adaptability of the process.

With all this behind us, we can move to the next step and confirm that the process and tools will work as expected.

Step 8: Test and Rework

In Chapter 8, you learned to create a test plan to test the process and the tools before introducing the process changes across the entire organization. In this phase of the work, you think about the who, what, where, when, and how of testing.

► **Whom** to involve in the testing
► **What** items to test
► **Where** to conduct the testing
► **When** to perform the testing
► **How** to conduct the testing

I use the same format of the test plan from Chapter 8 (Figure 8-2) for Pam's process. For the learning process, examples of our test items included:

► End-to-end business process (Microsoft PowerPoint process map; Microsoft Word detail document)
► Customer profile database (Microsoft Access)

- ▶ Offering profile database (Microsoft Access)
- ▶ Process performance profile database (Microsoft Access)
- ▶ Job aid covering the guidelines for entering data into the offering profile database (Adobe PDF file)
- ▶ Sample report that summarizes annual performance results of the learning process (Microsoft Excel)
- ▶ Class registration tool
- ▶ Resource management tool

By testing the learning process, I discovered the need to make the following changes:

- ▶ We had to do additional work on what constituted a match in the *match-potential-solutions* activity because it seemed too easy to credit a solution with addressing a performance goal.
- ▶ We had to train the customer performance consultants on how to use the offering database.
- ▶ We redefined the activity called *synthesize/evaluate refinements* because the process workers did not understand what this activity entailed.
- ▶ We modified how we set up the resource management application.
- ▶ We adapted the fields in the customer profile database to accommodate the customer performance consultants.
- ▶ We modified the process performance database to meet what Pam hoped to gain from this data.
- ▶ We changed the sample report that summarized the learning process's performance.

At the end of the testing phase, the project team made all the necessary changes. The training and development employees involved in the testing noticed we had made substantial changes to the process. They understood the reasons why and expressed excitement about the upcoming implementation.

Step 9: Implement Change

When I first started working with Pam, I created a project plan for the training and development business process improvement effort and continually adjusted the plan throughout the work, especially after deciding to redesign the process.

In Chapter 9, you learned that the implementation plan included phases and that a phase could include tracks. Three key tracks in the implementation phase include the:

1. *Communication track:* Developing a communication plan stating who has to know what when
2. *Training track:* Developing a training plan that tells who requires training on what
3. *Change management track:* The impact analysis that identifies whom to engage in the changes you want to introduce

Communication Track

The project team had to think about what communication needed to occur to verify everyone received the appropriate information to prepare them for the change. Figure 13-23 shows part of the learning process communication plan, in which I defined the audience, communication goals, key message points, the best communication vehicles to use, and the best timing to deliver the messages.

Figure 13-23 shows training and development employees and clients as the two main audiences that require communication about the process changes. A key challenge for training and development was to refocus the organization's mindset so that everything employees do revolves around the client.

Training Track

For the training plan, the project team had to think about what training needed to occur to ensure that all parties could perform their process responsibilities. They had to list the employees requiring training, identify what kind of training the employees required, and identify who owned the responsibility

Audience	Communication Goal	Key Message Points	Communication Vehicles (Method)	Due Date
All training and development employees	Engage the organization. Move toward client as number one.	■ What's changing and why ■ Importance of the client ■ More integrated process ■ Training plan and timeline	Department meeting Model Email follow-up	May 1
Client	Gain feedback and support.	■ Learning process redesigned to focus on their business objectives ■ Link new process to the results of the client interviews ■ Review the benefits of the new process including increased client interaction ■ Clarify training and development's charter (what is in and out of scope) ■ Contact resources for additional information	Email Model	May 10

Figure 13-23 BB&Z Learning Process: Communication Plan

to conduct the training. They also had to decide where the project team would hold the training, along with when and what methods they would use to conduct the training.

Figure 13-24 shows part of the learning process training plan. The figure shows that I designed the training approach to have employees attend training on the basis of how they relate to the four new business processes. This segregation was intentional to reinforce the importance of the new design. It also shows that the customer performance consultant will receive additional training on the client and on the offering profile databases (discussed earlier).

Change Management Track

The impact analysis for the new learning process captured the changes that had to occur to ensure the success of the

Audience	Training Objectives	Approach	Tools	Facilitator	Due Date
All training and development employees	■ *Define* how the learning process meets client needs. ■ *Describe* each step in the learning process. ■ *Explain* your role in the learning process. ■ *Illustrate* how the learning process model supports the business process.	Separate group meetings by the four new business processes: ■ Need/solution identification ■ Business direction/ measurement ■ Resource development and delivery ■ Promotion/ communication	■ Process documentation ■ Model ■ Job aids	Managers	May 30
Customer performance consultants	■ *Summarize* how to move to a proactive client relationship. ■ *Explain* the charter of the learning process and *demonstrate* the validation of a client need. ■ *Create* performance goals from a client need and *categorize* those needs.	Instructor-led training	■ Process documentation ■ Model ■ Job aids ■ Databases: client profile and offering profile ■ External data sources	Instructional designer	June 15

Figure 13-24 BB&Z Learning Process: Training Plan

new business process. In Chapter 6, as we built the new, improved process map, we created the impact analysis and identified the required changes.

Once Pam addressed the items in the impact analysis and after I developed the training and communication plans, Pam felt ready to introduce the new learning process. She now had confidence that the project team had considered the important items and felt ready to move ahead with implementation. Pam felt strongly about the next step, continuous improvement, because she now recognized how quickly a process may have to change. So the team had one last task to complete.

Step 10: Drive Continuous Improvement

During this step, Pam had another challenge she had to deal with: how to help the organization adopt a new mindset where they would always look for ways to improve the learning process. The continuous improvement cycle wheel in Chapter 10 (Figure 10-1) introduced some structure to this phase, and I led the project team in creating a plan to regularly evaluate, test, assess, and execute against improvements.

We developed a continuous improvement *plan* for each of the four business processes, and then developed the continuous improvement *schedule* to provide an overview of the timing for each of the business processes.

After the project team finished all the work, I included in the executive summary (1) the learning process model from Figure 13-21, (2) the process description summary shown in Figure 13-25, and (3) a process summary that included general assumptions, dependencies, job descriptions, and sizing algorithms.

At the end of our work, Pam Borzak had an organization that focused on the right areas. Her entire organization was client focused and regularly evaluated the effectiveness, efficiency, and adaptability of the learning process. I helped her develop recognition guidelines to reward employees for outstanding performance in support of the new business process.

Chapter Summary

Pam Borzak's story at BB&Z demonstrates how to apply the ten steps to business process improvement and how to adjust the steps as you encounter obstacles or bends in the road. The ten steps are:

1. *Develop the process inventory:* How to build a process inventory and process prioritization table for either an entire department or the business processes within a department.

Need/Solution Identification	Business Direction/Measurement
Overall description: This process is the focal point for the client *partnership*. It includes identification of needs and solutions, proposal creation, impact, and client acceptance. **Responsibilities:** ■ Defining the client needs entering the learning process ■ Validating and evaluating needs ■ Characterizing needs ■ Translating needs into performance goals and matching needs to potential solutions ■ Assessing the organization's capability to deliver solutions ■ Proposing recommendations ■ Signaling potential resources ■ Measuring solution results ■ Obtaining client acceptance ■ Consolidating common needs ■ Synthesizing and evaluating refinements ■ Ensuring the refinements of the solution and/or resources are integrated and made available throughout the process.	**Overall description:** This process sets the *foundation* for the business of training and development, the rules for running the business, measuring the overall performance of the learning process, and the development/coaching/reward of employees who work throughout the learning process. **Responsibilities:** ■ Creating and changing business rules ■ Creating decision support information ■ Developing business plans ■ Developing and conducting benchmarking and competitive analysis activity ■ Capturing, sharing, and applying learning ■ Analyzing process performance ■ Developing accountability and reward systems ■ Using the results of consolidated common needs on a strategic basis
Resource Development/Delivery	**Promotion/Communication**
Overall description: This process secures and develops resources (internal and external) to enable development and delivery of solutions. It includes managing vendor relationships, assembling the multiple components, and overall applied research and technology. **Responsibilities:** ■ Developing and acquiring resources ■ Assessing the organization's capability to deliver solutions ■ Assessing the delivery of products and services ■ Assembling resources ■ Initiating delivery of the planned solution ■ Refining delivery ■ Synthesizing and evaluating refinements ■ Ensuring the refinements of the solution and/or resources are integrated and made available throughout the process	**Overall description:** This process creates the promotional and/or communication strategy and evaluates the results of the strategy. It also manages the creation of the promotional materials and distributes that material. **Responsibilities:** ■ Developing a promotional/communication strategy ■ Developing promotional tools and materials ■ Collecting and analyzing promotional results ■ Implementing a distribution plan

Figure 13-25   BB&Z Learning Process: Process Descriptions and Responsibilities

2. *Establish the foundation:* How to develop the scope definition document for a business process.

3. *Draw the process map:* How to decide the level of detail for building the process map and how to create a map that spans multiple pages.

4. *Estimate time and cost:* How to calculate process and cycle time, how to incorporate frequency into the calculations, and how to include different types of employees.

5. *Verify the process map:* Ways to validate the accuracy of the process map.

6. *Apply improvement techniques:* How to incorporate benchmarking into the improvement phase and how to know when to design an entirely new process.

7. *Create internal controls, tools, and metrics:* How to develop internal controls, sample tools, and metrics. A reminder of the importance of building a model to explain a complicated process.

8. *Test and rework:* How to test all the components of a business process.

9. *Implement change:* How to develop the communication, training, and impact analysis plans.

10. *Drive continuous improvement:* How to create a schedule to keep track of all the different business processes.

What You Have Achieved

In this chapter, you have achieved the following:

▶ A grasp of how to adjust to bends in the road and adapt the ten steps

▶ An understanding of how to build a model to further explain a complex business process

▶ The ability to calculate employee costs when different types of employees are involved in the process

▶ The knowledge that you can build the process inventory and prioritization table at either the department or the process level

▶ An understanding of how to incorporate multiple frequencies in the cost analysis

▶ Insight into how to conduct a benchmark study

▶ Most important, the *power* to know that you can do it

CHAPTER 14

Case Study 2

Recruitment Process in Hong Kong

This case study focuses on a U.S.-based business expanding in Hong Kong. I chose this case because it introduces several different characteristics to business process work and shows how to adapt the ten steps. It skips step 1 because my client had already identified the process to focus on, and it skips step 6 because I had to design an entirely new process because no process existed. You can reference the preceding chapters in this book for clarification or for additional details as we move through this case study.

Background

Jim Mann, vice president of human resources for the Entertainment Park Group (EPG), asked my director if I could help him create the recruitment process for a new park the company planned to open in two years. The project started with a focus on hiring front-line hourly employees and later expanded to include salaried employees and third parties.

The only direction given to me included working with the senior management team to review current ideas, ask challenging questions, create a process map, and identify instances where they could leverage the company's existing enterprise resource planning (ERP) system.

As the first foray into the Asian market, senior leadership recognized that this expansion would put the company in the public spotlight and cause scrutiny on the hiring process. The company expected between 100,000 and 200,000 people to apply for about 5,500 jobs. Apprehension existed around the large number of applicants the company would not select. Even though the company may not hire an applicant, the company still wanted those applicants to visit the park. Thus, we made process decisions to make certain the applicants would have a positive experience.

In this case study, the requirement did not exist to build and prioritize a process inventory, as defined in step 1, because Jim had already identified the recruitment process as the focus. As a result, I started with step 2.

Step 2: Establish the Foundation

The scope definition document, as you learned in Chapter 3, establishes the boundaries for the business process. As you will see in this case, I changed the document to accommodate the requirements of the project. Jim included himself on the project team and two other participants: Brian Chan Siu Hong, director of recruitment, and Kim Li Mei Yan, a recruiter.

We had a difficult start writing the document. First, a 12-hour time difference existed because I was on the East Coast of the United States, while my three partners resided in Hong Kong, so I began the work in my evening. I asked to start the work at 8:00 p.m. for me, so we could work for two hours and end by 10:00 p.m. However, I learned that in Hong Kong the majority of citizens use public transportation and do not arrive at work until 9:00 a.m. As a result, we started at 9:00 p.m. for me and went until 11:00 p.m.

Second, we used a conference call for the first meeting. Jim did a decent job making introductions, explaining why he asked me to help, and identifying his goals. Jim and I had worked together before when he resided in the United States, and he understood my strengths (and weaknesses). I recall when we first discussed the project, Jim said that one reason he wanted me to help was so that I could "ask the hard questions in your typical Sue manner." Attempting to do business process work using conference calls proved more difficult than I imagined, and this included asking the hard questions. I had no opportunity to build personal rapport with Brian and Kim, did not have the advantage of making a face-to-face connection, and was worried that my questioning may appear as a personal challenge to them, which I wanted to avoid because of what I understood about the culture. I am guessing that the Hong Kong team probably wondered *who in the world is this person* and *why do we have to meet with her for two hours at a time*? The answer, of course, is that their boss told them to, and they would not openly disagree with Jim.

Third, I had a difficult time understanding Brian when he spoke. I had to ask him to repeat what he said several times, which I found embarrassing. I felt that I should be attuned to foreign accents, but I had to ask Jim multiple times to repeat what Brian said. I spoke with Jim after the first meeting and gained new insights. We agreed to use videoconferencing for future meetings so we could see each other and to help with the language difference.

We made limited progress during the first meeting and completed only a portion of the scope definition document. The team identified the purpose and boundaries for the process, which starts with *opening the position in the ERP system* and ends with the new employee *attending day 1 orientation*.

During the initial meeting, I started to capture terminology that the Hong Kong team used. I found that they seemed to imply something different when they used the words *applicant* and *candidate*. As I mentioned in Chapter 3, to me these terms had the same meaning, but not to the team. After we discussed the terms, I learned that an applicant signified a person who had completed a company application but who had not talked (and may never talk) to a company representative. A candidate, on the other hand, is a person the company will interview. As we worked through the process map, this distinction became crucial. You should always listen for different terminology as you lead process work because the meanings of words can easily derail a meeting.

After the initial painful start using conference calls, the use of video conferencing engaged the participants, enabled clearer communication, and speeded up the work. I found it easier to understand Brian when I could *see* him speak. Throughout this step, I had to balance facilitating the discussion and driving toward completion of the scope definition document. While I had the completed process map as my deliverable, I had to leave decisions to the team and permit them adequate time to come to conclusions. As in numerous Asian cultures, the Hong Kong team used silence as a form of communication, and I had to tolerate a degree of silence.

Figure 14-1 shows the completed scope definition document for this process. Notice the second measurement of success: how the Hong Kong population would view the company. The project team kept this at the forefront of our thoughts throughout the work. I deleted the client section and added a larger scope section because this process had numerous *in-scope* and *out-of-scope* elements. This figure again reinforces the flexibility of the scope definition document. Rework it so it meets your needs.

It took the team until the third meeting to have a completed document, which we reviewed at the start of the next meeting. Once the project team felt comfortable with the scope definition document, we moved to step 3 and began drawing the process map.

Step 3: Draw the Process Map

Drawing the process map in step 3 for a new business process gives the project team a model for the future, helps them understand where handoffs occur, and provides a tool to formulate decisions that address open matters.

In the EPG case, we chose to draw a cross between a high-level and detailed process map because:

▶ The business process is somewhat complex.
▶ The company will use the process often and look for opportunities to improve it over time.

Process Name: Recruitment Process

Process Owner: Brian Chan Siu Hong

Description (Purpose):

To select and hire hourly employees for the new park opening.

The main focus is to ensure that the selection process is well perceived by the general Hong Kong population.

Scope (boundaries):

Start Opening Position in Enterprise Resource Planning System

End Attend Day 1 Orientation (with area greeting)

Scope:

Within Scope	Outside Scope
How the AOP budgeting process for labor affects the recruitment process	AOP budgeting process itself
Opening job requisitions	Development of sourcing methods
Posting open positions	Form development (e.g., staffing requisition, job description)
Methods for applicant sourcing	Ongoing training after orientation
Screening and interviewing candidates	
Checking candidate references	
Offering employment	
Hiring employee	
Orientation and area greeting	

Process Responsibilities:

1. Website monitoring
2. Job seeker/applicant communications
3. Interviewing and employee selection
4. Mass transportation logistics
5. Orientation

Measurements of Success:

1. All hourly job openings filled two months in advance of park opening.

2. Hong Kong general population views the company in a positive light, even if an individual applied for an opening and was not hired.

Figure 14-1 EPG Scope Definition Document

▶ The company expects turnover as recruiters frequently rotate into and out of the job.

We also elected to draw a cross-functional process map to show clearly how the job seeker (or applicant or candidate) interacts with the process versus the responsibilities of human resources.

Figures 14-2 and 14-3 show a portion of the process map created for the new recruitment process and highlights human resources' role from creating the position in the company's ERP system through to running a report identifying possible applicants to interview.

Figure 14-2 shows that the company requires job seekers to visit the company's website to submit a resume and complete an online application. Figure 14-3 shows the job seeker turning into an applicant after completing the prerequisite online paperwork (15). The company instituted numerous guidelines in the process, preventing the applicant from applying for more than one job at a time; if not hired, he or she must wait three months before applying for the same job again. The position-based questions (17) varied based on the job. When hiring hourly employees, the company cared mainly about the applicants' availability to work any shift and their residency.

The remaining process map not included, covered scheduling interviews, managing mass transportation via train and bus, the logistics involved in moving a substantial number of applicants through various venues, conducting interviews, making the job offer, and creating an applicant record in the ERP system.

Figure 14-4 provides a subset of the detail document to accompany the process map. In reviewing this figure, you can see that the *job seeker* turns into an *applicant* after he or she completes the required online documentation (15); next, when human resources schedules an interview with the applicant, he or she turns into a *qualified person* (24), and eventually the person becomes a *candidate*. This distinction in terminology may seem odd, but the client felt strongly about this differentiation

(*text continues on page 348*)

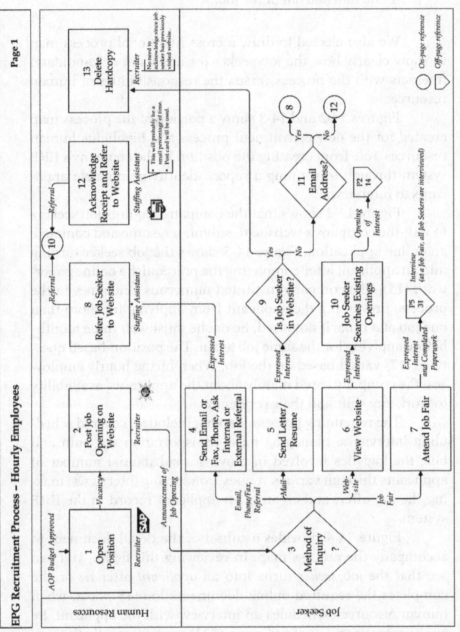

Figure 14-2 EPG Process Map: Part 1

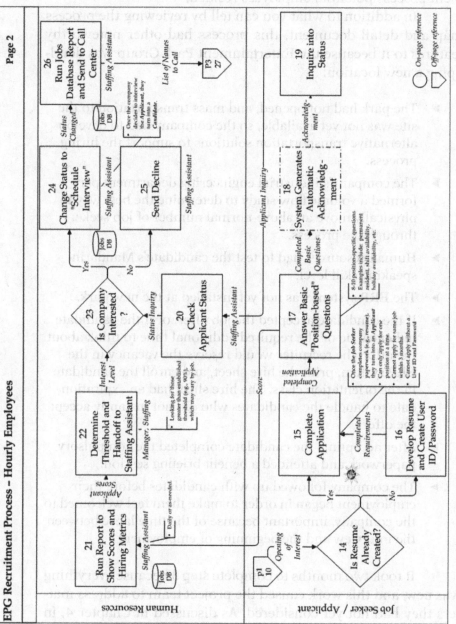

Figure 14-3 EPG Process Map: Part 2

because it allowed them to report on which stage of the recruit-ment process potential employees resided.

In addition to what you can tell by reviewing the process map and detail document, this process had other noteworthy features to it because the Entertainment Park Group was devel-oping a new location:

> ► The park had not opened, and mass transportation to the site was not yet available, so the company had to develop alternative transportation solutions to support the hiring process.

> ► The company's industrial engineering department per-formed a volume flow study to determine the best way to physically move an above-normal number of job seekers through the process.

> ► Human resources had to test the candidate's Mandarin-speaking skill level.

> ► The ERP system was not yet installed at the new park.

> ► If the candidate accepted the job offer, or if the candidate indicated he or she required additional time to think about the offer, the recruiter would reserve the vacancy in the ERP system, print the hire sheet, and enroll the candidate in the orientation class. The hire sheet had an expiration date to handle the candidates who did not instantly accept the offer.

> ► After accepting, the candidate completed the compulsory paperwork and attended a benefit briefing session.

> ► The company followed up with candidates before their employment began in order to make them feel welcomed to the company, important because of the time lapse between the interview and the beginning of employment.

It took two months to complete step 3 because everything was new, and this work caused the project team to address mat-ters they had not yet considered. As discussed in Chapter 4, in addition to updating the process map between meetings, I docu-mented the conversation as it went along in the detail document.

After drawing the process map and capturing the narra-

Activity Number	Activity Name/Description	Input(s) to Activity	Output(s) from Activity
1	**OPEN POSITION** This task denotes the beginning of the recruitment process. It assumes that all budgeting and head count approvals are resolved before the recruiter opens the position. This is the task of actually opening the position in SAP.	**None.** This is the first step in the process. It is assumed that approval of head count and budgets have already been given.	**Vacancy** The position has been created in SAP and flagged as an opening.
2	**POST JOB OPENING ON WEBSITE** This is the task of transferring the job information to the website. There may also be newspaper advertisements or other vehicles deemed necessary for the specific opening.	**Vacancy** The position has been created in SAP and flagged as an opening.	**Announcement of Job Opening** The availability of the opening is now public through whatever vehicles were identified (e.g., website, newspaper, etc.).
3	**METHOD OF INQUIRY** This is a decision point asking how the job seeker is approaching the company.	**Announcement of Job Opening** The availability of the opening is now public through whatever vehicles were identified (e.g., website, newspaper, etc.).	There are four possible outputs to this task depending on how the job seeker approached the company: 1. Email, phone, fax, or referral 2. Send letter or resume via external mail 3. View the website 4. Attend a job fair
10	**JOB SEEKER SEARCHES EXISTING OPENINGS** This task involves the job seeker using the company website to search for openings of interest to them.	**Expressed Interest** The job seeker has indicated that they are interested in working for the company.	**Opening of Interest** The job seeker has found an opening they are interested in applying for with the company.
11	**EMAIL ADDRESS?** This is a decision point after receiving an inquiry via external mail. The job seeker either has or does not have email access. The response differs based on the answer to this question.	**No** The job seeker has indicated that they are interested in working for the company by sending a letter and/or resume via external mail. The job seeker has not registered on the company website.	**Yes** If the job seeker has an email address, a response is sent to them via email telling them to visit the company website (8). **No** If the job seeker does <u>not</u> have an email address, then a postcard is sent via external mail telling them to visit the company website (12).
12	**ACKNOWLEDGE RECEIPT & REFER TO WEBSITE** This task occurs when the job seeker does not have an email account. As a result, a postcard is sent via external mail telling them to visit the company website. (This will probably be a small percentage of time.)	**No** Job seeker does not have an email address.	**Referral** The job seeker has been notified that they should apply for a job through the company website.

Figure 14-4 EPG Process: Detail Document

(continues)

Activity Number	Activity Name/Description	Input(s) to Activity	Output(s) from Activity
15	**COMPLETE APPLICATION** The job seeker is turned into an *applicant* once they complete the resume and apply for a job. This is the point in the process where the job seeker creates a User ID and password on the company website. Applicants can only apply for one position at a time and they cannot reapply for the same position within three months.	**Yes** The job seeker has already created a resume and it is stored on the website.	**Completed Application** Once the applicant hits the *Apply* button, they are automatically prompted to create a User ID and password.
17	**ANSWER BASIC "POSITION-BASED" QUESTIONS** Depending on the job or position an applicant is applying for, a different series of questions appears online. The applicant must go through the questions and answer each one. Typically, there will be 8–10 position-specific questions.	**Completed Application** Once the applicant hits the *Apply* button, they are automatically prompted to create a User ID and password.	There are two outputs to this task: **Completed Basic Questions** The applicant has answered the questions and will receive a system-generated acknowledgment. **Score** The answers to the questions generate a score that is sent to human resources.
Activity Number	**Activity Name/Description**	**Input(s) to Activity**	**Output(s) from Activity**
21	**RUN REPORT TO SHOW SCORES & HIRING METRICS** The staffing assistant runs a report on a *daily* basis to pull scores from the website. Human resources will look for scores greater than a particular threshold, for example 90 percent. The report includes the applicant name and position-based questionnaire score.	**Score** The applicant's answers to the questions will generate a score now available to human resources.	**Applicant Scores** The output includes all applicant scores for the position-based questions.
22	**DETERMINE THRESHOLD & HANDOFF TO STAFFING ASSISTANT** This is where human resources determines whether the threshold is 90 percent or something different. The threshold will vary based on the job. This threshold helps human resources preselect the top applicants based on how they answered questions. If the company does not secure sufficient applicants at the 90 percent threshold, they may lower the threshold to 80 or 85 percent.	**Applicant Scores** All applicant scores for the position-based questions.	**Interest Level** The percentage that is considered "passing." The applicants that pass the threshold are the ones who will be interviewed.
24	**CHANGE STATUS IN JOBS DATABASE TO "SCHEDULE INTERVIEW."** This task is manually updating the status information in the jobs database to indicate those applicants that will be interviewed. This task changes an applicant into a "qualified person."	**Yes** Human resources is interested in interviewing the applicant.	**Status Changed** The database is updated with the most recent applicant status.

Figure 14-4 (continued)

tive to accompany the map, the project team moved to step 4 where we added the process timing to the process map and identified the cost of the business process.

Step 4: Estimate Time and Cost

In Chapter 5, we discussed process and cycle times and how to use the process information to estimate the amount of labor a process requires and what a process costs. In the EPG case, the crucial work for us to do involved estimating how to staff the recruitment process. How many employees did EPG require to handle the expected 100,000–200,000 applicant volume?

During this step, I worked with the project team to add *process time* to the map for the newly designed recruitment process. At this point, we did not include cycle times, which as you recall is the time required for the end-to-end process including wait times. Process time told us the number of employees required to handle the applicant volume. In Chapter 5, you learned that calculating the labor cost of a business process entails four steps.

1. List Process Activities and Process Time

The cross-functional process map in Figures 14-2 and 14-3 included a human resource functional band and a job seeker/applicant band. To calculate process time, I included only the human resource band in the calculations because the time invested by the applicants does not add to the company's staffing requirement.

EPG's process map included a variety of activities, several *volume*-based and others *frequency*-based. I grouped the activities in the process map by three categories:

1. Logistics
2. Applicant communications
3. Evaluation/interview

Figure 14-5 provides a summary of the activities grouped by the three categories and also identifies whether the activity is a daily administrative task or one based on applicant volume.

Logistics			
Activity Number(s)	Activity Description	Minimum (hours) Based on Daily Tasks	Minutes Based on Applicant Volume
21, 26, 33	Run reports	30	
27, 28	Print train and bus schedules	10	
1, 2	Create requisition and post job		4.5
24	Change database status		.5
37	Create SAP record		2.0
	Subtotal	**40 (0.7 hour)**	**7.0**
Applicant Communications			
8, 12, 13, 20	Referring to website and status updates		5.0
27	Schedule interviews		3.0
29	Onsite spiel (4 times/day)	100	
34, 35	Offer or notification of no offer		5.0
	Subtotal	**100 (1.6 hours)**	**13.0**
Evaluation/Interview			
22	Determine threshold	60	
31	Conduct interview		20.0
	Subtotal	**60 (1 hour)**	**20.0**
	Grand total	**200**	**40.0**
		3.3 hours/day Daily Tasks	0.66 hour/ Applicant

Figure 14-5 EPG Process: Process Time

Figure 14-5 shows that applicant communications require the highest number of daily hours (100 minutes, or 1.6 hours), followed by evaluation/interview (60 minutes, or 1 hour), and then logistics (40 minutes, or 0.7 hour). When you look at the *volume* for the same three categories, evaluation/ interview appears to have the highest volume, followed by applicant communications and logistics. This figure shows an alternative method to explain process time from what Chapter 5 covered. In this case, we estimated process time to help us determine the number of employees the company had to hire to support the recruitment process. Like every tool in this book, adapt the process calculation tables to meet your need.

Now that we knew the hours required for daily tasks and applicant volume, we could move to the next step and identify the volume.

2. Identify Volume

In this case, we did not care about annual volume because this was a one-time, six-month recruitment process to handle the extraordinary volume of applicants. We opted to staff human resources to support the expected volume of 200,000 applicants. At the bottom of Figure 14-5, you see the total hours required: 3.3 hours each day to cover the daily activities and 0.66 hour for each applicant. The total hours required for both daily and volume tasks over a six-month period is 132,396 hours:

▶ **Daily:** In a five-day workweek, these activities required almost 66 hours a month, which equates to 396 hours over six months (3.3 hours × 20 days/month × 6 months).

▶ **Volume:** These activities require 132,000 hours based on the 200,000 applicants (0.66 hour × 200,000 applicants).

3. Determine FTE Formula

You will recall from Chapter 5 that the FTE number denotes the total number of hours that an employee can be paid for in a work year (Figure 5-8). This formula helps you to identify the number of employees required to support a business process. As in the majority of cases, I could not use 2,080 hours as a starting point for the FTE formula because I had to deduct benefited hours (e.g., vacation, sick, and holiday). Because Hong Kong has additional holiday hours, I used 1,840 as the labor calculation number. Figure 14-6 shows the formula I used to identify the number of FTEs required to support the *daily* hiring recruitment process, and Figure 14-7 shows the formula to identify the FTE requirement for the *volume* activities.

Daily Formula:

$$\frac{\text{Total labor hours}}{\text{FTE hours}} = \text{Total FTE required to support the business process}$$

Example:

$$\frac{396}{1,840} = 0.2 \text{ FTE required}$$

Figure 14-6 EPG Process: FTE Calculation—Daily Activities

Daily Formula:

$$\frac{\text{Total labor hours}}{\text{FTE hours}} = \text{Total FTE required to support the business process}$$

Example:

$$\frac{132,000}{1,840} = 72 \text{ FTE required}$$

Figure 14-7 EPG Process: FTE Calculation—Volume Activities

As you can see, the company had to hire 73 employees to support the six-month hiring process, considering both daily and volume-based activities. In looking at the 72 volume-based employees according to the three categories, the evaluation/ interview category requires the highest number of employees because it requires 20 minutes per applicant (200,000 × 20 minutes).

► Logistics: 12
► Applicant communication: 24
► Evaluation/interview: 36

These numbers include only the clerical staff and recruiters, not managers or other office staff. We could have reduced the volume number if we wanted to presume that the recruiters would not interview every applicant. For example, if we believed we would interview only half of the applicants, we could reduce the 36 employees conducting interviews to 18. In this scenario, the company would have to hire only 54 employees instead of 72. We elected to split the difference and hire 27 recruiters, bringing the total employees the company had to hire to 63.

4. Determine Employee Costs

Determining the employee expense for the clerical staff and recruiters was simple. The company agreed to pay the clerical staff between HK$116,335 and HK$139,602. In U.S. dollars, this salary equates to $15,000–$18,000, based on a 7.76 HKD/1 USD exchange rate. For recruiters, the company offered HK$349,006, which translates to US$45,000.

After the six-month hiring ramp-up was finished, the company planned to redeploy the clerical staff across the operations and the recruiters across human resources.

Step 5: Verify the Process Map

Jim, Brian, Kim, and I built the process map and identified process times, but the company had not yet hired other staff members. Since we had not hired process workers to fill the clerical and bulk recruiter roles, we did not have other process workers or stakeholders to validate our work. Instead, we asked two other business units in the company to review the process map and time estimates. This proved beneficial because the other business units offered to help the Hong Kong team with the interviewing process, which required us to hire fewer recruiters in the local market. This support reduced the size of the redeployment effort we faced after the park opening.

Step 6: Apply Improvement Techniques

We did not look at process improvements in the EPG case because this was a new process. However, we made minor changes after talking to the other business units in step 5.

After completing the mass hiring, our plan included revisiting the process map and making changes so the Hong Kong team could use the process for their ongoing business.

Step 7: Create Internal Controls, Tools, and Metrics

While we did not bother with internal controls at this stage of the process, we did have tools the team had to build. The team had to provide feedback on the website design and build the Microsoft Access jobs database they planned to use for tracking applicant status.

The first measurement of success was simple to measure: Did we or did we not have the required number of employees on board when expected?

The second one, though, required the team to spend time talking about how the company would know if the general population felt positive about the company doing business in Hong Kong. After discussing this measurement of success, we made changes to the process map. We made the decision to delete activity 13, "delete hardcopy," and have the staffing assistant call the job seeker even if he or she had already applied via the website. This seemed more respectful, and so we changed the *yes* output from activity 9 to route to activity 8.

Likewise, activity 25, "send decline," seemed rude for the Hong Kong culture, so we chose to have the staffing assistant call this group of applicants and explain why the company did not choose to pursue them and what next step(s) they could take to have the company consider them for another job. While this would be time-consuming, the team felt it appropriate because an applicant, who might not fit one job, could fill another position. This personal touch would also help the general Hong Kong population view the company in a better light.

Step 8: Test and Rework

This step also changed from what Chapter 8 covered because we did not plan to use this version of the recruitment process for the long term; thus we did not test the steps in the process map. However, we did test the tools including the website, reports generated from the job database, the applicability of the position-based questions, and the ERP transactions and reports. The company's industrial engineering group had conducted time studies on the train and bus schedules, and the team validated that we had planned the accurate number of departures in a day. Although the bus service existed, the train service did not, and the company expected the extended train service to finish six months before opening.

Step 9: Implement Change

The project plan covered in Chapter 9 showed how you can use phases and tracks to organize business process work. In this case, I did not include a change management track in the implementation phase because this was a new process, and the project team had already completed the design. However, I did include a communication track and a training track in the implementation phase to help the employees understand what they had to do in the new process. Kim Li Mei Yan took the lead on these two tracks. She created a communication plan like Figure 9-3 and a training plan similar to Figure 9-4. I also included a postimplementation design phase, which started after the mass hiring finished.

Step 10: Drive Continuous Improvement

I shared the continuous improvement cycle wheel from Chapter 10 and led the team through a discussion of how to evaluate, test, assess, and execute improvements to the business process. The team had trouble thinking about this at the time because they were putting their energy into the upcoming mass hires. This example shows how you, as the facilitator, have to demonstrate flexibility and understand the pressures your client may have on them today.

We did come back and revisit the recruitment process, but not until six months after the park had opened. I had added a postimplementation design phase to the project plan to start after the mass hiring finished in order to help Jim's team begin to adopt a continuous improvement mindset. After the mass hiring finished, I again shared the continuous improvement cycle wheel, and this time the larger recruitment team engaged in creating a continuous improvement plan and schedule.

Chapter Summary

Jim Mann's story at EPG demonstrates how to adapt the ten steps to a business process when you face a brand-new process. You can adapt each step to meet your business need, and you can skip a step you view as irrelevant. In this case study, we used eight of the ten steps. We skipped step 1, develop the process inventory, because Jim had already asked for my help with the recruitment business process. We also skipped step 6, apply improvement techniques, because we designed an entirely new process. However, we did finally move to step 6 after the park opened as part of the *evaluate* phase of the continuous improvement cycle.

What You Have Achieved

In this chapter, you have achieved the following:

▶ An understanding of how to design a business process for a brand-new process
▶ Clarity around how to estimate the labor required and the expense associated with staffing a process
▶ An understanding of how you can adapt the ten steps to meet your requirements
▶ Insight into how to work with international partners
▶ The knowledge that a business process is a business process, no matter where you live

► How to validate a process even if no process workers or stakeholders exist

► Insight into engaging a team in continuous improvement even if the timing has to vary

► Most important, the *power* to know that you can create an entirely new process

Index

account management process, 20
activities
  determining costs of, 122–123
  for process map, 80–81, 86–88
  in recruitment process case study,
    351–353
  time required for, 114–116
  tools used in, 95, 96
  in training and development case
    study, 305, 308–311
activity symbols (in BPMN), 277
adaptability, 6, 187
analytical tables, in executive
    summary, 260–265, 267–268
annotation symbol, 94–95
annual volume
  in cost estimates, 123–124
  in training and development case
    study, 309–313
appendix, in executive summary, 266
Apple, 244
approvals, required, 145–146
Aristotle, on the whole, 270
assessment phase, in continuous
    improvement, 243–245
audience
  for communication plan, 222
  for training plan, 226
automation, 161–164

baseline time, 114
benchmarking, 244–245, 316–322
Benefit/Return
  as prioritization criterion, 28, 29
  scaling for, 41–43
benefits costs, 126–127
Bosch, 244

boundaries of a process, 84, *see also*
    scope definition document
BPI, *see* business process
    improvement
BPM, *see* business process
    management; business process
    modeling
BPMN (business process modeling
    and notation), 273–280
BPMN 2.0, 279
Budgeting, 24–25
bureaucracy
  eliminating, 146–149
  incremental increase in, 2
business process improvement (BPI),
    1, 269
  advantages of, 2–3
  choosing names for efforts in, 287
  continuous improvement in, 15
  creating internal controls, tools,
    and metrics for, 13
  cross-functional teams for, 4
  definition of, 1
  drawing process map for, 10–11
  estimating time and costs in, 11
  evaluating need for, 4
  flexibility in, 323
  foundation for, 9–10
  implementation plan for, 14–15
  improvement techniques for, 12–13
  objectives of, 6
  process inventory for, 9
  roadmap for, 6–8
  testing and rework for, 14
  and understanding of processes,
    3–4
  verifying process map for, 11–12

business process management (BPM), 270–272
  definition of, 270
  drawing process map in, 80
  tools supporting, 277–280
business process modeling (BPM), 272–273
business process modeling and notation (BPMN), 273–280
Business @ the Speed of Thought (Bill Gates), 2

case study, *see* recruitment process case study; training and development case study
categorizing processes, 21, 23–24
Champy, James, 282–283
change management, 214, 283, *see also* implementation plan
change management process, 20
change management track, 14–15, 221
  activities involved in, 220
  in training and development case study, 334–336
checklists, as deliverables, 266
client-facing IT processes, 21, 23
Client Level affected
  as prioritization criterion, 24, 25
  scaling for, 31–34
clients, 5
  benchmarks for meeting needs of, 245
  benchmark study interviews with, 317–319
  measurements of success with, 72, 73
  in scope definition document, 69–70
communication
  definition of, 225
  in test plan, 200, 202
  vehicles for, 223
communication plan, 215, 221–224
  in continuous improvement cycle, 246
  as deliverable, 266
  time estimate for, 230
communication track, 15, 221–224
  activities involved in, 220

in training and development case study, 333–334
connector symbols
  off-page, 102, 299, 301
  on-page, 102, 300, 301
continuous improvement, 15, 234–251, 281
  assessment phase in, 243–245
  cycle of, 15, 236–237
  definition of, 235
  employee contributions to, 281
  evaluation phase in, 237–242
  execution phase in, 245–246
  mindset for, 236
  plan for, 246–249
  in recruitment process case study, 357–358
  schedule for, 250–251
  testing phase in, 242–243
  time estimate for, 250–251
  in training and development case study, 336
continuous improvement cycle wheel, 15, 236–237
continuous improvement plan, 246–249
  time estimate for developing, 250–251
  in training and development case study, 336
continuous improvement schedule, 250–251
  time estimate for developing, 251
  in training and development case study, 336
cost estimation, 11, 120–135, 139–140
  additional detail in, 130–132
  analysis of columns in, 132–135
  and components of total cost, 120–121
  for overhead costs, 129–130
  for people costs, 121–127
  in recruitment process case study, 351–355
  for tool costs, 127–129
  for total cost, 130
  in training and development case study, 302, 305–315
cost savings, hard vs. soft, 121–122

cross-functional process maps, 95, 97–99, 343, 345
cross-functional teams, 4
cultural changes, 158
Current State (of processes)
    as prioritization criterion, 27–28
    scaling for, 38–40
    weighting for, 45, 47
custom email forms, 178, 180–184, 196
Customer/Client Satisfaction
    as prioritization criterion, 27–28
    scaling for, 38–40
customers, 4–5
    benchmarks for meeting needs of, 245
    benchmark study interviews with, 317–319
    measurements of success with, 72, 73
cycle time, 11, 113–114, 116–120
    comparing process time and, 117, 119–120
    reducing, 158–161
cycle time symbol, 117, 118
cyclical/recurring symbol, 105, 106

Dalai Lama, on simplicity, 156
data integrity, 155
data sheets, 204–209
decision symbol, 88, 91–93
defining processes, 20–22, 58, 59
deliverables section, in executive summary, 265–266
Deming, W. Edwards, 282, 285
description of process
    areas out of scope in, 58, 63, 64
    defining the process in, 58, 59
    examples in, 63, 64
    in scope definition document, 58–64
    unusual or technical terms in, 61–63
design phase, 216, 219
detail document, 103–105
    as deliverable, 266
    in recruitment process case study, 345, 348
    and use of symbols, 277
detailed process maps, 83–84, 343, 345

development phase, 216, 219–220
Dhillon, Balbir S., 172
Disney, 244
DMAIC method, 285
documentation
    of internal controls, 176, 177, 326
    of process map development, 103–106
    of scope, 9–10, 52–77
drawing the process map, 10–11, 79–111
    approaches to, 79–80
    basic components in, 80–82
    between-meeting work on, 98–100
    boxes 4–7 in, 95, 96
    box 1 in, 85–89
    box 2 in, 89–93
    box 3 in, 92, 94–95
    for cross-functional maps, 95, 97–99
    documenting process of, 103–106
    entry point for, 84–85
    example of, 82–83
    in recruitment process case study, 343, 345–351
    software tools for, 105–107
    at subsequent meetings, 98–102
    time estimate for, 109–111
    in training and development case study, 298–304
dry-erase boards, 76–77
duplication, eliminating, 153–155

effectiveness, 6, 18–19
    balancing efficiency and, 272
    improvement driving, 269
    metrics of, 187
efficiency, 6
    with BPM, 271–272
    improvement driving, 269
    metrics of, 187
Einstein, Albert
    on simplicity, 156
    on things that count, 185
elapsed time, 114, *see also* cycle time
electronic boards, 76, 77
email, custom forms for, 178, 180–184, 196
email icon, 95, 96
employee costs, *see* people costs

enterprise-wide processes, 270–272
Entertainment Park Group (EPG),
    62, *see also* recruitment process
    case study
entry point, for process maps, 84–85
evaluation phase, in continuous
    improvement, 237–242
events symbols (in BPMN), 276–277
exclusive gateway symbol, 274
execution phase, in continuous
    improvement, 245–246
executive summary, 16, 253–268
    appendix of, 266
    deliverables section of, 265–266
    goals section of, 257–258
    key findings section of, 265
    project focus section of, 255–256
    sections of, 254
    summary section of, 258–265
    time estimate for creating, 267–268
    writing, 254, 268
expected volume, 353

face-to-face communication icon, 95,
    96
facilitators, training, 228
feedback, from testing, 200, 202, 209,
    211
finance processes, 21, 22
flexibility, 323
flow lines (in BPMN), 277, 278
forms, streamlining, 157
foundation for BPI, 52–53, 72–77
    in recruitment process case study,
        341–344
    time estimate for, 76–77
    in training and development case
        study, 294–297
    see also scope definition document
full-time equivalent (FTE) formula,
    124–125
    in recruitment process case study,
        353–355
    in training and development case
        study, 313–315
fully-loaded costs, 130
functional bands, on process maps,
    95, 97–99
Funding
    as prioritization criterion, 26, 27
    scaling for, 34, 35, 37

future state processes
    on process map, 89
    in scope definition document, 55

Gates, Bill
    on lousy processes, 2
    on technology, 162
gateway symbols (in BPMN),
    274–275
goals
    communication, 222–223
    performance, 321–322
    project, 257–258
    testing, 200, 201
    see also objectives

Hammer, Michael, 282–283
handoffs, 98, 154
hard cost savings, 121
health care, human error in, 172
Heraclitus, on change, 214
high-level process maps
    detailed maps vs., 83–84
    in recruitment process case study,
        343, 345
    in training and development case
        study, 298–302
horizontal functional bands, on
    process maps, 95, 97–98
Hoshin Kanri, 281–282
*Human Reliability and Error in
    Medical Systems* (Balbir S.
    Dhillon), 172
human resources processes, 20–22

IBM Blueworks Live, 278–279
icons, for process maps, 95, 96, *see
    also* symbols (for process maps)
iGrafx Flowcharter, 279
Impact (of business processes)
    as prioritization criterion, 24–25
    scaling for, 31–34
    weighting for, 43–45, 47
impact analysis, 158, 164, 166–168,
    215
    in continuous improvement cycle,
        246
    as deliverable, 266
    in executive summary, 261–262
    time estimate for, 230–231

Implementation (of processes)
  as prioritization criterion, 26–27
  scaling for, 33, 35–37
  weighting for, 44–47
implementation phase, 216, 220–229
  change management track in, 221
  communications track in, 221–224
  in recruitment process case study,
    357
  testing track in, 221
  in training and development case
    study, 333–336
  training track in, 224–229
  see also specific tracks
implementation plan, 14–15, 214–231
  components of, 215
  as deliverable, 266
  design phase of, 219
  development phase of, 219–220
  implementation phase of, 220–229
  phases in, 215–216
  in recruitment process case study,
    357
  time estimate for, 230–231
  in training and development case
    study, 333–336
improvement technique(s), 143–170,
    269–287
  automation as, 161–164
  business process management as,
    270–272
  business process modeling and
    notation as, 273–277
  business process modeling as,
    272–273
  continuous improvement as, 281
  eliminating bureaucracy as,
    146–149
  eliminating duplication as,
    153–155
  Hoshin Kanri as, 281–282
  impact analysis as, 164, 166–168
  kaizen as, 281
  Lean as, 285–286
  Lean Six Sigma as, 286
  in recruitment process case study,
    355–356
  reducing cycle time as, 158–161
  reengineering as, 282–284
  simplification as, 155–158

Six Sigma as, 284–285
  time estimated for, 168–169
  total quality management as,
    280–281
  in training and development case
    study, 316–326
  value added as, 149–153
  see also individual techniques
improvement techniques wheel,
    12–13, 144–145
inclusive gateway symbol, 274
information technology processes,
    22–23
inputs, for process map, 81–82, 87–88
internal control document, 176, 177,
    266
internal controls, 13, 171–176
  costs of, 172
  documenting, 176, 177
  identifying points of need for,
    173–176
  in recruitment process case study,
    356
  responsibility for, 172
  time spent on, 176
  in training and development case
    study, 326
internal control symbol, 105
internal-facing IT processes, 21
interoffice mail symbol, 90

job aids, 178–180, 327
Journal of Patient Safety, 172

kaizen, 281
key findings section, in executive
    summary, 265
key stakeholders and interests, in
    scope definition document,
    70–72
KISS philosophy, 157

labor costs, see people costs
laptops, for presentations, 76
lead generation process, 20
Lean, 285–286
Lean Six Sigma, 286
Lombardi Blueprint, 278
loops (in BPMN), 277

Malcolm Baldrige National Quality Award, 269–270, 281
measurement
    benchmark data for, 244–245
    of process time, 114–115
    see also metrics
measurements of success, 187–190
    in executive summary, 257
    in scope definition document, 72, 73
    in training and development case study, 329–331
message points, 223
metrics, 13, 185–190
    for adaptability, 187
    defining, 187–190
    for effectiveness, 187
    for efficiency, 187
    evaluating, 239–240
    for measuring success, 72, 73, see also measurements of success
    in recruitment process case study, 356
    in training and development case study, 329–331
    value vs. cost of, 185–186
Microsoft Access databases, 220, 326
Microsoft Excel, 184–186, 218
Microsoft InfoPath, 163, 164, 184
Microsoft Office Project, 216–219
Microsoft Office Suite, 191, 279
Microsoft Outlook, 178, 181–182, 196, 203, 204
Microsoft Visio, 99, 105–107, 277, 279
Microsoft Word, 218, 219
Motorola, 284

name of process, in scope definition document, 57
negative testing, 207
Number Affected (by a process)
    as prioritization criterion, 24, 25
    scaling for, 31–34

objectives
    of BPI, 6
    of testing, 200, 201
    of training, 226–228
    see also goals

Object Management Group (OMG), 273
off-page connector symbols, 102, 299, 301
on-page connector symbols, 102, 300, 301
optimization, 271–272
Outlook email icon, 95, 96
outputs, for process map, 81–82, 87–88, 91–93
overhead costs
    analyzing, 134–135
    estimating, 129–130
owner of process, see process owner

Pain Level
    as prioritization criterion, 27, 28
    scaling for, 38–40
parallel gateway symbol, 274
people (employee) costs
    analyzing, 133–134
    annual volume in, 123–124
    estimating, 121–127
    FTE formula for, 124–125
    and hard vs. soft cost savings, 121–122
    process activities and time in, 122–123
    in recruitment process case study, 355
    salary and benefits costs in, 126–127
    in training and development case study, 315
people/organizational processes, 21
per-course activities, 288
performance goals, 321–322
performance management process, 20
per-transaction activities, 289
phone icon, 90, 91
Plan-Do-Check-Act cycle, 285
policy development process, 20
pools (in BPMN), 275, 276
positive testing, 207
preventable adverse events, 172
prioritizing a process inventory, 23–47
    applying weighting in, 43–47
    Current State criterion for, 27–28

determining scale in, 29–43
developing criteria for, 23–24
Impact criterion for, 24–25
Implementation criterion for, 26–27
time estimate for, 48–49
Value criterion for, 28–29
problem statement, 255
processes
 categories of, 21, 23–24
 defining, 20–22
Process Exists? criterion
 in prioritization, 27, 28
 scaling for, 38–40
process inventory, 9, 18–23
 categories of processes in, 21, 23–24
 defining processes for, 20–22
 definition of, 19
 prioritization of, see prioritizing a process inventory
 steps in, 19
 subprocesses in, 21
 time estimate for, 48–49
 in training and development case study, 290–294
process maps
 changes to, 88, 90–91
 color coding of, 152–153
 components of, 80–82
 cost estimates for, 120–135
 cross-functional, 95, 97–99
 definition of, 80
 as deliverables, 266
 detail documents for, 103–105
 detailed, 83–84
 drawing, see drawing the process map
 example of, 82–83
 high-level, 83–84, 298–302
 paper vs. digital, 145
 review of, 100–101
 revising, 100–101, 166
 symbols for, see symbols (for process maps)
 time estimates for, 113–120
 in training and development case study, 298–304
 verifying, see verifying the process map

process name, in scope definition document, 57
process overview, as deliverable, 266
process owner, 48
 in scope definition document, 57–58
 verifying process map with, 137–138
process prioritization table, 19
 criteria on, 24–29
 scaling on, 29–43
 time estimate for completing, 48–49
 in training and development case study, 290–292
 weighting in, 43–47
process responsibilities, in scope definition document, 67–69
process time, 11, 113–116
 comparing cycle time and, 117, 119–120
 determining costs of, 122–123
 in recruitment process case study, 351–353
 in training and development case study, 302, 305, 308–311
process time symbol, 116, 118
process workers, verifying process map with, 136–137
project focus section, in executive summary, 255–256
project team meetings
 for drawing the process map, 109–111
 for improvement techniques, 168–169
 for internal controls, tools, and metrics, 191–192
 for scope definition, 76–77
 for time and cost estimates, 139
 for verifying process map, 139
Promapp, 279–280

qualitative value of processes, as prioritization criterion, 29

quantitative value of processes, as prioritization criterion, 29

recruitment process, 20
recruitment process case study, 340–358

recruitment process case study
(*continued*)
  continuous improvement in,
    357–358
  drawing process map in, 343,
    345–351
  foundation in, 341–344
  implementation plan in, 357
  improvement techniques in,
    355–356
  internal controls, tools and metrics
    in, 356
  scope definition document in,
    341–344
  testing and rework in, 356–357
  time and cost estimates in, 351–355
  verifying the process map in, 355
recurring symbol, 105, 106
redundancy, *see* duplication,
  eliminating
reengineering, 282–284
  and continuous improvement,
    235–236
  early popularity of, 269
  system impact of, 70
  TQM vs., 79, 80, 283
resources, for testing, 200, 201, 211
responsibilities for processes
  on process map, 86
  in scope definition document,
    67–69
retesting, 210
return from process, *see* Benefit/
  Return
reviewing process maps, 100–101
revising process maps, 100–101, 166
rework, 14, 209–210
  implementing, 211–212
  in recruitment process case study,
    356–357
  in training and development case
    study, 331–332
roadmap to BPI, 6–8, 294

Safe Harbor framework, 197
salary costs, in people costs, 126–127
Salary Planning, 24
sales and marketing processes, 20, 22
SALT requirement, 148
Sarbanes-Oxley Act (2002), 172

scaling, on process prioritization
  table, 29–43
  for Current State, 38–40
  for Impact, 31–34
  for Implementation, 33, 35–37
  for Value, 39, 41–43
scope, 63, 65
scope creep, 53–54
scope definition, in scope definition
  document, 63, 65–67
scope definition document, 9–10,
  52–77
  client and client needs in, 69–70
  as combination of current and
    future states, 55
  description of process in, 58–64
  importance of, 53
  key stakeholders and interests in,
    70–72
  measurements of success in, 72, 73
  process name in, 57
  process owner in, 57–58
  process responsibilities in, 67–69
  in recruitment process case study,
    341–344
  scope definition in, 63, 65–67
  sections of, 55–56
  time estimate for, 76–77
  in training and development case
    study, 294–297
Senge, Peter, 270
SharePoint, 223
Shewhart, Walter, 285
simplification, 155–158
Six Sigma, 271, 279, 284–286
SmartDraw, 99, 105–107, 277
soft cost savings, 121–122
SOR (system of record) icon, 95, 96
sponsor meetings
  for process inventory development,
    49–50
  for scope definition, 77
  for time and cost estimates, 140
sponsors, 48
  executive summaries for, 253–254
  gaining buy-in of, 231, 251
  impact analysis for, 166
  verifying process map with,
    137–138
spreadsheets, 184–186

stakeholders
  measurements of success with, 72,
    73
  in scope definition document,
    70–72
  verifying process map with, 137
standard deviation, 284–285
strategic thinking, 145
streamlining, *see* simplification
subprocesses, 21
success
  in communication, 224
  measurements of, *see* measurements of success
summary section, in executive
    summary, 258–265
  to familiarize a new department
    head, 258–265
  to identify changed responsibilities, 263–264
  to report how staff spends time,
    262–263
swim lanes, 97, 276
symbols (for process maps), 82, 95,
    96, 105, 302
  annotation, 94–95
  connector, 102, 299–301
  cycle time, 117, 118
  cyclical/recurring, 105, 106
  decision, 88, 91–93
  email, 95, 96
  face-to-face communication, 95, 96
  internal control, 105
  interoffice mail, 90
  off-page connector, 102, 299, 301
  on-page connector, 102, 300, 301
  phone, 90, 91, 95, 96
  process time, 116, 118
  system of record, 95, 96
  terminator, 82
  for warnings, 173
symbols (in BPMN), 273–277
  activity, 277
  events, 276–277
  flow lines, 277, 278
  gateways, 274–275
  loops, 277
  pools, 275, 276
  swim lanes, 276
system of record (SOR) icon, 95, 96
systems testing, 198, 207

tasks, for process map, 81
teams
  cross-functional, 4
  project, *see* project team meetings
technology, 162, 163
telephone icon, 95, 96
Terez, Tom, 148–149
terminator symbol, 82
terminology, in description of processes, 61–63
testing, 14, 195–121
  in continuous improvement cycle,
    242–243
  creating test plan for, 199–203
  developing test sets for, 203–209
  implementing test plan in, 207, 209
  in recruitment process case study,
    356–357
  and retesting, 210
  and rework, 209–210
  steps in, 198–199
  summarizing feedback from, 209
  time estimate for, 211–212
  in training and development case
    study, 331–332
  who, what, where, when, and how
    of, 196–198
testing track, 15, 220, 221
test plan
  creating, 199–203, 211
  implementing, 207, 209, 211–212
test scripts, 203–208
test sets, developing, 203–209, 211
time estimation, 11, 139–140
  for continuous improvement,
    250–251
  for cycle time, 116–120
  for drawing the process map,
    109–111
  for executive summary, 267–268
  for implementation plan, 230–231
  for improvement techniques,
    168–169
  for internal controls, tools, and
    metrics, 191–192
  for process inventory, 48–49
  for process maps, 113–120
  for process time, 114–116
  in recruitment process case study,
    351–355

time estimation (*continued*)
  for scope definition document,
    76–77
  in training and development case
    study, 302, 305–315
  and types of time, 113–114
  for verifying the process map, 140
time frame, in test plan, 200, 202
timelines, training, 229
timer event symbol, 276–277
time studies, 114–115
Time to Market
  as prioritization criterion, 26–27
  scaling for, 33–35, 37
Timing of Next Cycle
  as prioritization criterion, 26, 27
  scaling for, 34–37
tool costs
  analyzing, 134
  estimating, 127–129
tools, 13, 176–186
  for BPM and BPMN, 277–280
  custom email forms as, 178,
    180–184
  job aids as, 178–180
  in recruitment process case study,
    356
  spreadsheets as, 184–186
  for training, 228
  in training and development case
    study, 326–329
total costs
  components of, 120–121
  estimating, 130
  overhead costs in, 129–130
  people costs in, 121–127
  tool costs in, 127–129
total quality management (TQM), 79,
  80, 269, 280–283
total quality techniques, 235
training, 225
training and development case study,
  289–338
  continuous improvement in, 336
  drawing process map in, 298–304
  foundation in, 294–297
  implementation plan in, 333–336

improvement techniques in,
    316–326
  internal controls in, 326
  metrics in, 329–331
  process inventory in, 290–294
  scope definition document in,
    294–297
  testing and rework in, 331–332
  time and cost estimates in, 302,
    305–315
  tools in, 326–329
  verifying process map in, 315
training plan, 215, 224–229
  in continuous improvement cycle,
    246
  as deliverable, 266
  time estimate for, 231
training track, 15, 224–229
  activities involved in, 220
  objectives of, 226–228
  in training and development case
    study, 333, 334

Value (of processes)
  as prioritization criterion, 28–29
  scaling for, 39, 41–43
  weighting for, 45, 47
value-added techniques, 149–153
verifying the process map, 11–12,
  136–138
  with process workers, 136–137
  in recruitment process case study,
    355
  with sponsors, 137–138
  with stakeholders, 137
  time estimate for, 140
  in training and development case
    study, 315
vertical functional bands, on process
  maps, 98, 99

waiting time, in cycle time, 114
warning symbols, 173
weighting, in prioritizing a process
  inventory, 43–47
Welch, Jack, 146–147
workflow loop symbol, 105

CPSIA information can be obtained
at www.ICGtesting.com
Printed in the USA
BVHW082334160223
658713BV00008B/103